Pros and Cons

Pros and Cons: A Debater's Handbook offers an indispensable guide to the arguments both for and against over 140 current controversies and global issues.

The nineteenth edition includes new entries on topics such as the right to possess nuclear weapons, the bailing out of failing companies, the protection of indigenous languages and the torture of suspected terrorists. It is divided into eight thematic sections where individual subjects are covered in detail, plus a UK section. Equal coverage is given to both sides of each debate in a dual-column format which allows for easy comparison, with a list of related topics and suggestions for possible motions.

Providing authoritative advice on debating technique, the book covers the rules, structure and type of debate, offering tips on how to become a successful speaker. It is a key read for debaters at any level.

The English–Speaking Union (ESU) builds bridges between people and nations through the use of the English language. Its debate and public speaking competitions are among the most prestigious and the longest running in the debate calendar. The ESU's mentors also tour the world to coach and advise debate students of all ages. The ESU's path-finding speech and debate work is coupled with a worldwide programme of cross-generational education scholarships which places the English-Speaking Union in the van of thinkers, deliverers and facilitators in creating life-changing educational opportunities for people, whatever their age and social background.

Pros and Cons

A DEBATER'S HANDBOOK

19th Edition

Edited by

DEBBIE NEWMAN AND BEN WOOLGAR

The English-Speaking Union

Routledge
Taylor & Francis Group

LONDON AND NEW YORK

First edition by J. B. Askew, published in 1896

Nineteenth edition published 2014
by Routledge
2 Park Square, Milton Park, Abingdon, Oxon OX14 4RN

and by Routledge
711 Third Avenue, New York, NY 10017

Routledge is an imprint of the Taylor & Francis Group, an informa business

British Library Cataloguing in Publication Data
A catalogue record for this book is available from the British Library

Library of Congress Cataloging in Publication Data
A catalog record for this book has been requested

ISBN: 978-0-415-82779-9 (hbk)
ISBN: 978-0-415-82780-5 (pbk)
ISBN: 978-1-315-88603-9 (ebk)

Typeset in Bembo and Franklin Gothic
by Keystroke, Station Road, Codsall, Wolverhampton

Printed and bound by CPI Group (UK) Ltd, Croydon, CR0 4YY

CONTENTS

(C) International relations   **59**

(D) Economics   **89**

(E) Social, moral and religious   **107**

(F) Culture, education and sport   **159**

(G) Crime and punishment   **211**

(H) Health, science and technology   **241**

(I) United Kingdom issues   **271**

Appendices

FOREWORD

Writing the foreword for the last edition of *Pros and Cons*, Will Hutton commented: 'reasoned argument . . . is the stuff of democracy'. I agree, and the English-Speaking Union (ESU) has been aiding and abetting reasoned argument around the globe since 1918.

This book forearms the fledgling and the experienced debater alike with the tools not only to engage with the stuff of democracy, but also to experience the sheer fun of debate. It is, however, fun with a purpose. No matter how light or dark the subject, debate broadens the mind and develops the intellect – practitioners gain in confidence and self-belief and grow their critical thinking and social skills. The art of speaking – and, as importantly, listening – underpins civic and civil society.

This is the nineteenth edition of *Pros and Cons* – itself a testimony to its usefulness. Some of the topics it covers are radically different to those that have appeared in previous editions and some are similar – although the issues within the issues will have evolved and changed to meet new times and new realities. We at the English-Speaking Union are proud to continue our association with Routledge and proud to be associated with this publication. I urge everyone who reads *Pros and Cons* to get debating – it is an empowering feeling.

Peter Kyle, OBE
Director-General, The English-Speaking Union

PREFACE

This is the nineteenth edition of *Pros and Cons*, replacing the last which was written in 1999. In that time, much has changed in the world: 9/11 has reshaped the debates on international relations, while the growth of the Internet has changed the complexion of many of the social issues. About a third of the topics have changed; for example 'restricting Sunday shopping', 'easier divorce' and 'modernisation of trades unions' have been replaced with 'social networking has improved our lives', 'banning of violent video games' and 'torture of terrorist suspects'. With the remaining topics, some have needed little revision, but many have needed to be rewritten to reflect the world we live in. This edition has also attempted to be more international in its outlook, with the UK-specific issues in their own chapter and the other topics taking a more general approach. We hope that most of the topics here will remain relevant and largely unchanged, for a few years at least. For this reason, notable conflicts such as Israel and Palestine or Afghanistan have been omitted.

About the editorial team and acknowledgements

Debbie Newman, General Editor, is the director of The Noisy Classroom, which supports Speaking and Listening across the curriculum. She is a previous English national debating champion, president of the Cambridge Union Society and a coach for the World Schools Debating Championships (WSDC). She is a former head of the Centre for Speech and Debate at the English-Speaking Union, a fellow of the World Debate Institute and a qualified secondary school teacher.

Ben Woolgar, Assistant Editor, won the World Schools Debating Championships in 2008 when he was on the England Schools Debating Team. As a student at the

University of Oxford, he won the European Universities Debating Championships, reached the Grand Final of the World Universities Debating Championships and was ranked top speaker in the world. He is currently studying law at City University.

Many of the entries here have needed minimal revision due to the thorough and thoughtful work of the editors of and contributors to the last edition: Trevor Sather, Thomas Dixon, Alastair Endersby, Dan Neidle and Bobby Webster.

Thanks are due to Steve Roberts, Director of Charitable Activities at the English-Speaking Union, and his team for support with the project; and to Jason Vit who, when Head of Speech and Debate at the ESU, initiated the project. Thanks also to Paul Holleley.

INTRODUCTION

How can *Pros and Cons* help you to debate?

To debate well you need:

1 to have a range of good arguments and rebuttals
2 to develop these in a clear, detailed and analytical way
3 to deliver them persuasively.

Pros and Cons can help you with the first, and only the first, of these three. If you were to read out one side of a pros and cons article, it would not fill even the shortest of debate speeches. Each point is designed to express the idea, but you will need to flesh it out. If you know your topic in advance, you will be able to use these points as a springboard for your own research. If you are in an impromptu debate, you will have to rely on your own knowledge and ideas to populate the argument with up-to-date examples, detailed analysis and vivid analogies. But the ideas themselves can be useful. It is hard to know something about everything and yet debating competitions expect you to. It is important to read widely and follow current affairs, but doing that does not guarantee that you will not get caught out by a debate on indigenous languages, nuclear energy or taxation. *Pros and Cons* can be a useful safety net in those situations.

When using each article it is worth considering:

A Does each point stand up as a constructive argument in its own right, or is it only really strong as a rebuttal to its equivalent point on the other side? Where there are key points which directly clash, they have been placed opposite each other, but some points have been used to counter an argument rather than as a positive reason for one side of the case.

B Can the points be merged or split? Different debate formats favour different numbers of arguments. Check to see if two of the points here could be joined into a larger point. Or if you need quantity, sub-points could be repackaged as distinct arguments. If you are delivering an extension in a World Universities-style debate (or a British Parliament-style one), it is worth noting down the sub-points. It is possible that the top half of the table may make an economic argument, but have they hit all three of the smaller economic points? If they have not, then one of these, correctly labelled, could form your main extension.

C Look at *Pros and Cons* last, not first. Try to brainstorm your own arguments first and then check the chapter to see if there is anything there you had not thought of. The articles are not comprehensive and often not surprising (especially if the other teams also have the book!), so it is best not to rely on it too heavily. Also, if you do not practise generating points yourself, what will you do when the motion announced is not in here?

D Adapt the arguments here to the jurisdiction in which you are debating. The book is designed to be more international than its predecessor, but the writers are British and that bias will come through. The debate within your own country may have its own intricacies which are not reflected in the broader global debate. Some arguments are based on assumptions of liberal democracy and other values and systems which may just be plain wrong where you live.

E Is the argument or the example out of date? We have tried to write broad arguments which will stand the test of time, but the world changes. Do not believe everything you read here if you know or suspect it to be untrue! Things like whether something is legal or illegal in a given country change very quickly, so please do your research.

F What is the most effective order of arguments? This book lists points, but that is not the same as a debating case. You will need to think about how to order arguments, how to divide them between speakers, and how to label them as well as how much time to give to each. On the opposition in particular, some of the most significant points could be towards the end of the list.

Debating formats

There is an almost bewildering number of debate formats across the world. The number of speakers, the length and order of speeches, the role of the audience and opportunities for interruption and questioning all vary. So too do the judging criteria. On one side of the spectrum, some formats place so much emphasis on content and strategy that the debaters speak faster than most people can follow. On the other side, persuasive rhetoric and witty repartee can be valued more than logical analysis and examples. Most debate formats sit in the middle of this divide and give credit for content, style and strategy. Here are a few debate formats used in the English-Speaking Union programmes:

Mace format

This format involves two teams with two speakers on each side. Each speaker delivers a seven-minute speech and there is then a floor debate, where members of the audience make brief points, before one speaker on each team delivers a four-minute summary speech with the opposition team speaking first. The order is as follows:

First Proposition Speaker
First Opposition Speaker
Second Proposition Speaker
Second Opposition Speaker
Floor Debate
Opposition Summary Speaker
Proposition Summary Speaker

The first Proposition Speaker should define the debate. This does not mean giving dictionary definitions of every word, but rather explaining the terms so that everybody is clear exactly what the debate is about. For example, the speaker may need to clarify whether the law which is being debated should be passed just in their country or all around the world and specify any exemptions or limits. This speaker should then outline their side's arguments and go through the first, usually two or three, points in detail.

The first Opposition speaker should clarify the Opposition position in the debate; e.g. are they putting forward a counter-proposal or supporting the status quo? They should then outline their side's case, rebut the arguments put forward by the first Proposition Speaker and explain their team's first few arguments.

The second speakers on both sides should rebut the arguments which have come from the other team, support the points put forward by their first speakers, if they have been attacked, and then add at least one completely new point to the debate. It is not enough simply to expand on the arguments of the first speaker.

The summary speakers must remind the audience of the key points in the debate and try to convince them that they have been more persuasive in these areas than their opponents. The summary speakers should respond to points from the floor debate (and in the case of the Proposition team, to the second Opposition speech), but they should not add any new arguments to the debate at this stage.

Points of information

In this format, points of information (POIs) are allowed during the first four speeches but not in the summary speeches. The first and last minute of speeches are protected from these and a timekeeper should make an audible signal such as a bell ringing or a knock after one minute and at six minutes, as well as two at the end of the speech to indicate that the time is up. To offer point of information to the other team, a speaker should stand up and say 'on a point of information' or 'on that point'. They must then wait to see if the speaker who is delivering their speech will say 'accepted' or 'declined'.

If declined, the offerer must sit down and try again later. If accepted, they make a short point and then must sit down again and allow the main speaker to answer the point and carry on with their speech. All speakers should offer points of information, but should be sensitive not to offer so many that they are seen as barracking the speaker who has the floor. A speaker is recommended to take two points of information during a seven-minute speech and will be rewarded for accepting and answering these points.

Rebuttal

Apart from the very first speech in the debate, all speakers are expected to rebut the points which have come before them from the opposing team. This means listening to what the speaker has said and then explaining in your speech why their points are wrong, irrelevant, insignificant, dangerous, immoral, contradictory, or adducing any other grounds on which they can be undermined. It is not simply putting forward arguments against the motion – this is the constructive material – it is countering the specific arguments which have been put forward. As a speaker, you can think before the debate about what points may come up and prepare rebuttals to them, but be careful not to pre-empt arguments (the other side may not have thought of them) and make sure you listen carefully and rebut what the speaker actually says, not what you thought they would. However much you prepare, you will have to think on your feet.

The mace format awards points equally in four categories: reasoning and evidence, listening and responding, expression and delivery, and organisation and prioritisation.

LDC format

The LDC format was devised for the London Debate Challenge and is now widely used with younger students and for classroom debating at all levels. It has two teams of three speakers each of whom speaks for five minutes (or three or four with younger or novice debaters).

For the order of speeches, the rules on points of information and the judging criteria, please see the section on the mace format'. The only differences are the shorter (and equal) length of speeches and the fact that the summary speech is delivered by a third speaker rather than by a speaker who has already delivered a main speech. This allows more speakers to be involved.

World Schools Debating Championships (WSDC) style

This format is used at the World Schools Debating Championships and is also commonly used in the domestic circuits of many countries around the world. It consists of two teams of three speakers all of whom deliver a main eight-minute speech. One speaker also delivers a four-minute reply speech. There is no floor debate. The order is as follows:

First Proposition Speaker
First Opposition Speaker
Second Proposition Speaker
Second Opposition Speaker
Third Proposition Speaker
Third Opposition Speaker
Opposition Reply Speech
Proposition Reply Speech

For the roles of the first two speakers on each side, see the section on 'the mace format', above. The WSDC format also has a third main speech:

Third speakers
Third speakers on both sides need to address the arguments and the rebuttals put forward by the opposing team. Their aim should be to strengthen the arguments their team mates have put forward, weaken the Opposition and show why their case is still standing at the end of the debate. The rules allow the third Proposition, but not the third Opposition speaker to add a small point of their own, but in practice, many teams prefer to spend the time on rebuttal. Both speakers will certainly want to add new analysis and possibly new examples to reinforce their case.

Reply speakers
The reply speeches are a chance to reflect on the debate, albeit in a biased way. The speaker should package what has happened in the debate in such a way as to convince the audience, and the judges, that in the three main speeches, their side of the debate came through as the more persuasive. It should not contain new material, with the exception that the Proposition reply speech may need some new rebuttal after the third Opposition speech.

Points of information are allowed in this format in the three main speeches, but not in the reply speeches. The first and last minute of the main speeches are protected. For more information on points of information, see the section on ' the mace format'.

The judging criteria for the WSDC format is 40 per cent content, 40 per cent style and 20 per cent strategy.

The main features of the format as practised at the World Schools Debating Championships are:

- The debate should be approached from a global perspective. The definition should be global with only necessary exceptions. The examples should be global. The arguments should consider how the debate may be different in countries that are, for example, more or less economically developed or more or less democratic.
- The motions should be debated at the level of generality in which they have been worded. In some formats, it is acceptable to narrow down a motion to one example

of the principle, but at WSDC, you are expected to give multiple examples of a wide topic if it is phrased widely.

- The WSDC format gives 40 per cent of its marks to style which is more than many domestic circuits. This means that speakers should slow down (if they are used to racing), think about their language choice and make an effort to be engaging in their delivery.

World Universities/British Parliamentary style

This format is quite different to the three described so far. It is one of the most commonly used formats at university level (the World Universities Debating Championships use it), and it is widely used in schools' competitions hosted by universities in the UK.

It consists of four teams of two: two teams on each side of the motion. The teams on the same side must agree with each other, but debate better than the other teams on the same side in order to win. The teams do not prepare together. At university level, speeches are usually seven minutes long, whereas at school level, they are commonly five minutes. Points of information are allowed in *all* eight speeches and the first and last minute of each speech is protected from them (for more on points of information, see the section on 'the mace format'. The speeches are often given parliamentary names and the order of speeches is as follows:

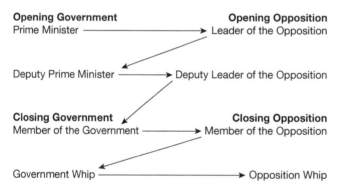

The speaking order in the World Universities or British Parliamentary debate format.

For the roles of the first two speakers on both sides, see the section on 'the mace format'. The roles of the closing teams are as follows:

Members of the government (third speakers on each side)
The third speaker should do substantial rebuttal to what has come before them in the debate if needed. They are also required to move the debate forward with at least one

new argument which is sometimes called an 'extension'. The closing team should not contradict the opening team, but neither can they simply repeat their arguments, having had more time to think about how to put them persuasively.

Whips (fourth speakers on each side)
The whips deliver summary speeches. They should not offer new arguments, but they can (and should) offer new rebuttal and analysis as they synthesise the debate. They should summarise all the key points on their team and try to emphasise why their partner's contribution has been particularly significant.

Debating in the classroom

Teachers should use or invent any format which suits their lessons. Speech length and the number of speakers can vary, as long as they are equal on both sides. The LDC format explained here is often an effective one in the classroom. Points of information can be used or discarded as wanted and the floor debate could be replaced with a question and answer session. Students can be used as the chairperson and timekeeper and the rest of the class can be involved through the floor debate and audience vote. If more class participation is needed, then students could be given peer assessment sheets to fill in as the debate goes on, or they could be journalists who will have to write up an article on the debate for homework.

In the language classroom or with younger pupils, teachers may be free to pick any topic, as the point of the exercise will be to develop the students' speaking and listening skills. Debates, however, can also be a useful teaching tool for delivering content and understanding across the curriculum. Science classrooms could host debates on genetics or nuclear energy; literature lessons can be enhanced with textual debates; geography teachers could choose topics on the environment or globalisation. When assessing the debate, the teacher will need to decide how much, if any, emphasis they are giving to the debating skills of the student and how much to the knowledge and understanding of the topic shown.

In addition to full-length debates, teachers may find it useful to use the topics in this book (and others they generate) for 'hat' debates. Write topics out and put them in a hat. Choose two students and invite them to pick out a topic which they then speak on for a minute each. Or for a variation, let them play 'rebuttal tennis' where they knock points back and forth to each other. This can be a good way to get large numbers of students speaking and can be an engaging starter activity, to introduce a new topic or to review student learning.

SECTION A

Philosophy/political theory

Anarchism

Like many of the views in this chapter, anarchism does not represent a singular or comprehensive ideological position, but a family of competing ones. The common thread that unites anarchist theories is a belief in the unjustifiability of the state and its authority over us. For example, some anarchists argue against the state on the grounds that its authority is not consented to, or that it produces worse outcomes for its citizens, or it unacceptably imposes the values or interests of a certain group upon all citizens of the state. Notably, anarchism can co-exist with many other philosophical positions. For instance, there are 'anarcho-capitalists', who believe that the absence of a state ensures a purer operation of the capitalist system with a truly free market. On the other hand, 'anarcho-socialists' believe that mutual co-operation is a naturally arising result in a stateless world, and will in fact bring about greater equality than any state mechanism could provide.

Pros

[1] Many anarchists' central claim is this: not everyone who must live under the state consents to it, and it is therefore an unacceptable curtailment of that individual's natural autonomy. Natural autonomy matters, because individuals need to make their own moral decisions, or because they are entitled to pursue their own self-interest. The state is no more than a randomly selected group of people which purports to be entitled to make those decisions for us, when in fact, they are not. By imposing its values, the state violates our natural autonomy.

[2] Anarchists recognise that even democracies are essentially repressive institutions in which an educated, privileged elite of politicians and civil servants imposes its will on ordinary citizens. Anarchists want to live in a non-hierarchical world of free association in which individual expression is paramount and all the state's tools of power such as government, taxation, laws and police are done away with. Voting rights and the separation of power are

Cons

[1] There is no doubt that not everyone consents to the state, but that is because to demand that they do would be an absurd requirement for the state's legitimacy. Rather, there is a need for everyone to play by a common set of rules, in order to ensure that basic outcomes like enforcement of the law and a fair distribution of goods can be achieved. Everyone should opt to act by the principle of 'fair play'. If anarchists purport to be moral, then they should favour the outcome of mutually beneficial co-operation. If they deny that they care about moral goods such as fairness and justice, then they are simply rejecting moral argument altogether. This is in itself a deeply defective position.

[2] The answer to the problem of undemocratic democracies is reform, not anarchy. Democracies can be made more representative through devolution, proportional representation and increased use of the referendum. The power relations that are the subject of complaint will inevitably also manifest themselves in the

insufficient tools to combat the power of the state, and democracy as a political system is incompatible with pure anarchy.

[3] Anarchism can produce stable political situations in which people are capable of flourishing while preserving their autonomy. We know that, on a small scale, anarchist co-operatives, usually blended with an element of distribution of wealth, are able to succeed and thrive. More generally, the state encourages us to think only in terms of our blunt self-interest, whereas actually, humans are capable of far greater co-operation, and have a natural predilection for it. This self-reliance of people is not manifested because the state creates the impression that everyone can rely on its structural presence and services.

[4] Even if anarchism is ultimately wrong, it represents a positive presence in political discourse. Because we accept that the state is generally legitimate, we also too readily accept the various impositions that the state makes on our lives. For instance, the 'Occupy' movement provided a valuable counterweight to the dominance of large banks in the aftermath of the global financial crisis (from 2008). The anarchist position opened people's eyes to the abuse of law enforcement and power which ultimately aimed to protect the powerful.

anarchic state. Rich elites will simply buy themselves private armies, or gather all means of production. This time, however, there will not be any means to temper those forces through the benevolent force of the state. The balance of power will be gone entirely. Rather than do away with the state entirely, less rigorous solutions are available to curb the power of the state.

[3] 'Free association' between people (perhaps local co-operation in agriculture or learning or trade), where successful, will be continued and eventually formalised in its optimal form. An anarchic 'state of nature' will inevitably evolve through the formalisation of co-operation on larger scales into something like the societies we now have. There will be an inevitable need for administrators, judges to decide on disputes, and law-enforcement bodies. Anarchism, therefore, is a pointlessly retrograde act – a state of anarchy can never last, because it will never be stable.

[4] Anarchism is often used as a political rationalisation of acts of terrorism and civil disobedience in the name of 'animal rights' or 'ecology'. Even if those are noble goals, these deeds should be seen for what they are – self-indulgent and anti-social acts passed off as an expression of 'anarchist' morality. A true anarchist would not eat, wear or use anything created by those who are part of the organised state. As long as these terrorists and eco-warriors use the fruits of the labour of the members of the hierarchical society they seek to subvert, they are acting hypocritically.

Possible motions

This House supports anarchism.

This House believes that there is no such thing as a legitimate state.

This House believes that citizens of democracies have no obligation to obey laws they believe to be unjust.

This House would require every generation to vote to ratify the treaties that bind them.

This House regrets that 'anarchism' has become a dirty word.

Related topics

Civil disobedience

Democracy

Social contract, existence of the

Terrorism, justifiability of

Animal rights

There are numerous debates about animal rights, ranging from vegetarianism, to the testing of cosmetics or medicines, to laws against animal cruelty in bullfighting. However, many of them share a common and underlying question: what rights, if any, do animals have? It is important to note that denying animal rights does not necessarily equate to saying that unrestrained cruelty to animals is acceptable; rather, it is the denial that they have the particularly strong moral weight afforded by rights. What a right is constitutes a difficult question, and partly one which the debate will inevitably focus on; that said, both teams must be careful to be precise about exactly what having certain rights would entail, rather than using the concept loosely.

Pros

[1] Although animals cannot verbally express their choices, they do form deep and lasting bonds with each other – relatively complex emotions such as grief, affection and joy. To argue that animals are simple beings not worthy of rights aimed to protect their well-being is a deep misunderstanding of their rich emotional life.

[2] Rights are not only granted to beings that contribute to society. They are deeper and more universal than that. For instance, people with severe disabilities, young children and visiting foreigners do not contribute to the state or society that gives and protects rights, but we still afford them certain protections. Similarly, we do not harm individuals who would not be able

Cons

[1] A core function of having a right is to be allowed to make autonomous choices, and to have those choices respected. When we say we have a right to 'free speech', what we really mean is that we can choose what we say and we cannot be forced to say something else. The choices we make define our individuality, and allow us to shape our own lives. Animals do not have the capacity to make choices; they are beings driven by basic urges, and do not have any level of reflective capacity to decide how to live their lives. It would simply be utterly pointless to give animals rights.

[2] Animals do not share in the network of duties and responsibilities that give people

to protest that harm, such as people with mental disabilities, or patients in a coma. On those grounds, animals, who are not part of social life and do not uphold civic duties, should not be excluded from having rights.

[3] One of the reasons for granting rights is the desire to protect sentient beings from cruel and unnecessary pain. Pain is a universally acknowledged bad state of being which we all seek to avoid. Animal pain, as experience, is no different from human pain. The ability to feel pain, however, varies according to the development of the nervous system of the sentient being. Granting rights can be perfectly compatible with that notion. To see this, consider that almost no one thinks that fish and seafood should have the same rights as mammals or birds; that is because their nervous systems are far less developed, so they simply do not feel pain in the same way. However, granting rights can be perfectly compatible with the level of potential pain experience and the rights necessary for protection from unnecessary pain.

rights. Rights are, after all, a human construct, and depend on others observing them; for that reason, to get rights, you must put something into the system that gives you those rights, and that requires contributions to society in the form of taxes, voting and so on. Animals do none of that, so cannot expect to benefit from it. It is simply misguided to think that the way in which we should relate ourselves to animals is to grant them rights in the same way as we grant rights to humans.

[3] Some say that what is relevant is not whether an animal can reason, but whether it can suffer. Whatever the case, animals do not feel pain in the same way as humans; their nervous systems are less developed, and so their pain counts for less than ours. That is particularly important given that animal rights are usually sacrificed to do some good for humans; for instance, to test potentially life-saving medicines. The pain we inflict on an animal through animal testing, for example, is far less devastating to a life than the pain we seek to cure in a human being's life. The animal's pain is 'worth it'. If granting rights to animals means we can no longer test medication on them, we are not weighing up harms and benefits in the right way.

Possible motions

This House would repeal all laws protecting animals.

This House believes that animal rights are a myth.

This House would not eat meat.

Related topics

Animal experimentation and vivisection, banning of

Blood sports, abolition of

Vegetarianism

Zoos, abolition of

Capitalism v. socialism

When the last edition of *Pros and Cons* was published (in 1999), it perhaps appeared as though the fall of the Berlin Wall had settled this topic for most right-thinking people. But since then, numerous developments have revived an interest in investigating the fundamental acceptability of capitalism as an economic system such as the development of 'Gross National Happiness' indexes to measure welfare as more than financial; a growing concern for capitalism's impact on the environment; and of course, the global financial crisis. An important point to remember is that in between the two polar opposites presented here, there is a spectrum of different systems which involve partial regulation by the state of the market and the use of market forces to deliver essential governmental functions.

Pros

[1] The fundamental driving force of human life, and of the natural world as a whole, is competition. Human nature is selfish and competitive, and by allowing this instinct to rule, we have survived as a species. Capitalism recognises this by letting the most successful individuals flourish through hard work and success in an open competitive market. Capitalism is an economic and social version of the 'survival of the fittest'.

[2] Capitalism recognises that it is not society at large but individuals who are the ultimate source of wealth creation and economic growth. It is people's effort which transforms the goods in the natural world into tradable projects or which offers valuable services. People's hard work should be rewarded with the fruits of their labour, instead of penalised with punitive taxes.

[3] The endeavours of the entrepreneur, the landowner or the capitalist in fact benefit not only those individuals but all those millions who work under them, or those who gain work due to their efforts, the so-called subsidiary economies. Individuals

Cons

[1] The natural and human worlds are characterised by co-operation as much as by competition. In nature, species flourish through the practice of 'reciprocal altruism' – mutual helping behaviour. Groups rather than individuals are the unit of selection. Socialism recognises these facts and proposes an equal co-operative society rather than an unnaturally harsh, individualist and competitive one.

[2] The capitalist belief in the autonomy of the individual is a myth. We are all dependent first on our parents, family and social circles, and more broadly on the education, resources, services, industry, technology and agriculture of fellow members of society. A truly 'autonomous individual' would not survive more than a few days. We are all reliant on and responsible for each other, and to encourage self-interest and competition destroys our natural network and capacity to develop ourselves and our projects.

[3] Rich people are not rich just because they have made choices which are more beneficial to themselves and others, but because they have been given numerous

who bring in investment from abroad and create successful enterprises are already benefiting the community at large by creating wealth, employment, better working conditions and an improved quality of life – they should not be required to do so a second time through redistribution of their private wealth.

[4] The socialist system encourages a sense of entitlement and welfare dependency. A capitalist system encourages enterprise and progress. People see that hard work and ingenuity are rewarded and thus they are motivated. In a socialist system where the state provides for all, there is no motivation to work hard, and the elimination of the market halts the processes of competition and selection.

[5] In purely economic terms, free competition is the only way to protect against monopolies. State-owned and state-run monopolies, in the absence of competition, become inefficient, wasteful and bureaucratic, and supply bad overpriced services to the consumer.

advantages which had nothing to do with their choices. Social position (and consequently education, contracts in industry, and good health) and natural attributes (like strength, intelligence and bravery) are in fact nothing but the arbitrary gifts of birth; indeed, ultimately, the propensity to work hard is not something chosen, but something we are born with. Those are not advantages that people deserve.

[4] Socialism is perfectly compatible with hard work, creativity and progress. In a socialist system where the ideology of co-operation is properly projected, no one will seek to be lazy and 'free-ride' off the achievements of others. Moreover, by giving people a basic safety net, socialism allows them to take the kind of risks that lead to great artistic or scientific advances and so makes society better off.

[5] Large-scale industries (such as a state-run health or education service) are more efficient than smaller ones through economies of scale. There is also a 'third way' compatible with socialist ideology, which allows some competition while still retaining ultimate state control of important services.

Possible motions

This House believes that capitalism is a force for good in the world.

This House believes that it is time for workers of the world to unite.

This House believes that capitalism is the best economic system.

Related topics

Marxism
Privatisation

Welfare state
State pensions, ending provision of
Salary capping, mandatory
Bonuses, banning of
Private schools
Inheritance tax at 100 per cent
University education, free for all
Failing companies, bailing out
Fairtrade, we should not support
Sport, regretting the commercialisation of

Censorship by the state

This topic will rarely be set as bluntly as a straightforward question of whether there should be any censorship or not, but rather reflects an underlying theme in numerous debates, about when and where the state should intervene in speech acts. It is important to adapt the arguments below to context; censorship of pornography, for instance, is quite a different question from whether racist political parties should be censored. However, the overarching theme is an age-old one, dating back at least to Plato, and remains very important.

Pros

[1] Freedom of speech is never an absolute right but an aspiration. It ceases to be a right when it causes harm to something we all recognise the value of; for example, legislating against incitement to racial hatred. Therefore, it is not the case that censorship is wrong in principle.

[2] Certain types of literature or visual image have been conclusively linked to crime. Excessive sex and violence in film and television have been shown (especially in studies in the USA) to contribute to a tendency towards similar behaviour in spectators. There is a direct causal link between such images and physical harm.

[3] Censorship acts to preserve free speech, but puts it on a level playing field. Those who argue for unregulated speech miss the point that it is not only state imposition that can silence minorities, but also their social denigration by racists, sexists, homophobes or other bigots. So it may be necessary, for instance, to outlaw racial epithets in order to ensure that black people are treated fairly in the public space and so have a chance to express their views.

[4] By censoring speech, we are able to stop new recruits being drawn over to the 'dark side' of racist or discriminatory groups. While it may 'drive them underground', that is where we want them; in that way,

Cons

[1] Censorship is wrong in principle. However violently we may disagree with a person's point of view or mode of expression, they must be free to express themselves in a free and civilised society. Anti-incitement laws can be distinguished on the grounds that the causal connection between speech and physical harm is so close, whereas in most censorship it is far more distant.

[2] In fact, the link between sex and violence on screen and in real life is far from conclusive. To say that those who watch violent films are more likely to commit crime does not establish the causal role of the films; it is equally likely that those who opt to watch such material already have such tendencies, which are manifested both in their choice of viewing and their behaviour. Moreover, such censorship might actually worsen their real-world behaviour, as they no longer have any release in the form of fantasy.

[3] The state simply cannot be trusted with the power to control what people can say, because it is itself often discriminatory towards minorities. If we give the state the power to, for instance, regulate the press, it might well misuse this to prohibit minorities from speaking out against the ways they have been abused by the government.

they are unable to get new followers, so their pernicious views cannot spread. This may entrench the views of some, but they were unlikely to be convinced anyway, so outright bans are a better approach.

Possible motions

This House believes that censorship has no place in a free society.

This House would allow anyone to say anything at any time.

This House believes that free speech is an absolute right.

Related topics

Protective legislation v. individual freedom

Pornography

Extremist political parties, banning of

Press, state regulation of the

Privacy of public figures

[4] Censorship such as legislation against incitement to racial hatred drives racists and others underground and thus entrenches and ghettoises that section of the community, rather than drawing its members into open and rational debate. This makes it harder to challenge their views, and thus to convince wavering members of such groups that their leaders are wrong.

Civil disobedience

Civil disobedience comes in many forms; the central point is that it is the refusal to obey certain laws to make a political point. Such disobedience can either be largely passive (for instance, a refusal to pay taxes) or can actively aim to disrupt a system of government (by sit-ins or property damage), and can be violent (arguably, for instance, the London riots in 2011) or non-violent (the 'Occupy' movement). The common aim, however, is to change the law. An interesting angle on the debate is to question some of the classic examples of 'success' for civil disobedience; for instance, were Gandhi's protests really as important as the canons of history have it in obtaining Indian independence, or did violent, more formalised efforts have a large impact?

Pros

[1] Democratic governments which are elected only every four to five years do not provide true or adequate representation of public interests. Once a government is elected, it may entirely ignore the will of the electorate until its term is finished. Therefore, civil disobedience is necessary as an effective method for the people's

Cons

[1] In fact, democratic means are much broader than a general election every few years. The election of local representatives takes place regularly. In Britain, MPs are available in 'surgery' with their constituents every week and will always respond to letters and bring matters of concern to the attention of ministers. Other countries

voice to be heard even in democratic countries – as a last resort. For example, the protests over student fees in the UK after the 2010 election were designed to reinforce the perception that Liberal Democrat MPs had 'betrayed' those who voted for them by changing their position.

[2] Historically, civil disobedience has triumphed over insidious regimes and forms of prejudice where other methods have failed; e.g. the movements orchestrated in India by Gandhi and in America by Martin Luther King. Riots and looting in Indonesia in 1998 protested against a corrupt and undemocratic regime, leading to the fall of President Suharto. Peaceful protests by minorities in undemocratic countries are often banned or quashed, or they can fail to bring about change. Nonetheless, civil disobedience movements can be entirely peaceful (e.g. Gandhi).

[3] Civil disobedience involving public confrontation with authority is often the only way to bring an issue to wider public and international attention. This tactic was successfully employed by the 'suffragettes' of the early women's movement, and also by supporters of nuclear disarmament, from the philosopher Bertrand Russell, who was arrested for civil disobedience several times in the cause of pacifism, to attacks in the USA and UK on military bases involved in the Iraq War (2003 to 2011). The student protests in Tiananmen Square (Beijing) in 1989 (and their brutal crushing by the authorities) brought the human rights abuses of the Chinese regime to the forefront of international attention and concern more effectively than anything else before or since; by contrast, during the 2008 Olympics, the Chinese government sought to close off opportunities for civil disobedience, to prevent a 'second Tiananmen'.

have comparable systems. Given this direct democratic access to government, through letter writing and lobbying, there is no need for civil disobedience.

[2] Peaceful protest is quite possible, even in an undemocratic society, without resorting to civil disobedience. A point can be made quite well without coming into confrontation with police, trespassing or causing disturbance and damage to people or property. Legal systems are the most effective way of protecting the vulnerable and minorities; once they break down, there is no way of protecting the most vulnerable. A good example of the unintended consequences of civil disobedience is Egypt's Arab Spring in 2011; while there is no doubt that President Mubarak's regime perpetrated significant crimes against women, the law and order vacuum after the revolution led to a significant spike in sexual abuse.

[3] There is no excuse for provoking violent confrontations with police, rioting, looting or trespassing. Such actions result in assaults, injuries and sometimes in deaths. For instance, while those who started the London riots in 2011 may have had a political or social message, they created a tidal wave of violence which the police were unable to restrain, that led to many people being seriously injured or killed.

Possible motions
This House supports civil disobedience.
This House would rage against the machine.
This House would break the law to protect the
    cause of justice.

Related topics
Anarchism
Democracy
Terrorism, justifiability of
Social movements: courts v. legislatures

Democracy

Those who live and have grown up in democracies tend to assume that it is the only viable system of government. It is important to question that premise, and challenge the system in which many of us live; there may be many circumstances in which we want to constrain democracy, or perhaps we should genuinely look to a completely different system of government, which leaves that behind altogether in favour of government by an expert elite.

Pros

[1] A country should be governed by representatives – chosen by every (adult) member of society – who are answerable to, and removable by, the people. This way, a minority, wealthy, landowning, military or educated elite will not be allowed disproportionate power. This ideal of the liberal democratic society was established by the French and American revolutions and is endorsed as the ideal method of government around the world.

[2] Certainly, modern democracies could be made more truly democratic, and this is happening through increased use of referenda (e.g. the French and Dutch referenda on the Lisbon Treaty (2005), the UK's referendum on the Alternative Vote (2011) and American states' referenda on gay marriage) and proportional representation (e.g. in the Scottish Parliament and the Welsh Assembly). Democracy is brought closer to the people by devolving power to local government. People also have a direct voice through access to repre-

Cons

[1] Modern 'democracies' are a sham. Such a system is impossible except on a very small scale. For a large country, decisive and effective leadership and government are incompatible with true democracy. Therefore, we have supposedly democratic systems in which the people have a say every four to five years, but have no real input into important decisions. Thus, the principle of democracy is not one we all really believe in at all.

[2] These measures are mere tokens – rhetorical gestures required to keep the people happy and to satisfy proponents of democracy. But the truth is still that real power is isolated within an elite of politicians and civil servants. It is the political parties that decide who will stand for election and who will be allocated the 'safe seats', thereby effectively, undemocratically, determining the constitution of parliaments. There are rarely provisions to 'recall' elected politicians if they fail to live up to their promises.

sentatives throughout their term of office (in Britain, through MPs' weekly 'surgeries'). A genuinely democratic system is very much a possibility, and not something we should eschew just because it cannot live up to an ancient idealised system.

[3] Democracy undeniably does not give the population absolute control of every decision made in a society, but that is an impossible ideal. Rather, democracy's value lies in the possibility of the populace removing the government every four or five years. This serves two purposes. First, it trims the worst excesses of government policy; if governments do truly unacceptable things, they will be stopped (for instance, George W. Bush's foreign policy, including the use of torture, was a key factor in America's swing to the Democrats in 2008). Second, it means that on a general level, public policy will reflect the will of the people, even if that is just a general choice between left and right.

[4] Democratic transitions are undeniably painful, but it is always a good idea to start on the road to democracy; imperfect democracy must always be compared with the human rights violations of a strong authoritarianism; it is not plausible that the Kenyan people are worse off now, even with the 2008 violence, than they were in the early 1990s under a one-party regime. It is also noteworthy that few of these problems lie with democracy itself; rather, they relate to the specific configurations of institutions adopted, which can rightly vary according to context to contain these problems. South Africa, for instance, after apartheid ended in 1994, adopted a well-designed Constitution that has prevented political competition falling back into violence.

[3] Modern politics is simply too complex for democracy to offer any meaningful choice to individuals. We do not select stances on individual issues, but pick from a predetermined 'bundle' of choices offered by a party or candidate, which means we exercise almost no choice over any given policy. This leads instead to a distortion by rhetoric, as politicians compete to position their 'ideology' in voters' minds, rather than actually engaging in honest debate. We would be better to seek alternative methods of accountability, rather than deluding ourselves that a modern, sound-bite-driven and highly financed electoral campaign works as one.

[4] On a more practical level, democratic transitions are often not a good idea for countries that currently have an alternative system of government. Democracy explodes political competition, and it may be that a society is simply not ready for it. Where institutions like the police and courts are weak, violence may ensue; the 'Ocampo Six' who were indicted in 2011 by the International Criminal Court (ICC) over electoral violence in Kenya represent the worst excesses of this tendency. In addition, where political parties and the media are weak, politicians turn to tribal ethnic groups, which can in turn spiral into violence and oppression; for instance, Malaysia, which is democratic in a formal sense, still hugely oppresses its minorities.

Possible motions

This House believes that democracy is the best system of government for every nation.

This House would prefer a benign dictatorship to a weak democracy.

This House believes that 'democracy is the worst system of government apart from all the others that have been tried' (Winston Churchill).

Related topics

House of Lords, elected v. appointed

Proportional representation

Referenda, increased use of

Monarchy, abolition of

Voting, compulsory

Voting age, reduction of

Term limits for politicians

Democracy, imposition of

Judges, election of

Social movements: courts v. legislatures

State funding of political parties

Marxism

In one sense, Marxism refers to the array of beliefs held by German philosopher and social critic Karl Marx, the intellectual founding father of communism. But as time has passed, clearly Marxist ideas have been put to a variety of different uses, many with obvious regrettable consequences (such as Soviet oppression). This debate should focus on retaining the core ideas of a Marxist theory, without simply harping on about the failures of certain past attempts to put them into practice. Another important point is that there are many sensible alternatives to Marxism that are themselves very different; this topic presumes that Marxism is being compared with a broadly egalitarian distribution of wealth favoured by philosophers such as John Rawls, who argued that we should only accept inequalities in so far as they benefit the least well-off in society. Marxism, however, favours a much more radical restructuring of society that goes well beyond redistributive taxation.

Pros

[1] The central tenet of Marxism is that the core of politics is class struggle; we should not accept redistributions of income that ultimately leave the central structures of the class system intact, and allow the rich access to large amounts of political power, as well as control of top jobs. Instead, we should move towards communal models of ownership where all such inequalities are abolished.

[2] Inequality is too deeply embedded in our social system for tinkering at the edges to effect any real change. The power of the

Cons

[1] The abolition of class is not a realistic or desirable objective. Inevitably, in any real communist system, certain elites will develop which in fact have considerable power, and will perpetuate this power through the same types of network as the upper classes do currently. Moreover, while we should undoubtedly seek to abolish the inequalities which lead to children being born into higher classes, that does not mean that class itself is damaging; rather, on a basic level, it simply means that people do the jobs that they are best suited for.

elite is perpetuated through political funding, educational institutions, cultural prestige and myriad other subtle techniques of social control. Therefore, the only way to change society sufficiently is a revolutionary abolition of private property and existing state institutions, so that we can start again from scratch.

[3] The free market is inherently unequal and exploitative. In particular, it allocates excess profits to those who control capital, and allows them to exploit their employees. Labourers become wage slaves who have no choice but to work for those who control society's resources, even though they receive far less than they are actually worth. Moreover, even with labour protection laws, they are still subject to the whims of their capitalist masters, easily hireable and fireable, with little power to control their own lives.

[4] No one deserves any advantages that they obtain under the capitalist system. Not only are their social advantages, such as education and inheritance, morally arbitrary and not chosen, but their natural attributes, like intelligence and strength, are also just things they are born with, and therefore they do not deserve advantages from them. Even the propensity for hard work can be seen as an arbitrary trait of birth, rather than a source of moral worth.

[2] Institutions do not encode any particular power structure; they are neutral tools that can be used to whatever ends the government of the day wants. We can perfectly well promote equality within a system that acknowledges private property; indeed, by having property assets that are divisible, we allow for their redistribution; in communal systems, the 'ownership' of such assets may be less transparent.

[3] Nothing about the market is inherently exploitative; markets are simply efficient means for allocating goods to people. If people want something enough, then they will be willing to pay for it, and this is the basic principle of the market. The same is true of employment; people are paid precisely what they are worth to others, providing they are willing to work for it. Where generous welfare systems exist, no one is truly compelled to labour.

[4] It ridiculously strips people of all of the attributes that make them unique and individual to say that they do not deserve anything based on their attributes at birth rather than things they have chosen. Attributes of birth are essential components of who we are, and we should be unwilling to sacrifice them.

Possible motions

This House believes that workers of the world should unite.
This House would abolish private property.
This House believes that modern politics needs more Marxism.

Related topics

Capitalism v. socialism
Privatisation
Welfare state
Monarchy, abolition of
Salary capping, mandatory

Pacifism

In one of the most famous debates at the Oxford Union, the motion 'This House will in no circumstances fight for its King and Country' was passed in 1933 by 275 votes to 153. It sparked off a national controversy in the press, and Winston Churchill denounced it as 'that abject, squalid, shameless avowal' and 'this ever shameful motion'. It is rumoured that the vote gave Adolf Hitler confidence that Great Britain would not militarily oppose his expansion in Europe. Pacifism is therefore a debating topic that is of more than passing interest, but of real historical significance.

Pros

[1] Pacifists are committed to the view that it is always wrong intentionally to kill. This view is obviously a difficult one to sustain in the face of certain dramatic counter-examples, but two things must be borne in mind. First, few, if any, modern wars are really wars of self-defence, national or personal; rather, they are about foreign expansion or intervention. Second, there is nothing wrong with the notion of absolute morality; it simply requires that some individuals are ready to accept bad consequences for themselves in order to remain morally pure.

[2] Pacifists such as the 'conscientious objectors' of the two world wars (some of whom were executed for their refusal to fight) have always served an invaluable role in questioning the prevailing territorial militarism of the majority. Pacifists say there is always another way. The carnage of the First World War and the Vietnam War in particular is now seen by many as appallingly futile and wasteful of human life.

[3] There are no true victors from a war. Issues are rarely settled by a war, but persist afterwards at the cost of millions of lives. There are still territorial and national disputes and civil wars in Syria, Sudan and

Cons

[1] Ultimately, pacifism is too absolute a stance; in the end, it reduces to the position that it is wrong to kill someone, even if they are attempting, very directly, to kill you. It could be argued that if a pacifist is unwilling to accept this, then they do not really believe in pacifism.

[2] Pacifism was a luxury that most could not afford during the world wars. There was a job to be done to maintain international justice and prevent the expansion of an aggressor. In those circumstances, it is morally wrong to sit back and do nothing.

[3] Often, disputes can persist after wars, but often also some resolution is achieved (e.g. the Second World War, or the Gulf War in 1991 – as a result of which Saddam Hussein withdrew from Kuwait). Violent conflict is a last resort, but is shown by evolutionary biology to be an inevitable fact of nature, and by history to be an inevitable fact of international relations. Nations should determine their own settlements and boundaries and this, regrettably, sometimes involves the use of force.

Southern Yemen despite the world wars and countless supposed settlements. War in these cases is futile and the United Nations (UN) should do more to enforce peace in these areas.

Possible motions

This House would be pacifist.

This House would never fight for King and Country.

Related topics

National service, (re)introduction of

Armaments, limitations on conventional

Dictators, assassination of

United Nations standing army

Military drones, prohibition of

Nuclear weapons, right to possess

Privatisation

Privatisation is the process of the state selling off its assets in certain industries and allowing a competitive free market to deal with those sectors instead. It spans largely corporate projects like nationalised mining, to utilities provision (electricity, water, gas, etc.), to public services (healthcare, education, etc.). The core of the debate remains the same, although the urgency of it may vary; for instance, we might be far more worried about the state selling off hospitals than about losing a government-owned car manufacturer.

Pros

[1] Privatisation is the most efficient way to provide public services. State-run bureaucracies will always be inefficient because they know that there is a government bailout waiting for them if they overspend, or fail to cut costs or sack staff. Moreover, governments tend to be more responsive to union pressure than private companies, and this prevents the mass sackings that are necessary to trim bloated government agencies.

[2] Private businesses in a free market are in competition and must therefore seek to attract customers by reducing prices and improving services. This means they cannot provide a sub-par service, because

Cons

[1] There is more to providing a good service than ruthless efficiency, free market economics and the drive to make profits. The vulnerable sectors of society will always suffer from privatisation. People in isolated villages will have their unprofitable public transport scrapped. Treating elderly patients will not represent an efficient targeting of medical resources. Public ownership ensures that health, education and the utilities are run with the underpinning of a moral conscience.

[2] It is misleading to identify privatisation with deregulation. Monopolies can be ended through deregulation without the government giving up its control of a

they will simply lose customers; a similar thing happens if they charge more than people are willing to pay. Businesses are motivated by profit, and so will work to ensure that they do not lose money by failing to improve service.

[3] Privatisation gives ordinary people a chance to be 'stakeholders' in the nation's economy by owning shares in services and industries. Privatised industries and services are answerable to shareholders. Having a real financial stake in a company gives people a direct interest and a say in the running of national services.

[4] Privatisation reduces the pressures on government finances; there is no longer the constant spectre of inefficient companies needing bailouts or making losses that the state cannot afford to sustain. Moreover, private companies can raise money for investment from the market rather than having to turn to their national treasury; in this way, they use private capital to serve the public interest.

Possible motions
This House would privatise.
This House would sell off its assets.
This House would trim the bloated state.

Related topics
Capitalism v. socialism
Marxism
Welfare state
BBC, privatisation of the
State pensions, ending provision of
Private schools
Arts funding by the state, abolition of

state-owned and/or state-run element within an open market. A state-run service operating within an open market, drawing finance from the private sector and giving ordinary people a chance to invest, can be highly effective in promoting competition without sacrificing the public interest; for instance, in South Africa, the state-owned airline SAA competes healthily against private sector competitors. In addition, the supply of certain services, like water or trains, is a 'natural monopoly', which means that no competition is really possible; in such cases, the state must control them to keep prices low, rather than allowing companies to overcharge consumers.

[3] It is a fantasy to suppose that private individuals who are shareholders or stakeholders exercise any power over privatised industries. The only way to guarantee accountability to the people is for utilities and services to be run by the government, which is truly open to influence through the democratic processes.

[4] Nationalised industries, if used properly, can be profit-making. For instance, when many governments nationalised banks in 2008, they did so on the basis that they would run them at a profit, and eventually sell them off; this plan is proving broadly successful, and the US and UK governments will almost certainly turn a profit on those nationalisations. Nationalised industry can be a gain for all.

Protective legislation v. individual freedom

This topic clearly underlies numerous other debates, and essentially focuses on the point at which the state should step in to prevent individuals from harming themselves. No one thinks that the state should protect us from all harmful choices; every activity includes a certain level of risk, which individuals must be able to assume to live a meaningful, enjoyable life. But there are many activities that the state does regulate on the grounds that they are 'irrational', such as smoking (by punitive taxation) or drug taking, which many think that the state should not interfere with.

Pros

[1] We all accept that, in essence, the state should be able to prevent harm to others arising from individual action; but so few dangerous actions are genuinely not at all harmful to others that this principle extends to allowing the state to prevent individuals from harming themselves. For instance, when individuals become addicted to alcohol or gambling, they do great damage to their families, both financially and psychologically. Because no one can extract themselves from the web of social relations that expose us to damage by those around us, the state must instead step in to make us safe from their behaviour.

[2] The state must also legislate to protect its citizens from self-imposed damage. It is the responsibility of an elected government to research the dangers of certain practices or substances and constrain the freedoms of its members for their own safety. In particular, the state is right to step in where individuals are imperfectly equipped to make choices, or risk destroying their capacity to make good choices later. For instance, where people will become addicted, or harm themselves in an irreparable way, the state should stop them so doing.

Cons

[1] Legislation is required to constrain and punish those who act to reduce our individual freedoms; for example, those violent criminals who threaten our freedom from fear and attack. Its role is to protect our freedoms, not to curtail them. Of course, many dangerous actions also have an impact to some extent on other people, but this misses the point; the question is whether the government should take any legislative action designed to prevent such actions.

[2] The libertarian principle is that people can do whatever they wish, as long as it does not harm others – and this must mean that they are allowed to hurt themselves. If consenting adults wish to indulge in sadomasochism, bare-knuckle boxing, or driving without a seat belt (which endangers no one other than themselves), then there is no reason for the state to prevent them. The role of the state is, at most, to provide information about the risks of such activities. Nothing about those choices needs to be irrational; indeed, even becoming addicted to smoking might be seen as a rational choice which individuals make, fully apprised of the risks.

[3] A further role of the state is to provide children with certain basic opportunities and protection. We allow the state to take it upon itself to make certain of these compulsory, in order to protect children from ill-informed decisions they may make themselves, or from irresponsible parents. In the past, parents would curtail children's schooling to utilise them as labour to bring in family income. In preventing this, the state curtails freedoms for the good of the individual children and for the long-term benefits to society of an educated and healthy population.

[3] The case is not the same with children, who do need to be protected and guided prior to full intellectual and moral maturity. However, the principle still applies that the freedom of independent morally mature individuals is paramount. The state has gone too far in making educational and medical opportunities compulsory. The parent is naturally, biologically, responsible for the care of the child. If parents wish to educate their child at home or not at all, or have religious objections to medical interferences with their child, then as parents, their views must prevail – those of certain Christian beliefs object to blood transfusions, and however harsh it seems, it must be their right to prescribe the same for their family.

Possible motions

This House believes that the state should not protect individuals from themselves.

This House would allow people to make bad choices.

Related topics

Welfare state

Drugs, legalisation of

Alcohol, prohibition of

Boxing, banning of

Smoking, banning of

Euthanasia, legalisation of

Polygamy, legalisation of

Social contract, existence of the

Obviously, the social contract is a metaphor, but it is relied upon with disturbing regularity as obviously being something which exists and binds all members of a society. That view is a bad one, and wrong; however, there may be other ways of arguing for a social contract which stand up to more scrutiny. Be careful, however, to establish what exactly it is that this 'contract' might sign us up for; many social contract arguments only aim to legitimate any kind of state, not a specific set of government policies.

Pros

[1] Without a state to govern us, we would all live in a 'state of nature', which would be violent, unco-operative and unproductive – ultimately not beneficial for anyone. Thus, if we were to be in such a state of nature, we would all agree to sign up to a state, because it would definitely be in our interests to do so.

[2] Humans did in the past consent to live in states. Not everyone alive today consents to the state, but that is because it is totally impractical to have a new consensual state-building process every time a new person enters the world. Rather, we are bound by the consent of our ancestors; that is what made the state legitimate in the first place.

[3] Citizens, in fact, consent to their states on a daily basis. They pay taxes, vote in elections, and use the state's services. All of these choices amount to consent to the state, because they provide it with the means to operate.

[4] Citizens do not leave their states; this amounts to 'tacit consent'. There are many places around the world that closely resemble a state of nature (conflict zones, or places like Somalia where the state has collapsed almost completely). If the state is so terrible, anarchists are welcome to go and live there, but they choose not to.

Cons

[1] Even if all of this were true, it is unclear what work the idea of a 'contract' is doing. No one actually agreed to anything; it is simply argued that they would have done, because certain goods and interests are protected by the existence of a state that would not be protected otherwise. But in that case, there is no need to appeal to the idea of consent; we can just argue for the state on the basis of those goods directly. Indeed, the attempt to smuggle in a consent argument aims to give the state an air of legitimacy that it does not deserve.

[2] This is simply an absurd historical fiction. States came about because powerful people wished to own land and exert violence in support of that landowning; there was no 'contractual moment' in the history of our states. In any case, if there were, why should it bind us today? The point of the social contract argument is about consent; that presumably requires our consent, rather than somebody else's.

[3] Voting does not represent consent to the state for two reasons: first, because we might think the state was totally illegitimate while desiring some control over how it is run; second, because many people vote for the losing side, so how do they 'consent'? Similarly, use of public services is, in many cases, something out of which we cannot opt (clean air, national defence); and in other cases (such as healthcare), we may still want it, even if we wish it were not provided for us by the state.

[4] Not leaving a coercive force does not amount to accepting it. First, for many people, the cost of emigration is simply prohibitively expensive, and the demand

that is made on them by asking them to leave their states is an unreasonable one, because they have families and lives built up there. Second, the world is covered entirely in sovereign states; even the worst examples have notional governments with police forces and law courts to enforce them. We can only hop from state to state, but we cannot go and live somewhere without one, which is the option that would be required to establish tacit consent.

Utilitarianism

Utilitarianism is almost certainly the best known moral framework, but it is often used imprecisely. That is perhaps the fault of the slogan coined by Jeremy Bentham (1776) in *A Fragment on Government*, advocating the 'greatest happiness of the greatest number'. But as a moment's reflection shows, that is not one principle, but two. There might be some hypothetical situations where we can, for instance, increase 20 people's happiness by one unit, or 10 people's by three units; in such a case, the 'greatest happiness' would commend the latter, but the 'greatest number' would commend the former. Put simply, utilitarians believe in creating the greatest amount of happiness possible. That may sound like an intuitively plausible claim, but as the following arguments show, it is far from obvious that utilitarianism is the correct moral worldview. This raises a final important point; utilitarianism may be deployed in many debates, but it must be argued for. Simply to say 'According to John Stuart Mill's principle of utilitarianism . . .' does not advance the debate.

Pros

[1] The great advantage of happiness as a benefit to promote is that it is universal. Everyone knows what happiness feels like, and everyone feels it at least some of the time; thus, we are not simply encoding some people's desires as being the things which matter, but working off a physical human good. Moreover, in essence, the pursuit of happiness guides all human action; for that reason, we should

Cons

[1] The truth is that while we can all say 'I am happy', we have no idea whether the good experienced is the same for all people, or in fact radically different. Conceptions of exactly what happiness is diverge hugely. Is it short-term pleasure, or is that a life, as Mill said, 'fit only for swine'? Or is it long-term satisfaction in doing well at your job and in your life? And if so, how are those things to be

seek to promote it for others as we do ourselves.

[2] Utilitarianism allows us to make trade-offs. A rights-based or duty-based ethical theory may leave us with unsolvable conflicts; when the right to life and the right to bodily autonomy conflict in the case of torturing a terrorist for potentially life-saving information, how are we to decide which one is more important? By contrast, utilitarianism is simply a matter of totting up the numbers, and this, at least in principle, gives us an answer. Moreover, work in behavioural economics and psychology has given us a much better idea of how actually to measure happiness; now, more than ever, utilitarianism can guide real-world choice making.

[3] Utilitarianism is a highly egalitarian doctrine; it treats happiness as of equal worth, regardless of who possesses it. Moreover, because people who are worse off tend to gain more happiness from small incremental increases in their resources, utilitarianism is also radically redistributive, requiring us to give money to the poorest until each transfer does not make them more happy than the corresponding loss of happiness for the rich.

[4] Utilitarianism simply does not allow these kinds of abuses with any regularity, because their impact on happiness is so severe. 'Rule-utilitarians' believe that rights can be justified on the grounds that rules need to be imposed on human action to maximise happiness, because otherwise biases and the difficulties of decision making in any given case overwhelm us. Moreover, if torture is, in the end, the utility-maximising act, then so be it; that does not mean it is not what we should do.

prioritised? The truth is that utilitarianism is just as guilty as other philosophies of simply taking one group's preferences and treating them as universals.

[2] In theory, utilitarianism might allow for easy trade-offs; but in practice, that is absurd. We do not know how to value happiness; we do not know if everyone experiences it with the same intensity, or whether some people can get happier than others. We also do not know how to measure it; as such, it is not at all useful in making real-world choices.

[3] If we want our moral theories to care about equality, then we can build equality into them. The problem with utilitarianism is that it has no interest at all in equality. In the classic thought experiment of the Utility Monster, we imagine that some person can generate infinite happiness from society's resources; we would therefore be obligated to give all the resources to that monster. Obviously there is no real-life monster, but there are many people who cannot benefit from resources in the same way as others, especially people with severe disabilities; utilitarianism might require us, in fact, to deprive them of resources.

[4] Utilitarianism imposes no limits whatsoever on what may be done to a person in pursuit of the greater good; it erodes individual rights. No one would want to live in a world where it is possible for anything to be done to them by the state; torture, murder, etc. all become fair game. While they may rarely be the utilitarian course, the fact that they are in principle not barred is deeply troubling, as it shows that we are sacrificing personal bodily autonomy altogether. Utilitarianism errs by having only one value.

Possible motions
This House would maximise happiness.
This House would be utilitarian.

Related topics
Capitalism v. socialism
Welfare state
Terrorist suspects, torture of

Welfare state

The essence of the welfare state is that it provides benefits and services to everyone in a country, regardless of their ability to pay. It is founded on a belief that everyone deserves equal quality of certain essential public services, regardless of how much they earn. Objections can be both ideological (it rewards the undeserving) and practical (it provides poor outcomes). There are major definitional issues in this debate; teams should attempt to broadly agree on an expansive but imperfectly defined mass of things that the welfare state covers, ranging from schools to unemployment benefits.

Pros

[1] Society should provide free education (arguably including university education), healthcare, unemployment and sickness benefits, and old age pensions for all. These are fundamental rights in a humane society (and the yardstick of a civilised society is sometimes said to be how well it looks after its pensioners).

[2] State-owned and state-run welfare services are the property of the nation and therefore should be available to all. They are a physical manifestation of the responsibility of society to each of its members. Everyone pays tax, and so everyone should receive free welfare.

[3] In the interest of equality, there should be no private education, health services or pensions. The state should have a monopoly on the welfare state in order to ensure truly efficient welfare – through economies of scale and centralisation – which is also egalitarian. The best resources can be distributed within the public system rather than being creamed off for the elite who

Cons

[1] State welfare should be provided not as a matter of course, but only in cases of extreme need. The welfare state should function only as a safety net. Even in communist countries and in post-war Britain, where there was great enthusiasm for these ideas, economic realities have made free welfare for all an unrealisable dream.

[2] Society is responsible to all its members, but equally, its members should not all receive welfare if they can afford private healthcare, education and pensions. All state benefits should be means-tested so that only the truly needy receive them.

[3] It is fair that those who are hard-working and successful should be able to buy superior education and better healthcare, since these are not rights, but luxuries or privileges which may be paid for. Privatisation of healthcare, education and pensions means competition on the free market and therefore better and cheaper services.

can afford private schools and private healthcare.

[4] More equal societies almost always do better on a wide range of metrics of well-being. Reduced stress and increased community cohesion lead to hugely positive outcomes for individuals, including longer life expectancies, reduced crime and greater reported levels of happiness.

[4] While welfare states may make many people better off, they do so by unacceptably lowering the quality of life of the most successful people within society. Those people should not be used as a social safety net for the failings of others; rather, they should be allowed to live in peace and enjoy the property they have worked for without state interference.

Possible motions

This House believes in the welfare state.

This House believes that only the desperately poor should receive state benefits.

Related topics

Capitalism v. socialism

Marxism

Privatisation

State pensions, ending provision of

Private schools

University education, free for all

SECTION B

Constitutional/governance

Churches in politics

In an increasingly secular world, does the Church still have anything left to say about social and political issues, or should it be confined to the realm of private spirituality? And if it does have anything to say about political matters, will anybody listen? Or is it the case that, in a multicultural society, only democratically elected politicians should have the authority to shape social and economic policy?

Pros

[1] Religion and politics cannot be compartmentalised. The idea that there is a clear line between religion and politics is recent in origin and wholly artificial. From the Hebrew prophets, through Jesus to Mohammed, religious leaders have always linked spiritual progress with social change. The fight against poverty, disease, social injustice and economic inequalities as practised and preached by Jesus, for example, is an explicitly political agenda. It is right that churches should continue to take political stands. There is no such thing as 'private' morality or religion – these are inherently social phenomena.

[2] Religion has played a progressive role in society through history and retains it today. The first attack on the divine right of kings can be found in the Book of Kings in the Bible. Slavery was first prohibited by Jewish religious leaders 2,500 years before Lord Wilberforce. From Martin Luther King to the Beveridge Report, it has been religion that has inspired society's betterment.

[3] Religious leaders do not rely on the support of companies, organisations or political parties. In times of political consensus, we need such people to defend those in society who have no voice. Religious leaders can fulfil a unique role as genuine critics of the abuses and wrongs

Cons

[1] Politics and religion are separate spheres of life. Religious leaders can seek to influence people's private moral and spiritual needs and politicians should be left to deal with broader social and political matters. Church attendances are plummeting. Standards of private morality are at an all-time low. These are the priorities that religious leaders should be tackling, leaving debates about health service reform, social security systems, defence spending and international aid to the politicians who are elected to make decisions on these matters.

[2] The encroachment of religion into politics is inherently dangerous in the modern world. The accountability of political leaders is essential to avoid corruption and self-interest – yet religious leaders can by their very nature not be accountable in the same way. It is true that in the past, religion and politics were inextricably linked, but that is no longer the case. In the modern democratic world, there are secular political mechanisms to ensure representation for the poor and underprivileged without religious interference.

[3] The potential political power of religious leaders is vast. For this reason alone, they are open to 'hijacking' by political extremists. The extremes and certainties of

of the secular world – a position that no secular figure could take without being accused of hypocrisy. This is the traditional role that was played by Biblical prophets such as Jeremiah and Hosea.

religion have no place in a political life that must be about compromise and pragmatism. Democratically unaccountable religious leaders straying into politics can be responsible for whipping up public outcry by peddling their extreme and zealous views (e.g. in favour of the death penalty or against homosexual marriages). Religious leaders should restrict themselves to preaching to their flocks about religion and morality.

Possible motions

This House believes that religion is and should be a political force.

This House believes that religion and politics should mix.

Related topics

Disestablishment of the Church of England

Monarchy, abolition of

God, existence of

Religious teaching in schools

Extremist political parties, banning of

An extremist political party could come from the extremes of the political left, but at present the most prominent are on the far right. Many European countries, such as the Netherlands, have seen a rise in support for far-right parties. Is the correct response to this to ban them? Can the restriction of democracy be justified by the harm these parties cause? A Proposition team may wish to consider how they define 'extremism' and who would make the ultimate decisions about which parties to ban.

Pros

[1] Extremist political parties harm minorities within society by allowing prejudice and discrimination to be openly peddled. This makes minorities feel marginalised and often unsafe. Allowing the British National Party (BNP) to stand with a manifesto underpinned by racial hatred makes immigrants feel unwelcome in the UK. Banning these parties shows our desire to protect minorities and is a sign of being a civilised, inclusive society.

Cons

[1] Everyone has the right to freedom of speech. People may feel offended by the rhetoric of the far right, but a democracy should be tolerant of their views. Many countries have laws preventing the spread of racial hatred and political parties have to stay within these limits. This is a better way of controlling hate speech than banning the parties outright.

[2] Extremist political parties do not increase prejudice; they reflect prejudice in

[2] Extremist political parties increase the amount of prejudice within society as they legitimise these views and give a platform for the dissemination of prejudice. If the National Front has the chance to campaign alongside the Socialist Party, then it appears their views are respectable and a genuine choice. As the rhetoric of the far right is often very seductive, it will use this to win support. The National Front won 17 per cent of the vote in the first ballot of the French elections in 2002, beating the Socialist Party.

[3]Extremist political parties can affect the whole political discourse. It is not possible to assume that they will not attract any popular support. In Austria, the far-right Freedom Party won 28 per cent of the vote in 1999 and formed a coalition government. Even a party which wins very few seats can find itself holding the balance of power after an election. This means they can win important concessions to join a coalition. Their presence on the ballot paper can also lead to mainstream parties being forced further to the right on issues such as immigration in an attempt to win back votes.

[4] Banning extremist political parties will be effective. A small hardcore group of people will try to continue to peddle their ideas, but it will be easy for the police to target them. Most people will not choose to break the law and will leave the party.

[5] It is possible to identify extremist parties that should be banned. Although the exact line may be blurred, there are plenty of examples of far-right parties which clearly fall over it. Concerns about the level of immigration a country can support are not the same as anti-immigration and repatriation policies underpinned by racism and xenophobia.

society. They may allow us to tackle racism by acting as a barometer which gives society a warning that there is a problem. They also allow for these views to be torn down in public debate. If they were to be silenced, and spread their ideas privately, then they would never be refuted. The National Front was roundly defeated in the final ballot of the 2002 French election and France was given the chance to examine why so many people had voted for them.

[3] In a democracy, people have the right to vote as they choose. If choices are limited, it is no longer a real democracy. Mainstream parties need to listen to people's concerns and work hard to win their confidence.

[4] If extremist parties are banned, they will not disappear; they will become underground groups where they are likely to become more extreme in views, rhetoric and behaviour. A political party needs to remain respectable and within the law to be legitimate and so their existence has a moderating effect.

[5] It is difficult to decide which parties count as extreme, and dangerous to give anybody the power to do so. Clearly it is not the case that any party that wishes to curb immigration is extreme, and so where do we draw the line? In 2012, a local council in England removed foster children from a family because they were members of the UK Independence Party; UKIP believes that the UK should leave the European Union (EU) and is not considered by most to be an extremist party, so this highlights the potential problems.

Possible motions

This House would ban extremist political parties.
This House believes that the far right under-
    mines democracy.

Related topics

Censorship by the state
Democracy

Monarchy, abolition of

Britain is one of the oldest surviving hereditary monarchies. Several other European countries are monarchies (Denmark, Sweden, Norway, the Netherlands and Spain) along with other countries around the world such as Morocco and Lesotho in Africa and Bhutan in Asia. Arab sheikhs and the Japanese emperor are also examples of hereditary rulers. Historically, a partially elected parliament was seen as a mechanism to check the power of the monarch. As centuries passed, more and more real power passed to parliaments and away from monarchs, in some cases through violent revolution (as in France and Russia). In other cases, such as Britain or the Netherlands, the process was more gradual and the monarch has simply been left with only ceremonial duties and nominal powers. Is there any point in maintaining this institution or is an elected president the only appropriate head of state in the modern world? The arguments below use examples from the British monarchy, but can be replaced with details of the particular monarch or with multiple examples if necessary.

Pros

[1] It is thoroughly anti-democratic to have a head of state whose position is decided on birth rights. The people of a country should choose their head of state through an election. Just as important is the lack of accountability in birth rights. Unlike the case of a head of state who can be voted out, a monarch cannot be. Inherited power is an out-of-date idea that has no place in the twenty-first century with its merito-cratic and anti-elitist ideals.

[2] An hereditary monarch will always be from the same race and class. This harms representation and tells members of minorities and the working classes that however hard they work, nobody from their background will be the head of state. This harms inclusivity and aspiration. In contrast, the election of a black US presi-

Cons

[1] The monarch has no real power, so is not needed to allow the day-to-day run-ning of a modern democracy. The role is ceremonial and in this role their inde-pendence is an advantage. An elected head of state may feel justified to wield power or to interfere with the government and this would be undesirable. The media does a good job of holding the monarchy to account, and changes such as the Queen paying taxes show that she does listen and respond to criticism.

[2] Electing a head of state brings no guarantee of representation. Britain has only ever had white prime ministers. In the US, in recent decades, one sees power concentrated in political dynasties such as the Kennedy, the Bush and the Clinton families.

dent, Barack Obama, is inspirational for minorities.

[3] The monarchy can appear to be embarrassing and out of touch with society. Their cosseted upbringing means they have little in common with those they lead. With the British monarchy, Prince Philip's racist remarks and Prince Harry's nude photos and Nazi fancy-dress costumes are examples of behaviour that the public would rather not have associated with the country.

[4] The monarchy is hugely expensive. The taxpayer is funding lavish lifestyles in palaces with banquets and overseas travel. In 2011/12, the Queen's official expenditure totalled £32.3 million. Spending on royal residences and other buildings totalled £12.2 million. The campaign group Republic have claimed that taxpayers are spending five times more on each member of the Royal Family than on a frontline soldier in Afghanistan.

[5] Constitutionally, in the UK, the monarch is both pointless and dangerous at the same time – the worst mix. The convention that the monarch would never interfere in legislative matters means that there is an important check missing on the prime minister's power. On the other hand, if the monarch were to use their veto, it would be an outrageous abuse of an unelected power.

[6] The monarchy serves as a reminder of our imperialist and elitist past. We should cast off these shackles and embrace modernity. It would send a powerful message to the descendants of all those oppressed and slaughtered in the name of the crown to dispense with this tainted institution.

[3] The monarchy is a symbol of a nation and something to be proud of. It is a rallying point for the nation in times of both trouble and celebration. It offers a positive image of the country abroad. Royal family members are no more out of touch or embarrassing than politicians. In Britain, the younger members are positive role models. All members of the royal family get out into the community and do large amounts of charity work, more so than politicians. Many of them serve in the armed forces.

[4] The monarchy raises money through attracting tourism revenue to the country. It also raises money for charity, pays tax and advances British business interests abroad. Historic buildings would have to be maintained even if the monarchy were abolished.

[5] The system of a constitutional monarch offers the perfect balance; they do not interfere with the sovereignty of parliament, but there is an ultimate check there if it were needed in extreme circumstances. Other heads of state would expect more power and this would weaken parliament.

[6] The Queen is the head of state of many Commonwealth nations and is a unifying figurehead. The monarch is part of the traditions and culture of a country and that heritage should be celebrated.

Possible motions

This House would elect its head of state.

This House would abolish the monarchy.

Related topics

Democracy

House of Lords, elected v. appointed

Disestablishment of the Church of England

Political candidacy, age of

In the USA, a candidate must be 25 to stand for the House of Representatives, 30 for the Senate and 35 for president. In Italy, a candidate must be 50 or more to stand for president; and in Germany, the age limit is 40 to stand for chancellor, though the country allows 18 year olds to stand for other positions. Are all these restrictions ageist and should the age of candidacy for all positions be the same as the voting age? In countries such as Australia and Denmark, 18 year olds may stand for any office. In Britain, the minimum age to stand for parliament was lowered from 21 to 18 in 2007. Is this more democratic and representative or is it reckless?

Pros

[1] There is no logical reason to prevent 18 year olds standing for parliament. They can marry and they pay taxes and so are fully fledged members of society. If the democratic system is designed to reflect the views of those aged 18 and above (the electorate), then it is only proper that 18 year olds should be allowed to be representatives. It is ageist and discriminatory to exclude them from that role. It implies that they are second-class citizens.

[2] Being an MP or representative is not the same as being a business person. An elected representative merely needs to present an open and articulate channel of communication for those whom he or she represents. Intelligence, listening skills, openness, integrity and articulacy are all skills that can be well developed by the age of 18. If the electorate does not want to trust a particular 18 year old, it will not vote for that person.

[3] Elected assemblies are too often stuffy, pompous and out of touch with the public, especially with the needs and interests of the young. Allowing 18 year olds to be democratic representatives will give a voice to those concerns and do something to bring the democratic process closer to

Cons

[1] It is misleading to present standing for parliament and voting in an election as comparable democratic functions. Being a representative, unlike simply voting for one, requires a level of life experience and maturity that an 18 year old cannot possibly possess. Many complex issues and different groups need to be understood and represented. A democratically elected assembly is required to *represent* the views and interests of the electorate, but not to *resemble* that electorate in every detail of demography, such as age.

[2] The electorate of a constituency cannot be expected to trust an 18 year old to fulfil such a demanding role. People aged 18 with little or no experience of life or work are not given highly responsible jobs in industry and commerce; nor should they be in politics. Local parties would probably not select them and the electorate would probably not vote for them.

[3] There is no significant sense in which 18 year olds are more 'in touch' with reality than 21 year olds or indeed 61 year olds, or more idealistic or dynamic. This is just ageist rhetoric. The sort of 18 year old who wanted to run for office would most likely be a precocious and pompous young per-

real people. Even if very few, or none, were elected, their voices during the election would change the campaign and put pressure on other politicians to appeal to young voters. The idealism of young people would be a benefit in an ever more cynical political world; 18 year olds could bring dynamism, idealism and values to bear in the political system.

[4] It is undemocratic to have arbitrary restrictions on the choice of the electorate. If an electorate wishes to have a 20-year-old parliamentarian or a 28-year-old president, why should it be denied its choice by the constitution? If it values age and wisdom, it will vote elsewhere, but a younger candidate should be given the opportunity to see if they can win the electorate's vote.

[5] Students in schools, colleges and universities are already involved in politics and representation at a high level through student unions. Through these organisations, 18 year olds could have accumulated much relevant knowledge and experience, campaigning on educational, social and environmental issues.

[6] Lowering the age of candidacy would not change the issue of career politicians as at present, young people start as political aides until they are old enough to run for office, so do not gather experience of the wider world during this time. At least if they are campaigning, they will be meeting 'real' people on the doorsteps.

son who might be out of touch with youth culture. It is also questionable whether wide-eyed naïve idealism is truly an attractive trait in a representative when what is needed is political pragmatism, informed by worldly experience and deep thought.

[4] There are other restrictions on candidacy which vary between jurisdictions. but include nationality, place of residency and whether the candidate has registered as bankrupt. A minimum age is in line with this. The logic behind this policy of exclusions, besides, would suggest there should be no minimum age at all in case the voters want to support a 13 year old.

[5] The narrow range of issues that concerns student unions (mainly education and its funding) is not sufficient experience for the broad issues and challenges of being a representative. The sort of people who would want to be elected politicians at the age of 18 would most likely want to go to university – this would not be compatible with the huge demands on time and commitment of being an elected politician.

[6] Reducing the age of eligibility would only fuel the problem that many countries are seeing of career politicians. If an 18 year old has a desire to be a politician, they should go out into the world first to get some experience of life.

Possible motions
This House would allow 18 year olds to stand for office.
This House would give the young a voice.

Related topics
Term limits for politicians
Voting age, reduction of
Mandatory retirement age

Politicians' outside interests, banning of

This debate looks at whether being an elected representative should be a full-time job, or whether politicians should be able to balance it with other paid work. Do we value politicians more if they devote their time while in government solely to politics, or do we welcome the idea of elected representatives having business interests outside their political role?

Pros

[1] Politicians are elected to serve their constituents full time, and for this they are well paid. When members of parliament continue their past employment or accept new directorships or posts as consultants, they are short-changing and insulting their constituents, who expect their representatives to be working solely for them.

[2] Countries should not be ruled by 'pressure group politics', where the most important decisions are made by small interest groups which influence the most important politicians. This subverts natural democracy where all members represent their constituency and the people who elected them.

[3] It is impossible to police outside interests. We can never know precisely what a politician has promised to do in exchange for money, even if that money is declared in the Register of Members' Interests. The only solution is outright abolition.

[4] It is wrong in principle for any individual or group to be able to buy political power and influence. Even if lobby groups are allowed to influence politicians, they should not be allowed *financial* arrangements with them. Otherwise only the wealthy groups paying the most (e.g. major corporations selling tobacco, arms,

Cons

[1] The recent trend for politics to be populated by career politicians is deplorable. Few 'normal' people would enter politics if they had to abandon their previous life, especially as the salaries of most politicians are actually very small. It is far better to allow outside interests and attract, for example, experienced business people or lawyers to parliament.

[2] Politicians are elected to represent the population of the country, which must include interest groups as well as geographical constituencies. They will always represent the special interests of vocal groups of constituents with particular grievances (e.g. cases of alleged miscarriages of justice), but that need not totally exclude representing broader interest groups. A politician's own constituents must always be his or her first concern, but need not be the only concern.

[3] Political lobbying is acceptable so long as politicians declare their pay-masters. It is not the fact that finance is involved at all that is objectionable – a politician's job is to persuade the government to pass legislation, so why should they not profit from doing their job? – but the fact that, if the arrangement is concealed, their motives are unclear. Declaration of outside interests is sufficient – they need not be banned.

cars, etc.) would be able to win legislation in their favour; smaller, poorer factions (e.g. animal rights' defenders) would have no say. If money is removed from the equation, then each opinion has a more equal chance of being heard.

Possible motions

This House would ban politicians from having outside interests.

This House believes that elected representatives should represent their constituents, not lobby groups.

Related topics

Capitalism v. socialism

Privacy of public figures

State funding of political parties

Term limits for politicians

[4] Politicians do not have the time to listen to every opinion and weigh them up against each other. By the very nature of capitalism, some groups will wield more power and may be able to influence parliament directly; but there are many other methods which smaller parties can use to make themselves heard. These include petitions, use of the media, direct action and so on.

Proportional representation

Some countries including the USA and the UK use an electoral system called 'first past the post' (FPTP) in some of their elections. This is where the candidate who receives the most votes wins the seat and the other votes count for nothing. Should such countries reform this system to a more proportional one where the number of seats won is more in line with the popular vote received? There are many models of proportional representation such as Single Transferable Vote or Alternative Vote. A Proposition team may wish to research these models and choose a system to support since they all have slightly different pros and cons, but the debate can also be had on the principle.

Pros

[1] Britain and America's current electoral system is winner-takes-all, 'first past the post' democracy. Whichever single candidate gains the most votes wins the constituency, and votes for the other parties are ignored, even if the winner only won by a couple of votes. Thus, parties with a

Cons

[1] All electoral systems are unfair in one way or another. Across the globe, no uniform democratic system has emerged, and different countries all have very different ways of electing representatives democratically.

slight lead in the country can get a vastly disproportionate majority in legislature. For example, in the 1997 UK general election, Labour won less than 45 per cent of the popular vote but 64 per cent of the seats in parliament. It is even possible for a government or a president to be elected with a minority of the popular vote, as happened with George W. Bush in 2000. This is undemocratic.

[2] Small parties are not represented at all. In the 1997 UK election, the Liberal Democrats' 17 per cent of the vote gave them around 7 per cent of the seats and the Referendum Party's 2.5 per cent gave them no MPs at all. This cannot be fair. Introducing PR is the way to end this unfairness and allow small parties to get the recognition they deserve. Proportional representation also frees the electorate to vote for smaller parties knowing that their vote will not be wasted.

[3] It is right that we should be governed by coalitions, since in reality there is no majority opinion on most issues. The art of social harmony and fair government is the ability to reach compromises. This is the most mature and civilised way to govern. 'Strength of government' seen another way is simply the minority steam-rolling their views through over the majority. A coalition government does not have to mean instability: in Germany, Gerhard Schroeder's Social Democratic Party governed in coalition with the Green Party from 1998 to 2005.

[4] Members of parliament often get elected with a minority of the vote. In 1997, the Liberal Democrats won Tweeddale in the Scottish Borders with 31 per cent of the vote; seats won with under 35 per cent of the vote were by no

[2] Proportional representation creates governments that are at the mercy of the whims of tiny parties with negligible electoral support. Such small parties can hold larger parties to ransom if it is their support that makes the difference between a coalition government maintaining an overall majority or losing it. Proportional representation leads to instability and disproportionate power for small parties. It is not more democratic to have a small party decide who the government of the day is.

[3] Proportional representation creates weak coalition governments, as in Italy where the Communist Party, despite a low level of support, frequently holds considerable sway by offering to form coalitions with larger parties and thus form a majority government. Elections there are far more frequent than in Britain, for example, because the coalition governments that PR produces are weak and unstable and frequently collapse. No system is perfect, but the current one at least guarantees some continuity and strength of government over a sufficient period of time to instigate a legislative programme.

[4] Systems that count a voter's second choice force political parties to bargain with each other for each other's second-place recommendations. Back-room dealings like this do not aid democracy. Would the public be happy to be ruled by a party that was everyone's second choice – as, for example, the Liberal Democrats could well be in Britain? Systems which allow for multi-member constituencies dilute and devalue the representation and accountability of the constituency system. Forms of PR which use party lists to top up – adding representatives to an elected body based on

means uncommon. So the people's so-called representatives normally represent only a minority of their constituents. Some forms of PR ensure that a representative has at least 51 per cent of the vote, while others allow multiple winners in each seat to ensure greater representation. This in turn leads to a stronger mandate for politicians.

[5] In 'safe' seats, there is hardly any incentive for people to vote. In seats in the North West of England where Labour regularly wins 80 per cent of the vote, it is often said that a root vegetable with a red rosette would be elected. In the USA, there is a congressional seat in Tennessee that the Republicans have held since 1869. People feel their vote is wasted, since the result is a foregone conclusion. With a PR system, everyone's vote counts even if they are in the minority in their particular constituency. Proportional representation also stops the situation where a whole election and all of its campaigning is really happening in only a handful of marginal seats. It equalises people's votes so that parties have to try to have a wider appeal across the country.

a political party receiving a certain share of the vote across a wider area – break the constituency link, creating two tiers of politicians and putting too much power in the hands of the central party machine.

[5] Many of the systems proposed are hugely complex. If the public does not understand the political system, then results can seem arbitrary and accountability is lost. The uncertainty and confusion this creates can cause disillusionment with the democratic process. Some voters will understand and use tactical voting to their advantage, whereas others will not know how to play the game. The transparency of the 'first past the post' system is one of its many virtues.

Possible motions

This House believes in proportional representation.

This House believes that the 'first past the post' system is undemocratic.

Related topics

Democracy
Referenda, increased use of
Voting, compulsory

Referenda, increased use of

Do referenda have a place in representative democracies? Some countries' constitutions demand referenda on certain (often constitutional) issues. In other cases, it is up to the government to call the referendum. The most common referenda deal with either moral questions or constitutional issues which are seen as needing direct public involvement. Europe has seen a number of referenda on economic packages, such as bailouts, since the 2008 global financial crisis. In some countries such as Switzerland, the public can trigger a referendum on any issue with a certain number of citizens backing it. The UK held a referendum on the Alternative Vote system in 2011. Would a move towards further use of this participative model be beneficial, or is the reliance on elected representatives to legislate on our behalf sufficient?

Pros

[1] The first democracy, in ancient Athens, did not rely on elected politicians and parliaments. Instead, the citizens met on the Pnyx hill to debate and vote on every issue of policy. Modern democracy and the size of the modern electorate have removed this participative element from day-to-day politics and distanced people from decision making. We should return to a more direct form of democracy to re-engage voters and increase participation. Referenda might work particularly well at the level of local government; e.g. in making transport, environmental and planning decisions.

[2] Modern technology gives us the power to return to the Athenian ideal. It is now entirely practicable for every major policy decision to be made by referenda via the Internet.

[3] Political systems often fall out of touch with the public. There are many issues where the will of the public is simply ignored because the major parties agree; e.g. the British public would almost certainly vote for capital punishment if their politicians allowed them to. Genuine democracy would circumvent the parties' prejudices and put power back in the hands of the people.

[4] When important constitutional decisions need to be made which it would be hard for future governments to undo, such as a country's involvement in the European Union (EU) or devolution of power to a region, these should automatically go to referendum to avoid one parliament binding all future parliaments. This could also extend to matters such as party funding, electoral reform, crime and

Cons

[1] Government involves more than individual decisions. There has to be an underlying strategy, one that is not blown with the wind from day to day. Government by constant referenda does not allow this. California holds dozens of referenda every year. The reams of paper voters have to read through result in widespread apathy, low turnouts and consequently, freakish results.

[2] The vast majority of people are not interested in politics on a day-to-day basis. Government by constant referenda would become government by the politically obsessed – government by zealots and extremists. A system based on Internet access would disenfranchise the most disadvantaged in society who do not have access to the technology, while at the same time making it too easy for the majority to express an ill-informed decision on a matter which they neither know nor care about.

[3] The phrasing of the question to be asked in any referendum has a significant impact on the result. The timing can also be crucial. The politicians who control the wording and timing are retaining significant power, and in a way that is insidiously unaccountable. So, in fact, referendum results are often simply manipulated by the media machines of the political parties involved. Furthermore, it is a strength of representative democracies that they are not just versions of mob rule. Capital punishment has not been reintroduced in Britain despite much popular support because the question is settled by elected representatives with a higher than average amount of information, experience and intellectual ability at their disposal. Using

punishment, and privacy laws. Switzerland provides a model of effective direct democracy where referenda are frequently held to determine policy decisions.

Possible motions

This House calls for more use of the referendum.

This House believes that true democracy is direct democracy.

Related topics

Democracy

Voting, compulsory

Written constitution

Social movements: courts v. legislatures

referenda may be superficially more democratic, but will lead to mob rule as opposed to enlightened government.

[4] Elected representatives must be trusted with decisions. It is they, especially ministers and civil servants, who have the time, information, expertise and authority to make well-informed decisions. There is no need for any increased use of referenda. Referenda may be appropriate on some constitutional issues, but sometimes even on these, the level of complexity means that we need experts rather than laypeople to decide. For example, the public cannot be expected to read and understand the whole of an EU treaty on which it may be asked to vote. Referenda are not needed for any issues other than major constitutional change.

Social movements: courts v. legislatures

Many of the great landmark moments for liberal social movements that live in the popular imagination today are decisions of the US Supreme Court; *Brown* v. *Board of Education of Topeka* abolishing school segregation, *Roe* v. *Wade* legalising abortion, or *Lawrence* v. *Texas* striking down Texas's anti-sodomy laws. Yet plenty of other countries achieved the same things through legislative change: the Wolfenden Report, for instance, which led to decriminalising homosexuality in the UK; or the Irish referendum on divorce in 1996. Precisely which social movements are at issue will vary across countries; gay rights will be an issue in many, but some still have illegal abortion, issues over women's rights or racial discrimination. An interesting new area for this debate is socio-economic rights, such as rights to housing and education; these were placed, for example, in the 1996 South African Constitution, which has led to a series of judgements there.

Pros

[1] Courts are not susceptible to electoral pressure, and as such, even when populations may have regressive views, they can introduce liberalising measures. For instance, long before the Civil Rights Act of 1964 in the USA, the Supreme Court banned segregationist measures. Even though support for abortion in Ireland today is minimal, courts have upheld a woman's right to choose. They are thus especially good enablers of social movements.

[2] Many countries have constitutions which encode the basic value of equality between persons, and are made their guardians. But often these general pronouncements need filling out with specifics, and elected politicians are slow to do so. Courts then fill this gap by deciding on specific rights.

[3] Once courts have made a decision, they tend to stick to it; 'legal' answers are much less variable than political ones. Moreover, courts tend to command a degree of respect not held by elected leaders, and so their decisions are more likely to be abided by. For all the public excitement over the abortion issue in the USA, the right is basically undisturbed today.

[4] A court battle, because it involves convincing only a small number of judges, is much cheaper than a democratic campaign, and so is more likely to succeed as a strategy for a small, under-resourced organisation. Thus the Californian gay rights movement could not defeat the well-funded church groups campaigning for Proposition 8 against gay marriage, but were able to win a court battle on the same issue.

Cons

[1] Courts may well be more regressive than their electorates. Judges come from a small elitist cross-section of society, and have often been appointed for their political views; for instance, the justices of the US Supreme Court are highly politicised and sectarian, and only reach liberal decisions when liberals are in the majority.

[2] Courts do not have unlimited power to just 'be liberal'; they are bounded by what the law allows them. Some countries do not have constitutions, and others do not have any kind of substantive Bill of Rights that allows judges to extend equality. Indeed, often, as in the case of abortion in Ireland, the regressive measure is actually built into the constitution. As such, there is nothing courts can do; only the legislature can act.

[3] Legal answers may be more durable, but they are less respected precisely because they are seen as judicial 'impositions' on the people. In such cases, the measure may be overturned by the electorate, or judges may be stripped of their powers; Franklin D. Roosevelt's plan to stack the Supreme Court with his supporters when it struck down several New Deal measures in the mid-1930s is a key example. Moreover, without changing attitudes, changing the law matters little; the judicial decriminalisation of homosexuality in South Africa has not prevented widespread 'gay bashing' and 'corrective rape' of lesbians.

[4] Lawsuits are very expensive, especially when the other side can hire armies of well-paid lawyers. Moreover, campaigning to change the public's mind and getting them to put pressure on their representatives form a virtuous circle. When public support grows, so do donations.

Possible motions

This House believes that social movements should pursue change in courts rather than legislatures.

This House believes that change is more likely in the courtroom than in parliament.

This House believes that Britain should withdraw from the European Court of Human Rights.

Related topics
Democracy
Civil disobedience
Judges, election of
Written constitution

State funding of political parties

Some countries, such as Australia, fund their political parties through taxpayers' money. Other countries, including the UK, require their political parties to fundraise to meet their costs. Which system is fairer and more democratic? The different models for state funding are complex, but it may be worth a Proposition team giving some details about the system they would use as it can affect the arguments. It is possible, however, to have the debate in principle and this article looks at the arguments as they work across various models. There is an interesting related debate on capping campaign expenditure which also seeks to create a more transparent political system.

Pros

[1] As long as parties have to raise their own funds, rich individuals and interest groups who donate will have disproportionate influence in society. Remove the need for money and you remove the influence of the funders and level the playing field for all voices to be heard. There is evidence that politicians are swayed by the views of those who fund them, be they oil companies, trades unions or millionaires who are essentially buying favourable legislation. A famous example of this was in 1997 when Tony Blair's government exempted Formula One racing from a ban on tobacco advertising after receiving a significant donation from its president, Bernie Ecclestone.

Cons

[1] We have to protect people's freedom to participate in the political system and giving money to political parties is one way of doing this. It is a step down from standing for office oneself and on a par with giving one's time for campaigning. It is not just millionaires who donate; many working people donate small amounts to parties through unions and it is the number of them that make them significant. Parties do not change their policies as a result of donations, but rather, donations follow policies; e.g. big businesses give money to the party they would like to see elected because they support their policies. There is nothing corrupt about this.

[2] How do you decide which party gets what funding? There is no good way;

[2] State funding makes elections fairer in two ways: first, it prevents a party from effectively being able to buy an election due to their fuller coffers allowing them significantly more publicity; second, it makes it easier for small or new parties to make an impact on the electorate as they are not priced out of the system.

[3] State funding leads to a reduction of the total amount of money in elections. This is a positive thing as it decreases flashy television advertisements in favour of an increase in cheaper grass-roots campaigning, thereby engaging the voter more directly and focusing on policy rather than image.

[4] State funding of political parties reduces public cynicism about politics as it leads to a fairer and more transparent system. The public find it hard to trust in politicians who they believe can be bought.

[5] This system allows politicians to focus on politics rather than fundraising. Parties are under huge financial strain and must devote large amounts of time and energy to staying solvent. They must often prioritise attending a fundraising event with rich donors over a charitable, civic or cultural event which needs their support and from which they could gain a wider understanding of the needs of their constituents or the country at large.

[6] An effective democracy is worth spending money on. State funding would represent a tiny amount of government spending and would be in line with money already spent on democratic processes such as elections and referenda.

either you give an advantage to the incumbents and entrench the status quo of the big parties by giving them the most, or you disproportionately support small fringe parties, which is unfair and could lead to the taxpayer funding extreme parties' campaigns.

[3] State funding limits the overall amount of money which is spent in campaigns. This is bad in principle as it curtails freedom of speech, and bad in practice as it makes it harder to engage votes and leads to more voter apathy.

[4] It is not necessary to go so far as state funding to have transparency. An open register of donations allows the media to hold parties to account and prevents corruption.

[5] The need to fundraise leads to responsive parties. If they are automatically bankrolled by the state, then they could soon become isolationist and introspective elites.

[6] State funding of political parties is a waste of taxpayers' money and there is little public support for it. Most people believe that there are better things to spend their taxes on than political parties.

Possible motions
This House supports state funding of political parties.
This House believes that state funding of political parties enhances democracy.

Related topics
Democracy
Term limits for politicians
Politicians' outside interests, banning of

Term limits for politicians

This debate addresses the question of whether we need to take any action to counteract the perceived dominance of older and more established figures in political life. It also raises the question of whether politics should be perceived as a career in itself. At present in the UK, there is no limit to the number of terms in office that an MP can serve, whether as a back-bencher, a minister, or even as prime minister. In the USA, there is no limit for members of the House of Representatives, but an individual may only serve as president for a maximum of two terms. A definition should clarify whether the debate is only about executive positions or also about members of the legislature. It will probably also want to set the number of terms and whether the limits are consecutive or lifetime.

Pros

[1] A regrettable trend in recent years has been the development of the 'professional politician'. Politics should be a brief interlude in a career, not a career in itself. Politics is enriched by life experience and career politicians narrow the perspective of government. Young people are diving into student politics, emerging as full-time political organisers and resurfacing as political candidates a few years later without ever having done a 'real job'. This produces bland politicians with no experience of the real world. Term limits would mean that people would be more inclined to accumulate experience before entering the political system for their one chance as an elected representative. Limiting members of parliament to a set number of terms (two or even one) would therefore be healthy for democracy.

[2] Politicians in their last term can be brave and principled as they are less afraid of the opinion polls, thus allowing them to be bolder in their decision making. For example, Bill Clinton continued to push for a peace settlement in the Middle East and began important negotiations with

Cons

[1] This is a perfectly valid view – but it is not valid to force this view onto the political system. If people want to prevent someone standing two or three times, they can vote against them. If we want to re-elect a veteran politician, we should be able to. The experience and wisdom gained within politics can be as valuable as that learnt in business. To attempt to remove elected representatives by legal means is undemocratic as it restricts voter choice. Americans voted in Franklin D. Roosevelt to take a third term and prospered because of it.

[2] Term limits create 'lame duck' politicians in their last term who know they will never face the electorate again. This has the double disadvantage of reducing their moral authority and eliminating their motivation to keep in touch with their public. Term limits would produce less effective representatives.

[3] There are plenty of examples of incumbent politicians being beaten in elections. Being in the spotlight highlights mistakes and unpopular policies and characteristics as well as successes; this is how accountability works.

North Korea in the final months of his presidency. '

[3] Once elected, politicians enjoy a significant 'incumbency factor'. The publicity that their post affords them and the apparatus available to them provide a significant advantage to them and a disadvantage to their opponents; this is unfair and undemocratic.

[4] Like introducing a mandatory retirement age, limiting the amount of time a person can serve as a representative will create regular openings for talented people at the bottom end of the scale. Term limits would increase the number of younger and more energetic representatives and relax the stranglehold on power enjoyed by the career politician by virtue simply of his or her age. In practice, an experienced politician is never deselected in favour of a younger candidate, however out of touch he or she has become, and this perpetuates an ageing and ageist legislature. Legislation must be passed to force local party selection committees to select new candidates, say every 10 years, to counteract the current inequitable system and prevent stagnation.

[5] Term limits prevent a stranglehold on power. In turn this can reduce corruption, lessen the influence of special interest groups and produce a more open and accountable system. In countries with safe-seat constituencies or party lists, many senior politicians are untouchable and term limits can perform an important constitutional check.

[4] It is ageist to assume that younger politicians will be more dynamic and talented, and it is foolish to throw away the experience and skills of older politicians. In a system where politicians are under unprecedented pressure both from the executive and from lobbyists, inexperienced novices are ill-equipped to cope. Experienced legislators benefit both their constituents and parliament. Term limits would effectively abolish the experienced politician at a considerable loss to the nation. Even more power would then be concentrated in the hands of unelected civil servants and functionaries. This is particularly acute at times of crisis where continuity can be valuable. It is down to the political parties to select their candidates, and down to them to decide whether to value youth over experience or vice versa. This is not a decision that should be forced upon them by legislation.

[5] There are other checks against abuse of power in a democratic system – the legislature, the media, the courts and the electorate themselves. If all of these bodies are happy with the work of a politician, why should they not be allowed to continue to serve?

Possible motions

This House would limit the term of politicians.

This House regrets the rise of the career politician.

This House favours youth over experience in its politicians.

Related topics

State funding of political parties

Political candidacy, age of

Democracy

Politicians' outside interests, banning of

Voting age, reduction of

Most countries, including the UK, have a minimum voting age of 18, but many countries, including Brazil, Austria and Nicaragua, have a voting age of 16. There is a lobby in the UK to lower the voting age to 16 and so this article deals with changing the voting age from 18 to 16. The arguments could be adapted to support a lower voting age; e.g. the start of high school or the age of criminal responsibility.

Pros

[1] In society today, young people reach social and intellectual maturity at a younger age than ever before. By the age of 16 (and possibly 14), young people are well-informed and mature enough to vote.

[2] In the UK, at the age of 16, young people can have a job, have sex legally and get married. It is absurd for a married person with a job and children not to be recognised as an adult who can vote. Voting is an important decision, but so is getting married. Such a person is a full adult member of society and should be treated as such. In some countries, the age of consent and/or the school leaving age are even younger, making the discrepancies greater still.

[3] Because of the advances in information technology over recent decades, teenagers are now more aware of political issues than ever before. The broadcast media and the Internet in particular ensure that everyone, including 16 year olds, is familiar with the issues of the day. There is no need to wait for young people to be 18 in order for them to have a fuller understanding of politics.

[4] Even if one takes a pessimistic view of the ability of some 16-year-old school-leavers to make a well-informed and well-

Cons

[1] It is not true that young people are more mature than ever in today's society. They masquerade as adults by mimicking traditionally adult behaviour (drinking, smoking, using drugs, having sex, swearing, fighting) at younger and younger ages, but that does not make them mature. If anything, the voting age should be raised to give these immature would-be adults a longer time actually to grow up and mature *intellectually*.

[2] It is perfectly acceptable for different 'rites of passage' to occur at different ages. In the UK, for example, the ages for leaving school, being allowed to have sex legally, smoke, drive, drink and vote are staggered over three years (16, 17, 18). In many countries, the school-leaving age and the age of consent are also 18 and so the voting age is more in line. In the USA, you have to be 21 to buy alcohol which shows that there is debate even about whether 18 year olds can make mature decisions. Voting is a responsible act that requires more than a year or two of adult experience of life and politics. The age for voting should stay at 18 or be raised to 21 – as indeed should the age for marriage, another momentously important decision that should not be made by adolescents.

[3] The rise of broadcast media and information technology has led to a ridiculously

thought-out democratic decision, it is not clear that the passage of two years will make any real difference to such people. Many people are politically unsophisticated or uninterested in politics, but there is not a significant difference between the ages of 16 and 18. The same proportion of 16 year olds as of 18 year olds will be apathetic, uninterested or ill-informed. The extra two years without a vote is a case of arbitrary discrimination.

[5] In any case, voters are not required to be fully informed or highly intellectual – such a requirement would be elitist and anti-democratic. People aged 16 are, in many other respects, adult members of society.

[6] Many voters will have to wait two, three or even four years for their first national election after they turn 18, so may actually be as old as 22 when they have the opportunity to vote for the first time. In the same way, if the voting age were lowered to 16, half of voters would still have to wait until they were 18. Evidence shows that those who vote when young are more likely to continue voting through their life and so we should set the habit early.

simplistic and superficial political world emerging – a world in which real political argumentation has been replaced by the 'sound bite'. This is a reason to demand that the voter be older and be wiser to the tricks of the media spin-doctor. A 16-year-old voter would be putty in the hands of media managers.

[4] There is a significant difference between the levels of analysis of which a 16 year old and an 18 year old are capable. At 16, people are still children mentally. The voting age could be raised to 21, to allow for fuller mental development.

[5] While some people think there should be a test for a voting 'licence', as long as that does not exist, we need to put an age limit on voting. Teenagers are less likely to follow the news and care about politics as the issues do not directly affect them. Where laws do affect them directly, they are represented through their parents' votes.

[6] Young people are one of the demographic groups with the lowest turnouts in elections. Most will not vote in their first available election, and so bad habits will be set. If they are older when the right is granted, they will value it more and be more likely to use it.

Possible motions
This House would reduce the voting age to 16.
This House believes that the voting age should be the same as the age of criminal responsibility.

Related topics
Political candidacy, age of
Voting, compulsory

Voting, compulsory

Voting is compulsory in a number of jurisdictions including Australia, Belgium, Brazil and Bolivia. In Australia, failure to vote is punishable by fines or even by imprisonment, whereas in other countries the sanction can be a withholding of benefits or services. A definition may wish to consider which type of sanction the Proposition team wish to endorse and what level of elections this applies to. It is also possible to include a 'no vote' box on the ballot paper to allow for a rejection of all candidates.

Pros

[1] The electoral turnout in many established democracies is distressingly low. We should adopt compulsory voting to secure greater democratic involvement of the population. Proxy voting and postal voting will be available for those who cannot physically get to the polling station – voting by the Internet should also be investigated to improve ease and access.

[2] Low participation rates are doubly dangerous. They mean that our politicians are not representative of the population as a whole. Since the poor and disadvantaged are far less likely to vote than any other socio-economic group, they can safely be ignored by mainstream politicians. In turn, this leads to greater disillusionment with politics and a sense of disenfranchisement. The only way to break this cycle is mandatory voting as politicians then have to target policies to all sections of society. This would also end biases like that towards pensioners. At present, they are the group most likely to vote and so politicians must pander to them. In the austerity drive in the UK after 2010, pensioners have been largely immune from the cuts suffered by other groups.

[3] Liberal democracy relies upon a balance of rights. The above argument shows that our democracy is endangered

Cons

[1] There are many reasons why people do not vote. Up to 10 per cent of the population is not on the electoral register at any one time. Many people cannot get away from work, or find someone to look after their children. Some cannot physically get to a polling booth; others are simply not interested in politics. None of these motivations can be affected by forcing people to vote – those who cannot, will continue not to. Increasing turnout by making access to voting easier is a good idea, but it does not need to be linked to compulsion.

[2] Forcing people to vote is not the same as forcing them to make an informed choice based on a detailed understanding of manifestos. Those who were apathetic before will continue to be so. They will vote randomly or may be seduced by image, prejudice or by fringe or extreme parties. In turn, this means that there is not much extra motivation for mainstream parties to turn their attention away from pensioners and the professional classes who are more likely to vote based on political record and promises.

[3] Abstention from voting is a democratic right. To deny the right to abstain in a vote is as dictatorial as to deny the right to support or oppose it. Just as the right to

through a lack of participation in elections. The resolution of such a crisis may in a small way restrict some personal liberties, but it is in the interests of society as a whole. We compel people to take part in other civic duties such as serving on juries and paying taxes and we should not be afraid to do the same in the case of voting. Besides, anyone wishing to register an abstention can do so by spoiling the ballot paper, leaving it unmarked or crossing the 'no vote' box, if available.

[4] Especially after the suffering of and sacrifices made by women and minority campaigners in the pursuit of universal suffrage, we owe it to our ancestors and to history to exercise our democratic right to vote. If people are so apathetic that they will not do this freely, we must make it compulsory. Such apathy also affects the moral authority of the West which is seen to preach democracy and sometimes impose it, while its own democracies are sick.

Possible motions

This House would make voting compulsory.
This House believes it is a crime not to vote.
This House believes that voting is a duty.

Related topics

Democracy
Protective legislation v. individual freedom
Democracy, imposition of

free speech is complemented by the right to silence, so the right to vote is balanced by the right of abstention. Refraining from the democratic process is a democratic statement of disenchantment. Forcing those who are disenchanted with politics in general to go and spoil a paper is a pointless waste of resources. Their right to register dissatisfaction should not be taken away by politicians who want to hide the fact of their unpopularity and irrelevance in society. The analogy with jury service does not hold since we do not *need* people to vote in order for an important social institution to function (in the way that we *do* need a jury to turn up for the justice system to function). Elections do not need a 100 per cent, or even an 80 per cent, turnout in order to fulfil their function. Nobody is harmed if an individual chooses not to vote, and so their freedom should not be curtailed.

[4] Suffragettes and other suffrage campaigners sought to make voting a right rather than a privilege, but they did not seek to make it a *duty*. In the same way, campaigners for equality for blacks, homosexuals or women have ensured that they have *access* to higher education, political power and the professions, but members of these groups are not now *forced* to attend university, stand for parliament or become soldiers. It is the freedom and lack of state compulsion in democracies that countries are espousing abroad.

SECTION C

International relations

Armaments, limitations on conventional

There are many obvious arguments against nuclear, chemical and biological weapons, but we are much more accustomed to a ready acceptance of the acceptability and desirability of large stocks of conventional weapons. This debate focuses on the possibilities of reducing those stocks of weapons, either by a refusal to trade in them, or gradual reductions of stockpiles and non-renewal of weapons programmes. Such a debate does not require a country to leave itself with no defence systems whatsoever, but allows it to retain measures to defend itself; it mainly limits its capacity to launch offensive wars.

Pros

[1] Horrific though the effects of nuclear, biological and chemical weapons are, the vast majority of deaths and injuries are caused by conventional arms. Action must be taken to engineer peace where possible and stop the proliferation of weapons. The existence of large stocks of arms ultimately makes it much more likely that nations will end up using them; large stockpiles of arms encourage aggressive foreign policies, which put states in the situation where they might need to be deployed. A unilateral end to arms sales is thus a logical first step to the achievement of long-term peace.

[2] Even if a unilateral end to arms sales would not stop others selling them, we should end our complicity in wars and violence. By selling arms, we facilitate great atrocities, and it would be an act of moral leadership to refuse to do so. Even if individual states are unable to engineer a significant reduction in global content, they can put pressure on others to do so by their example, and so start the ball rolling on a process of disarmament.

[3] Arms may be supplied to oppressive, non-democratic regimes which use them for internal repression (e.g. Saudi Arabia).

Cons

[1] 'Perpetual peace' is not a realistic goal. States' interests and ideologies will always collide with each other, and so there will always be situations in which they may wish to go to war. In consequence, there will also always be a demand for arms, and a willingness to supply them. Given that war is inevitable, there will always be a large international economy based on weaponry in which we may justifiably be involved.

[2] The global arms market is highly diffuse, and there is simply no way that individual states can be expected to have any impact on what others do. In particular, because Russia and China can produce large quantities of highly developed weaponry, and have shown no signs that they will stop, this move is pointless.

[3] Foreign policy is about promoting our national interests, a process which is not always compatible with 'whiter-than-white' ethical considerations. At least if we are on friendly terms with such regimes, they are more likely to listen to our human rights message; if we ignore them, they will side with other countries with no such considerations. For example, Saudi Arabia is a vital British ally in the

It is hypocritical to argue for the respect for human rights while supplying the means to suppress them. This was made particularly clear when, in 2008, Britain's Serious Fraud Office halted an investigation into bribery over arms sales to Saudi Arabia on foreign policy grounds; it was made abundantly clear that national interest will always trump ethical considerations in British foreign policy.

[4] The threat to defence industry jobs cannot justify our involvement in bloodshed, and the government could support the redeployment of industries and workers. The need to defend one's country would continue to support most of the arms industry.

region, on whom Britain is highly dependent for oil and regional military bases; it would be naïve to alienate the Saudis.

[4] The arms industry is a large and successful one providing many jobs and economic benefits. It would be wrong to throw this away for a gesture of pointless symbolism.

Possible motions
This House would end the arms trade.
This House would not sell arms for export.

Related topics
Pacifism
Nuclear weapons, right to possess
United Nations standing army
Military drones, prohibition of
Private military corporations, banning of

Commonwealth, abolition of the

The Commonwealth of Nations (or 'The British Commonwealth' until 1949) is a voluntary association of 54 nations (as of 2013) – each (except Mozambique and Rwanda) having once been a colony, protectorate or dependency of Britain, or of another Commonwealth country. In 1991, the Commonwealth Heads of Government issued the Harare Commonwealth Declaration stating the principles and purpose of the Commonwealth – co-operation in pursuit of world peace, commitment to the United Nations' Universal Declaration of Human Rights, opposition to all forms of racial oppression, commitment to the removal of disparities in living standards among member nations, equal rights for women, the rule of law and democratic government. In recent years, Nigeria, Pakistan, Zimbabwe and Fiji have all been suspended – one of the Commonwealth's strongest sanctions – over military coups. Additionally, newly independent or only semi-recognised states, such as the Republic of South Sudan and Somaliland, have applied to join, welcoming the Commonwealth's support and stamp of approval.

Pros

[1] The Commonwealth is founded upon an outdated and oppressive colonial system. Now that the European empires have been dismantled, we should base international co-operation on truly international foundations, not on the imperial maps of the past. The Commonwealth fosters neo-colonialism and blinds its members to non-English-speaking culture. If there is a need for an international talking shop and network of trade and technical support for developing nations, it should be truly global, not based on the historic British empire, with the present British monarch as its head.

[2] International organisations (notably the UN and Amnesty International) already exist to promote education, human rights and equality worldwide. The Harare Declaration is simply an empty repetition of these organisations' principles. Trading blocs such as the North American Free Trade Agreement (NAFTA), the EU, and the Association of Southeast Asian Nations (ASEAN), which are based on real economic and political interests, foster international trade. In all its supposed roles, the Commonwealth is merely duplicating functions performed better by other international organisations.

[3] The Commonwealth is a sham. Its members, especially powerful ones such as Britain, will always act in accordance with self-interest rather than in alliance with their Commonwealth colleagues. In 1986, Britain refused to place sanctions upon South Africa even though the Commonwealth voted in favour of sanctions, and Rwanda was allowed to join in 2009 in spite of its dubious democratic and human

Cons

[1] The British Commonwealth is a lasting testimony to how injustice and oppression can be transformed into co-operation and harmony, using the linguistic and historical links of post-colonial nations in a positive way. The nations of the Commonwealth share English as a first or major language and are almost all independently governed by parliamentary systems modelled on the British one. Moreover, Rwanda's accession in 2009 points towards a new future for the Commonwealth as an organisation based on those values, but without the historical baggage of colonialism.

[2] There is room in the world for many such organisations with particular emphases and interests. Membership of the UN and membership of the Commonwealth are not mutually exclusive. Moreover, the Commonwealth performs numerous functions that are simply more about 'soft power' than economic or military might; for instance, the Commonwealth Games bring nations together, and the Commonwealth Foundation funds valuable inter-cultural exchanges.

[3] Powerful countries such as Britain can afford to ignore the policies and interests of the rest of the Commonwealth, and they sometimes do, unfortunately. But the real beneficiaries are the less developed and less powerful countries (e.g. Saint Kitts and Nevis, Sierra Leone, Tonga, The Gambia), whose heads of state can negotiate with the big world players at Commonwealth Heads of Government meetings, and can foster bilateral trade agreements and programmes of technical co-operation and education through the NGOs of the Commonwealth network.

rights credentials, just because of Britain's alliance with it.

[4] The Commonwealth is indecisive and impotent. Despite declarations in Singapore in 1971 and Harare in 1991, asserting obvious moral truths about the iniquities of oppression, racism, sexism and so on, the Commonwealth has no means of enforcing its principles or curtailing human rights abuses. The leaked memo in 2010 showing that the Secretary General had banned staff from speaking out about human rights abuses is a perfect example; it is so preoccupied by not offending anyone that it fails to take decisive actions.

Moreover, Britain does also sometimes offer assistance to Commonwealth member states, such as its highly successful intervention in Sierra Leone in 2000.

[4] It is acknowledged that the Commonwealth is not an agency for the enforcement of international law – it is a low-budget network of mutual co-operation. The principles of democracy, equality, rule of law and individual freedom are not at all obvious in many developing countries – e.g. in the case of women's rights or child labour, which the Commonwealth combats through educational programmes. Moreover, suspension from the Commonwealth is a powerful indicator of international disapproval that can also rally other international organisations to take action.

Possible motions

This House would abolish the Commonwealth.
This House believes that the Commonwealth is a hangover from history.

Related topics

Immigration, limitation of
United Nations, failure of the
Should Britain leave the EU?

Democracy, imposition of

This debate focuses on whether democracy can and should be imposed by military, diplomatic or economic action. However, it is often hard to disentangle such interventions from their other possible motives; for instance, while many think that the intervention in Iraq (from 2003) was essentially to impose democracy, cynics say that it was more about obtaining oil, and the official line remains that it was to prevent Saddam Hussein's development of Weapons of Mass Destruction. Both teams must avoid descending into 'example ping-pong', in which they simply list case studies, but must deconstruct the actual reasons that those particular instances have succeeded or failed.

Pros

[1] Democracy is desirable in itself as the best system of government. Despite its obvious flaws, any other system is bound to be worse. It ensures that governments are accountable to their people, guards against corruption, protects individual liberty and allows flawed policies to be corrected. Economies are more likely to be open, competitive and prosperous. If we believe in these benefits, we should promote them vigorously to others.

[2] Democracy is not a purely domestic issue, as it tends to produce governments that co-operate internationally. There has never been a war between two democracies.

[3] Democracy carries with it a self-correcting mechanism; if Western pressure leads to the replacement of a dictatorship with democracy, then the electorate can always choose to return to dictatorship – an unlikely prospect. So-called Western cultural imperialism actually consists of trusting the people to choose for themselves.

[4] As well as imposing democracy through force, it should also be promoted peacefully through diplomacy, trade and aid. In such cases, countries can choose whether to listen to us, but we can make their people well aware of our commitment to democracy and the reasons for it; for instance, through the BBC World Service. Choosing only to trade with or give aid to other democracies is sensible as their economies are more stable and any use of aid can be openly monitored.

Cons

[1] It is one thing to believe our system to be the best, and quite another to impose it on other countries. This is a breach of the UN policy of non-intervention in the domestic affairs of independent nations. Just as Western citizens fought for their political institutions, we should trust the citizens of other nations to do likewise if they wish to. Moreover, some countries may not have the prerequisites for a successful democratic system, such as a strong rule of law, and to impose democracy on them would not produce beneficial outcomes.

[2] There has also never been a war between two countries with a McDonald's (although the Georgia versus Russia example has weakened the 'Golden Arches' theory); democracy is not necessarily the causally important factor here. In fact, economic development may explain both why countries are more prosperous and why they are more peaceful, which would not make the case for forcing democratisation. In any case, India and Pakistan, Peru and Ecuador, and Greece and Turkey are all examples of pairs of democratic states with violent and nationalistic histories.

[3] The differing types of democracy make it impossible to choose which standards to impose. Britain, the USA and European countries all differ in terms of restraints on government and the balance between consensus and confrontation. Moreover, there is a serious risk of imposing superficial democracy, which in fact leads to the same single party simply using elections to legitimate its rule; almost no country does not bother with the pretence of elections.

Possible motions

This House would impose democracy with the barrel of a gun.

This House believes that democracy is so good we should force it on everyone.

Related topics

Democracy

Dictators, assassination of

Non-UN-sanctioned military intervention

Sanctions, use of

[4] We should be prepared to engage constructively with countries and pressurise them to hold elections, or in some cases boycott them, but this is not the same as imposing democracy. The use of force against other countries, other than in self-defence, is fundamentally incompatible with the qualities inherent in democracy.

Dictators, assassination of

In spite of the general move towards democracy around the world, there are numerous dictatorial regimes worldwide. In general, military intervention in them would be impossible or impractical, but it is possible that targeted assassination might be more successful. The development of technology, and the greater use of assassination as a strategy for other targets including terrorists, makes assassination a more plausible route for ridding the world of them.

Pros

[1] Murder is rightly seen as wrong in all societies, but the specific circumstance of a dictatorship, where one unelected individual rules a state through force and fear, means that there are no other ways of removing the dictator from power. If the harm that dictators cause is great enough, and their deaths would remove clear and present dangers, then assassination may be justifiable as a last resort – the end justifying the means.

[2] Dictators pose a danger to international peace. Their unpopularity at home frequently causes them to launch foreign wars as a distraction (e.g. the Argentine military junta invaded the Falkland Islands in 1982, and Saddam Hussein invaded

Cons

[1] Assassination is simply unjustifiable as murder is always wrong. A soldier killing in war is a special case, justified by the rules established by the Geneva Convention, but the cold-blooded killing of a political leader is not. The ends may not always justify the means; dictators are usually replaced by other members of their military regime, and should the attack fail, it would only make them more bloodthirsty and vengeful than before.

[2] Dictators may threaten their neighbours, but so do leaders in democracies such as India and Pakistan, Egypt and Israel, and indeed the USA in wars from Vietnam to Iraq. Moreover, human rights abuses are far from being confined to

Kuwait in 1990). The removal of one individual through assassination may prevent thousands from dying and millions from suffering. Moreover, dictators often present a clear danger to their own populations; for instance, the massacres of Bashar al-Assad's regime in Syria.

[3] Dictators often promote terrorist activity against other states, as in Iraq, Iran, Syria or Libya, to strike at former domestic enemies now in exile or as revenge against governments which have supported their opponents.

[4] The security with which dictators surround themselves and the climate of fear that they create make it virtually impossible for either popular or elite (i.e. army) opposition to remove them from power, as the career of Saddam Hussein showed. If widespread suffering and death of their citizens are commonplace, this justifies removing them from power in the only way left. Even during the Arab Spring of 2011, it was primarily the fact that militaries switched sides, not mere people power, which overthrew Arab dictators.

dictatorships; for instance, the treatment of the Kurds in Turkey is endorsed by the democratic process. Even under a dictatorship, such conflicts may be very popular with the people for patriotic, territorial or ideological reasons. Assassinating dictators will not, therefore, prevent international conflict.

[3] Even the world's greatest democracy, the USA, has employed terrorist activity, notoriously against Nicaragua in the early 1980s. Assassination itself is a form of terrorism in any case and to use it is to descend to the level of dictators.

[4] The internal security of a dictator can be destabilised by isolating the regime diplomatically and economically, while keeping the people informed through global communication. Constructive engagement remains the best solution; history has shown that authoritarian regimes do not survive when a wealthy middle class is opposed to them. Creating the middle class through economics is our best attack on dictators.

Possible motions
This House would assassinate foreign dictators.
This House believes that targeted assassination is the only way to bring down despots.

Related topics
Civil disobedience
Democracy, imposition of
Military drones, prohibition of
Non-UN-sanctioned military intervention
Sanctions, use of
Terrorism, justifiability of

European Union, expansion of the

From the six members who signed the Treaty of Rome in 1957, to Croatia becoming the 28th member state on 1 July 2013, the EU's history has been one of continuous expansion, as new states see the merits of the European project and seek to gain benefits of membership. Equally, some think that whatever the merits of past expansions, it is no longer viable for the EU to expand further; it has simply reached the limits for a viable institution that is so closely integrated. However, the requirement that new member states join the euro has deterred many prospective entrants, given its recent instability; perversely, however, the global financial crisis appears to have encouraged other new entrants, especially Iceland, whose own currency problems were so bad that even the euro seemed preferable.

Pros

[1] The European Union has had great success in reuniting a continent shattered by the Second World War. Members get clear benefits from co-operation and avoiding confrontation. Trade and prosperity are promoted, and citizens have increased opportunities to travel and work abroad. Through demonstrating liberal democracy to Eastern Europe, it may also have helped to win the Cold War. All of these benefits should be extended to others.

[2] The idea of global free trade is a distant dream; in the meantime, the world increasingly divides into regional free trade blocs (NAFTA, Mercosur [Common Market of the South], ASEAN, etc.). So the only way to grow the economies of Europe is to expand their trading frontiers further and further, to find new markets for products, and achieve specialisation and economies of scale.

[3] The EU has now adapted its institutions sufficiently to be highly capable of adapting to large numbers of new entrants. For instance, the reforms in the Lisbon Treaty (2007) relating to the man-

Cons

[1] The extent to which the EU was actually causally important in preventing conflict in post-war Europe is contestable; it is simply not in fact plausible that Europe would have gone to war again after the devastation of the Second World War. Moreover, whatever its successes in the past, the EU is no longer primarily about that task, but about a broader project of economic liberalism. If anything, that produces more conflict and political disenchantment; for instance, the EU's enforcement of austerity on Greece (from 2010 to 2013) was heavily responsible for the rise of neo-Nazi party Golden Dawn.

[2] The answer to the need for increased trade is not expansion of the geographical scope of the EU, but better deals to lower trading barriers with different global economies. For instance, the EU's round of 'Open Skies' agreements with Canada and the USA to expand access to each other's airline industries is a perfect example of how a smaller EU, acting in concert, can still liberalise trading relations without admitting new members.

agement of the European Commission and the budget process mean that new members can now be absorbed in a flexible manner. Thus, new members do not present serious institutional problems.

[4] One of the EU's great achievements is acting as a redistributive scheme for the European continent; in particular, it has succeeded in transforming Portugal, Poland, Spain and Ireland from relatively poor countries into developed economies on a par with the rest of Europe. It is now a moral imperative that the economic benefits of membership be spread to states in Southeastern Europe in particular.

Possible motions

This House would expand the EU indefinitely.

This House would welcome the countries of the Balkans into the EU.

This House would remove all geographical requirements for EU membership, and admit countries based purely on political and economic criteria.

Related topics

Immigration, limitation of

Commonwealth, abolition of the

United States of Europe

Euro, abolition of the

Should Britain leave the EU?

[3] The EU is simply not built to continue expanding indefinitely. First, every time new members join, the institutions have to be adapted; for instance, the number of Commissioners has risen from 15 to 28 in spite of the fact that there are no new competences assigned to them. Second, many EU policies depend on a system of enforcement that only works when there are a small number of states, such that trust is maintained easily; for instance, the common currency depends on the ability to limit government spending under the Stability and Growth Pact, but as the recent euro crisis has shown, the EU's accountability mechanisms are simply not built strongly enough to prevent states breaching it.

[4] The EU was able to make a small number of states grow rapidly by doing that process incrementally; when they were a small percentage of the EU economy, it was easy to reallocate funding to them. But the 2004 expansion has meant that poorer states are now a much larger proportion of the EU's population, and it is no longer reasonable to expect the core of the EU to pay for them. Moreover, such generosity is a sham; in fact, the single largest item in the EU's budget is the Common Agricultural Policy which favours French farmers, not the genuinely poor. It is not growth-enhancing to force states to contribute to that scheme.

Military drones, prohibition of

The concept of an unmanned military aircraft is almost as old as the use of air power itself; one was first tested in 1916 for the Royal Air Force's use in the First World War. However, they have, naturally, developed hugely in recent years, and are now in widespread use in military operations around the world. They are also used for numerous purposes; sometimes they are simply for intelligence gathering, but they are also often deployed as part of the USA's programme of covert assassination of terrorist leaders in Pakistan, Afghanistan and Yemen. Drones began as a tool to support conventional operations on the battlefield, but in 2002, a Predator drone was used by the CIA to kill alleged terrorists in Yemen, and they are now regularly used off the battlefield. Worries that they might fall into the wrong hands were crystallised in 2011, when Iran captured an American RQ-170 drone which had been spying in its airspace. There are question marks about their legitimacy in international law, given that they are typically used for targeted assassinations, but there are no express rules governing their use at present.

Pros

[1] Drones give militaries lethal capabilities that they did not previously possess. In particular, they are able to conduct military operations that would previously have been unacceptable because of the risk to human life involved. The possibility of losing troops and the political costs that come with that are the main restraint on powerful militaries – and particularly the USA and China – that tempers their behaviour in combat. Using drones leads to escalation in conflicts and the deaths of large numbers of civilians which would be prevented by this ban.

[2] Drones, by removing the human element of killing in war, encourage trigger-happy behaviour and so increase the likelihood of civilian casualties. When a person who will bear direct moral responsibility for the consequences of a bombing has to launch a powerful explosive device, they are more likely to adequately balance the need to achieve strategic objectives

Cons

[1] Drones do not create new military operations; rather, they are an alternative to fighter-bombers on missions which would otherwise have had to take place anyway. In its Kosovo bombing campaign (1998/99), NATO instructed planes to fly at 45,000 feet to avoid pilot casualties, which is above the height at which it is possible to distinguish civilians and combatants. Drones, because they can fly lower and so get better images of their targets, are actually more able to be discriminating, and so are less likely to kill civilians.

[2] There is nothing necessarily dehumanising about simply being far away from the target; fighter pilots also do not see the pain or suffering they cause, but watch it on a camera from far away. There are many advantages to the 'pilots' being on the ground rather than in the plane. The most important one is that, because pilots are not in personal danger, they are less likely to lash out and fire in panic, but

with the avoidance of civilian death. This is removed completely when the 'buck stops' with a technician who clicks a mouse thousands of miles away, totally divorced from the situation, and who is more likely to fire on groups of people whose identity is unknown.

[3] Drones are intimately connected to the broader policy of extra-judicial assassination of terrorists outside war zones, which is a highly damaging one. Drones make that policy possible because they do not create the risk of a pilot being shot down over a non-combatant state (who would therefore not be protected by the laws of war), and also because they do not require air bases or carriers in the region. The policy of extra-judicial assassination is a clear violation of international law, and radicalises populations and governments which were not previously involved at all in the 'War on Terror'.

[4] The harms of drone warfare are inherent to the drones themselves. No one seriously believes that drone 'regulation' would do much to limit their usage. Rather, a total ban in international law would make it easier to control them; they could then be impounded or shot down if found, and sanctions could be imposed on countries seeking to develop them to inhibit those countries from getting the relevant technology. Regulation simply represents a tacit acceptance by the international community that drones are acceptable.

can instead remain cool-headed about their strategies. Moreover, because they can be supervised more readily by commanders and given information by analysts who know what the target looks like, in consequence, civilian deaths are much less likely.

[3] Extra-judicial assassinations are not enabled by drones, and would continue regardless of them. The USA has determined that many of its greatest threats lie outside its borders, and is determined to pursue them, regardless of national sovereignty. If it were unable to use drones, it would simply turn to more dangerous methods, such as manned aircraft or on-the-ground Special Forces teams, which risk higher casualties and more damage. Moreover, drone attacks may not be in violation of international law, as they specifically target those who threaten terrorist acts, and are often used in areas where there is little or no meaningful governmental control.

[4] It is inevitable that some countries will seek to use drone warfare, regardless of whether others ban it, or even if they are expressly prohibited in international law. Given that, it is better that a system be established for monitoring and regulating drone warfare, with clear protocols as to acceptable usage, rather than allowing total free rein. If, for instance, all drones had to be registered, there would be less danger of them being unsafe or falling into criminal or terrorist hands. Moreover, it might be possible to prevent Russia, China and Iran fitting them with extreme weapons to make them more destructive.

Possible motions

Related topics
Pacifism
Armaments, limitations on conventional
Democracy, imposition of
Dictators, assassination of

Possible motions
This House would ban the use of drones.
This House believes the use of drones is inhuman.

Non-UN-sanctioned military intervention

As a formal matter of international law, military actions not in self-defence must be approved by the United Nations, or they are illegal. This debate proposes changing that position in order to encourage humanitarian interventions. It is worth noting that as sanctions for breaches of those rules are minimal, this debate takes place on the basis that actual sanctions for breach will be rare, although the International Criminal Court (ICC) has now agreed to prosecute the crime of aggression, so that may change in the future. Iraq will obviously loom large in this debate, but there are numerous other examples that are relevant.

Pros

[1] The UN is not the global moral arbiter that it claims to be; the fact is that the UN Security Council is an accident of history, and its permanent members frequently abuse human rights and go to war illegally themselves. It is nothing but the rankest hypocrisy for them to seek to control who may go to war, and on what grounds.

[2] The requirement of UN approval often needlessly delays much-needed intervention in these countries, which in turn costs lives. The UN's inaction over Rwanda in 1994 left French troops on the ground, powerless to act. Allowing unilateral intervention speeds this up by allowing states to act as soon as they have the relevant logistical capability; this saves lives.

[3] It is wrong to think that the need for the UN's approval should override the strong moral and cultural links that particular countries have with other regions of

Cons

[1] The UN is imperfect, and the UNSC is in need of reform. But the UN is, as it were, the best moral arbiter available to us. It represents the collective will of the world and an important check on powerful nations. Iraq, an unjust war, is what results when states ignore the UN.

[2] If America had intervened in Libya without the need for Russia not to veto, it would have launched a disastrous ground campaign, rather than its careful, surgical air strikes. The requirement for negotiation and consensus makes interventions better than if they are hot-headedly launched by a single constituency.

[3] The legacy of colonialism is one that should be expunged, not promoted. States intervening in their former colonies are just as likely to provoke resentment and bad memories as to be welcomed. The world should instead strive for a sense of

the world. For instance, former colonial powers regularly intervene in their former colonies, because they know them well and have strong ties; this leads to effective interventions, as with Britain in Sierra Leone or France in the Ivory Coast.

[4] The UN does not need to authorise an intervention to have some oversight of it. This is the distinction between *ius ad bellum* (the law of whether going to war is just) and *ius in bello* (law during war). Abuse can still be prosecuted at the International Criminal Court.

communal responsibility for atrocities and declining spheres of influence.

[4] The UN is not just an arbiter of the law of going to war, but also law in war. In order to effectively prevent war crimes and crimes against humanity, the UN must control the manner of these interventions. One of the reasons that the Iraq war was so brutal was the lack of rules of engagement established by the UN.

Possible motions
This House believes that humanitarian interventions should not require UN approval.
This House would go to war without the UN.

Related topics
Pacifism
United Nations, failure of
United Nations standing army
Democracy, imposition of
Military drones, prohibition of

Nuclear weapons, right to possess

The Treaty on the Non-Proliferation of Nuclear Weapons limits the possession of nuclear weapons to the five permanent members of the UN Security Council: the USA, the UK, France, Russia and China. When it was signed in 1968, they were the only nuclear-armed nations, but since then, India, Pakistan and North Korea have openly joined the nuclear club. All are outside the NPT, as is Israel, which is widely accepted to have nuclear weapons in spite of official denials. Iran has also attempted to join the nuclear club, and states including Libya and the United Arab Emirates (UAE) have made much more preliminary attempts to do so, while South Africa remains the only state to have voluntarily given up its nuclear weapons. This debate is principally about the moral question of whether any such right exists, but it is also partly about the merits of acknowledging it in international law.

Pros

[1] It cannot be denied that the consequences of a nuclear weapon being used are horrific, but we should not preclude the possibility that they might occasionally become necessary. If a state needs to defend itself and its very existence as an independent nation, or to prevent mass atrocities against its population, then those interests are so fundamental that nothing should be ruled out in defending them, including the use of a Weapon of Mass Destruction. We always have to weigh the loss of civilian life on one side with the equally potent potential loss of civilian life on the other side, but states are entitled to care more about their own populations, and because of that, they must be given a margin of discretion in deciding how to defend themselves, which extends to nuclear weapons.

[2] In any event, the point of nuclear weapons is not to use them, but to maintain a credible threat that they might be used. In practice, no state will ever be called upon to fire them, so a right to *possess* them can be established very easily. As long as states never actually fire them, then none of their harmful consequences ever come about, and so they are merely used as a bargaining chip, which is essential in a world where other states possess them and so can use that bargaining chip too.

[3] It is telling that the only times nuclear weapons have been fired in anger were in Japan in 1945, when there was only one nuclear power in the world (the USA). Since then, the nuclear states have always kept each other in check through the principle of Mutual Assured Destruction, or MAD. As long as there is a risk of

Cons

[1] The use of nuclear weapons is never acceptable. When A-bombs explode, every living organism for miles around is instantly incinerated; they have incomparable destructive potential, which should never be used. They rely on indiscriminately targeting populations, rather than attempting to avoid civilian casualties, which dissolves all of the normal rules of war. Moreover, radiation remains lethal for many, many years afterwards, which means that people who cannot possibly have been legitimate targets (as they have not yet been born) will be affected. It is not possible to have a right to do something fundamentally immoral.

[2] The consequences of a nuclear weapon ever being deployed are sufficiently catastrophic that anything which raises the risk of their ever being used is immoral. States cannot guarantee that they have adequate command-and-control structures in place to prevent these weapons being fired in the wrong circumstances; nor can they prevent a change of government that makes them less restrained. So it is never acceptable to possess nuclear weapons, even if they are ultimately never intended for use.

[3] There is a reason it is called MAD; this principle is a precarious means of preventing potentially catastrophic consequences for the world. Unless the suggestion is that every state will come to possess nuclear weapons (which is near-impossible given the enormous costs of developing and maintaining a weapons programme), there will be some countries against which nuclear powers can always use aggression. Moreover, while it may be the case that relatively stable and advanced states have

retaliation in nuclear form, that risk is great enough to prevent states from firing a nuclear weapon. Moreover, as more states acquire nuclear weapons, there are more potential nuclear retaliators, so MAD is reinforced, and the risk of nuclear attack decreases.

[4] Acknowledging a right to possess nuclear weapons allows for the establishment of a proper system of regulation and tracking; for instance, states could sign up to regular International Atomic Energy Agency (IAEA) inspections, and register all their weapons, both to ensure high safety standards and to make sure that they would never fall into the hands of terrorists or criminal gangs, and that if they did, it would be easier to get them back. At the moment, the large number of nuclear weapons outside state control is a cause for huge concern.

not fired nuclear weapons in anger, that principle weakens as governments which care less about their population's welfare gain control of these weapons.

[4] Regulation does not alter the real problem; when nuclear weapons are more plentiful, it is more likely that they will fall into the wrong hands. Extending the right to nuclear weapons extends it to governments which do not have the capacity to deal with the enormous task of managing a nuclear arsenal. Even in the existing structure, many former Soviet nuclear weapons are thought to have passed to terrorists or, more often, the mafia, who do not know how to handle them (or intend to handle them maliciously), increasing the chance of nuclear disaster. This can only be prevented if the number of nuclear weapons overall is reduced.

Possible motions
This House believes that every state has a right to a nuclear weapon.
This House would repeal the Treaty for the Non-Proliferation of Nuclear Weapons.
This House would give every country a nuclear weapon.

Related topics
Pacifism
Armaments, limitations on conventional
Military drones, prohibition of
Nuclear energy

Private military corporations, banning of

Private military corporations (PMCs) first came to global attention when Blackwater, a PMC to which the US military had contracted out many of its operations in Iraq, was involved in a 2007 incident in which its employees shot dead 17 Iraqi civilians in a roadside bombing incident. However, PMCs have been around for much longer, with many being heavily involved in African civil wars over resources in the 1990s. Their staff are often recruited from the ranks of former Special Forces soldiers, and so tend to be highly trained. However, there have also been significant questions about their accountability; Paul Bremer, the head of the American provisional administration in Iraq, signed 'Order 17', which removed Iraqi authority over the employees of PMCs. However, more recently, the American government has ordered that they be subject to the Uniform Code of Military Justice, and has scaled back their use in foreign operations, but many problems undoubtedly remain. Private military corporations fulfil a range of functions, from protecting ships and oilfields in danger zones for large companies, to guarding embassies and prisons, to essentially replicating the functions of ordinary soldiers.

Pros

[1] It is wrong that military operations be conducted for profit. All armies must balance operational efficiency in achieving their objectives with the need to protect civilians and the reputation of their fighting force more broadly. While ministers and commanders can give orders, much of this is ultimately dependent on individual soldiers and the choices they make. Their motives best balance these concerns when they act out of a sense of honour, rather than being purely profit-driven, possibly even with incentive-based pay; all this makes soldiers more likely to take risks with civilian lives in order to achieve mission objectives.

[2] Private military corporations cannot be trusted on the battlefield because they lack accountability. They are not subject to courts-martial, and are often also able to avoid the legal systems of both their employing country and the country they

Cons

[1] Incentives improve performance, and this is as true on the battlefield as anywhere else. If protection of civilians is an important objective, then governments can and will build these into the contracts that they sign with PMCs. Public outcry at mass civilian deaths – as happened in September 2007 when Blackwater killed 17 Iraqi civilians – will force governments to discontinue contracts with any firms that do not live up to ethical standards. This will then be reflected in the orders that the PMCs give their workers.

[2] Private military corporations do not lack accountability. Their accountability simply takes the form of pay-based incentives and the prospect of renewed contracts, rather than conventional military punishments. But even if they were less accountable than professional militaries, this would be compensated for by their increased professionalism; PMCs tend to

are in. This means that their incentive structure is even more strongly geared towards self-protection at the expense of observing the rules which are essential for ethical conduct on the battlefield. There is thus a much greater risk of their attacking civilians and even committing crimes against humanity.

[3] Private military corporations and their employees are often not bound by national and international law, and are also far removed from the PR issues faced by military forces; this allows the nations employing them to get them to do things that would be unacceptable if done by national armies. For instance, whereas British soldiers are now subject to the European Convention on Human Rights, the same does not apply to PMCs. They were heavily involved in the Abu Ghraib prison torture scandal in Iraq, as many operations there had been contracted out to PMCs.

[4] Many dangerous and evil governments are able to use PMCs for their nefarious purposes, even when their militaries are weak. This is because they will act for anyone, regardless of the morality of their cause.

draw from the highest ranks of former Special Forces, and so their staff are all highly trained and committed.

[3] Private military corporations did formerly exist in something of a legal black hole, but these gaps have now been closed. For instance, contractors are now subject to the US Uniform Code of Military Justice, and when operating in Iraq, the laws of the host country. Blackwater has been subject to numerous lawsuits and criminal charges for its actions in Iraq, and in 2010 paid out US$42 million to settle claims that it had acted illegally in smuggling weapons overseas.

[4] Dictators and warlords will always be able to hire mercenaries or recruit people with the promise of a commercial pay-off, whether PMCs help them or not. Regardless, most PMCs which operate with Western governments will not also work with more dubious governments, because this might create conflicts of interest or expose them to bad press, and such work is much less lucrative than their core contracts.

Possible motions

This House would ban private military companies.

This House believes that governments should not hire mercenaries.

Related topics

Pacifism

Armaments, limitations on conventional

National service, (re)introduction of

Women fighting on the frontline

United Nations standing army

Sanctions, use of

Sanctions refer to any measures (economic, cultural or diplomatic) which target a country for specific policies or institutional structures (such as dictatorship). In the past, sanctions were applied on a broad-brush basis, to prohibit or severely limit all contact with a country (such as funnelling nearly all the money that went into Iraq through the UN Oil-for-Food programme; or the international prohibition on trade with Burma), but increasingly, those are being replaced by 'smart sanctions', which shut down the bank accounts and companies of specific individuals within a regime (such as the sanctions on Robert Mugabe's Zimbabwean regime), and often for a specific purpose (for instance, the prevention of Iran's nuclear weapons programme).

Pros

[1] Economic sanctions are the best method available to the international community for altering the behaviour of unpleasant regimes. Bloodshed is avoided and direct intervention into another country's affairs is eschewed. By linking sanctions to specific behaviour that we wish to change, we can send a clear message to regimes which abuse human rights, defy democratic election results and proliferate nuclear weapons.

[2] There are limited examples where economic sanctions have been conclusively effective, but that is because sanctions have seldom been applied effectively by the whole international community. However, China's acceptance of sanctions against Iran and, more limitedly, in Sudan suggests that they are adopting a new turn towards a 'moral foreign policy', and it will be easier to get their agreement to sanctions in future.

[3] Sanctions can be designed in such a way that the suffering of the people is minimised, and pressure on the leadership is maximised. Oil-for-Food did weaken Saddam Hussein's regime substantially, and sanctions on North Korea managed to

Cons

[1] As with all intervention in dictatorial regimes for whatever purpose, sanctions are fine in theory, but can have serious unintended consequences. The standard example of success against South Africa is questionable; many factors were at work there and change was a long time in coming. Iraq was under sanctions for many years without liberalisation; the same applies to Cuba. It is unclear that sanctions work. But worse still, they can entrench dictators' powers by allowing them to paint the West as evil interferers, while Western states are just trying to prevent popular suffering.

[2] It will always be difficult to obtain full international consensus on sanctions; and the targets are usually more insular states which depend less on wide trade links in any case. Even when potentially effective, they may be circumvented by smuggling, corruption and other forms of sanction breaking. For instance, there is substantial evidence that many Western companies are still trading with banned Iranian groups through offshore accounts.

[3] Too often the sanctions hurt the people they are meant to help; the poor will

minimise the consequences of famine without expanding the powers of the regime there.

[4] Even if sanctions are often ineffective, to continue to trade with 'nasty' regimes represents complicity in their actions. Too often in the past we have sold them arms, trained their soldiers or bought their oil, diamonds, gold or crops; that makes us directly involved in their actions in an unacceptable way.

Possible motions

This House believes that sanctions do more harm than good.

This House believes that sanctions are always preferable to war.

Related topics

Democracy, imposition of

Dictators, assassination of

always be a last priority in times of economic crisis, while the ruling elite will take first pick of available resources. We simply lack the ability to monitor how and where this money is actually spent, because dictators hide it in Swiss bank accounts.

[4] To claim the moral high ground in this way is pure hypocrisy. Sanctions have invariably been used selectively, putting national interests first – despite their questionable behaviour, China and Nigeria have not been targets for heavy sanctions because they are seen as valuable strategic and economic partners. Serbia, Kenya and Cuba – which are targeted more seriously – are seen as of little value to the West. Perhaps the clearest example of this was the Oil-for-Food scheme in Iraq, which focused on maintaining the flow of oil to the West.

Terrorism, justifiability of

The popular imaginary of terrorism might now mainly focus on Al-Qaeda and the mass destruction of 9/11, the London and Madrid train bombings and associations with the Taliban, but there are many terrorist groups with arguably far more just aims; historical examples include the African National Congress (ANC) or the Irish Republican Army (IRA), and current ones include ETA (the Basque nationalist movement) and Palestinian terrorism. The point of the debate is not to argue about whether specific causes are just, but whether, assuming they are, violence against civilians would then be legitimate to pursue those aims. Equally, while the Proposition team must defend some specific acts of violence, they need not support, for instance, the blowing up of kindergartens.

Pros

[1] Sometimes minorities under oppressive regimes have no other means of expression, as they are denied access to media, the political system or the outside world, as were the ANC in South Africa under apartheid. As a last resort, it may be defensible to resort to violence.

[2] The end justifies the means; it may be that the eventual outcome of a terrorist campaign is beneficial and this outweighs the harm done in achieving it. History will be the judge, as when terrorism in East Pakistan helped to bring about the creation of Bangladesh in 1971, or the Jews forced the British out of Palestine and this led to the creation of Israel in 1948.

[3] Terrorist attacks are justifiable in the same way that just wars are; the only thing that deprives terrorists of the right to fight conventional wars is their lack of a state, which is usually exactly what they are fighting for. But given that we allow a sensible level of civilian death in wartime, we should also do so when it arises from terror.

[4] Terrorism is about causing fear. Although some civilians will usually have to die, much of the campaign may not actually involve violence, but merely the exploitation of existent fear. In 1997, the IRA threatened to blow up several railway stations in South East England without doing so; and they have used 'phony' warnings to evacuate buildings, exploiting the fear caused by previous explosions. The level of violence can be – and often is – kept to the bare minimum necessary to be taken seriously.

Cons

[1] Having no other means of expression is no justification for harm done to innocent civilians. Mahatma Gandhi and others have shown the potential success of peaceful protest. A noble cause is devalued if it is fought through violence; the ANC were for a long time painted in a bad light because of their violent actions, perpetuating apartheid. Moreover, it is simply false to claim that groups have no other access to the outside world; if you can launch a terrorist attack, you can also stage a sit-in.

[2] There are very few cases of terrorism actually working. In some cases, the satisfactory outcome is only achieved once the terrorists are forced to renounce violence; but in most cases, the fighting continues and nothing is achieved. The IRA won no concessions from the British government in 70 years of violent campaigning, and the Palestine Liberation Organization (PLO) was forced to renounce terrorism before negotiations began.

[4] Terrorist attacks are not like war in numerous ways. First, one side is not wearing uniform, which makes it very hard to fairly identify when you will be attacked. Second, they do not have fixed installations that can be retaliated against. Third, and most importantly, they do not have internal disciplinary procedures that can be used to enforce the laws of war against their members. As such, they cannot be protected by those rules.

[4] The bare minimum is unacceptable – 'phony' warnings still serve as reminders. The more often a terrorist exploits the fear from a previous attack, the more the public will begin to see through it and the terrorist must attack again. Moreover, fear

Possible motions

This House believes that terrorism is justifiable in pursuit of a just cause.

This House supports Palestinian/Basque/Tamil terrorism.

Related topics

Civil disobedience

Pacifism

Dictators, assassination of

Terrorists, negotiation with

Terrorist suspects, torture of

is simply not credibly created unless it is supported by a real risk of attack, which in turn requires that at some point an attack takes place. A terrorist group that only ever made threats would hardly be feared.

Terrorists, negotiation with

Unlike the 'justifiability of terrorism debate', this debate does become more definitional. That is because there are some terrorist groups with whom negotiation seems almost inevitable (Hamas, for instance, is also the elected Palestinian government), but others with whom it seems absurd (Al-Qaeda does not have a set of well-defined aims that lend themselves to a sensible compromise, but demands a restoration of Islamic law stretching from Spain to China). This debate, therefore, rests on the ability of both sides to move away from reductive examples and focus on the general principles of the debate, rather than simply trading case studies.

Pros

[1] Negotiation may lead to lives being saved, and this must be any government's first priority. Hostages tend to be civilians, who are not the property of the government to be sacrificed for other matters. If the price to pay for their safety is the release of 'political' prisoners, it is cheap. For instance, Israel's trading of Gilad Shalit for 1,100 Palestinian prisoners (in 2011) was ultimately worth it, because it saved a life.

[2] Negotiation in its simplest form means 'talking to'. We must keep an open dialogue with terrorist groups, to understand them and encourage them to take part in

Cons

[1] 'Political prisoners' tend to be imprisoned terrorists who will kill again on their release, so any hostages saved in the present must be weighed against probable future casualties. Second, there is no guarantee that hostages will not be killed anyway once the terrorists' demands are met. The Gilad Shalit swap will ultimately lead to loss of life; Israel had been highly successful in removing Palestinian terrorists' bomb-makers, many of whom have now been sent back to start their work again.

[2] Keeping an open dialogue with terrorist groups gives them political legitimacy

the political process without arms. Negotiation does not automatically require concessions, but can simply offer a basis on which to air grievances, which may lead to greater understanding.

[3] In many cases, terrorists are simply an unavoidable part of the political reality of engaging with a particular group which may have legitimate grievances. Where are the Palestinian leaders who have had no involvement with terrorism? Or the Tamil ones? It must be possible to make peace with these broad ethnic groups, and that requires engaging with their terrorist leaders.

[4] Negotiating with terrorists helps to improve their conduct after a peace deal, and make them into more viable political forces for power sharing. If a terrorist organisation needs to negotiate, it must also form a political wing, and start thinking about its policy priorities, rather than mere violence. Thus, when peace comes, it is a more effective partner and representative of a certain set of interests.

that they do not deserve. It is better to have no relationship whatsoever with them until they renounce violence, in order to show that they are voluntarily excluding themselves from democracy.

[3] By negotiating with terrorists, we reduce the political power of leaders on the other side who do renounce violence. One of the reasons that it often feels like the only leaders of a particular cause are terrorists is that a policy of negotiating with them means they are the ones who get results. When that is stopped, non-violent actors become more powerful, because they too can get concessions.

[4] Terrorist groups never focus their efforts on politics; they always remain primarily about violence, because that is ultimately what they think they require to win concessions. Their engagement with politics is superficial. It is far better to require them to give up arms altogether first, so that they may then genuinely transfer energies towards coherent policy formation.

Possible motions

This House would negotiate with terrorists.

This House would require all terrorist groups to renounce violence before negotiation.

Related topics

Civil disobedience

Terrorism, justifiability of

Terrorist suspects, torture of

United Nations, failure of the

The UN has certainly not been an unqualified success, but it has hardly been an unmitigated disaster either. The central point in this debate is to identify some theoretical framework or set of criteria in which to fit the numerous examples on both sides. For instance, the UN might be compared to its initial aims, or it might be said that those have evolved over time, or that the original charter is an overly demanding metric to use. As this debate is so fact-heavy, it is particularly important to be up to date on the UN's work. There is also some confusion about exactly what counts as 'the UN', because organisations like the International Monetary Fund (IMF) and the World Bank are notionally connected to it, but financially and operationally separate; generally, these can be excluded as there is plenty of material without them.

Pros

[1] The United Nations was founded in the aftermath of the Second World War, in an attempt to preserve peace and to build a better world founded upon respect for human rights. There have been so many conflicts, with so much loss of life, in the past 50 years that it is clear that the UN has not satisfied the hopes of its founders. Not only do many regimes still abuse basic human rights, but the UN has been powerless to prevent ethnic cleansing and genocide in Central Africa and the Balkans.

[2] While there has not been a Third World War, this is nothing to do with the UN: rather, for 45 years, it was prevented by Mutual Assured Destruction (MAD) between the Cold War powers, which has now given way to economic common sense; war is simply too expensive for interconnected and globalised economies to engage in it.

[3] Many of the UN's failures stem from its intrinsic bureaucratic shortcomings, such as the ability of any permanent member of the Security Council (UNSC) to veto decisions. The selection of these

Cons

[1] To a large extent the UN has fulfilled its remit, helping to prevent a global war, standing up to aggression (especially in North Korea and Kuwait) and making human rights a powerful worldwide concept which states can flout but not ignore – or else why would China have tried to justify its record as better than that of the USA? Some UN failures are tragic, but it cannot be expected to succeed in every case; it should be judged against the outcome were it never to have existed.

[2] Mutual Assured Destruction may have prevented nuclear warfare, but the UN has been the global focus for negotiation and co-operation in the way its predecessor, the League of Nations, never was. Both formal and informal compromises can be reached in tense situations. The end of the Cold War made co-operation via the UN even easier, and it was later a focal point for Western intervention in the Ivory Coast, Libya and Mali.

[3] There are plans to make the UNSC more representative, such as by expanding the number of permanent members, and including a more diverse set of countries

members is looking increasingly arbitrary and is not dependent on commitment to the UN ideals (China, for example, sells arms and nuclear technology to dangerous regimes, while the USA refuses to pay its contributions to the UN). Some resolutions passed by large majorities in the General Assembly (e.g. against Israel) have not been implemented, in large part due to obstruction by the USA and other Security Council members.

[4] Perhaps the UN's most serious failing is that it has not prevented genocide in numerous instances; its inaction in Rwanda (1994), and then at Srebrenica (1995), points to a deep and systematic inability to tackle the most heinous crimes on earth. Moreover, the UN record has not improved; massacres in Syria by Bashar al-Assad and in the Ivory Coast by Laurent Gbagbo show that the UN remains largely powerless to protect the world's most vulnerable people.

on it; suggestions include Japan, India, Brazil and South Africa. In addition, the veto power could be revoked or reformed such that, for instance, two permanent members had to wield it to have effect.

[4] An organisation cannot simply be blamed for the fact that terrible atrocities happen in the world; genocide is horrendous, but it is a fact of the modern world, and when armies are amassing in such numbers to commit genocide, the UN could hardly step in easily to stop them.

Possible motions

This House would abolish the UN.
This House believes that the UN has failed.

Related topics

Democracy, imposition of
Sanctions, use of
Non-UN-sanctioned military intervention
United Nations standing army

United Nations standing army

The United Nations, by Chapter 7 of its Charter, gives the Security Council the task of identifying all threats to and breaches of global peace and acting accordingly to end them, but it is still entirely dependent on the co-operation of states with its interventions and peacekeeping missions to do so. This debate instead proposes that the UN should recruit a permanent standing army, which would be able to respond quickly to potential atrocities and threats to peace. There are some practical problems with this idea, but what is even less clear is who would run such a body; the Proposition team must make a definitional choice as to whether the Security Council, General Assembly or the Secretary-General would ultimately command it.

Pros

[1] Many of the threats that the UN has to deal with require urgent responses. Genocides and invasions do. At the moment, the UN must recruit *ad hoc* forces for every mission, which means that they cannot respond straight away, so conflicts get more advanced and harder to solve before intervention. For instance, during the First Gulf War (1990/91), preventing Saddam Hussein from defeating the Kuwaiti military with an instant airborne response would have reduced bloodshed in the long run.

[2] Increasingly, a global consensus is developing around the need for humanitarian intervention, as reflected in the UN's intervention to assist the Libyan rebels in overthrowing Muammar Gaddafi. As such, there will be an international willingness to use such a force when needed.

[3] The types of intervention that the UN makes are highly specialised, as peacekeeping is a difficult and complex task. Normal military forces train for pitched battles, not for counter-terrorism operations, disarmament or aid delivery. By creating a permanent force for these tasks, we massively increase the UN's operational effectiveness.

[4] The current system of funding for UN peacekeepers pays a flat fee of just over US$1,000 per month per peacekeeper to contributing states. This gives incentives to countries that run their military forces cheaply (in particular, Pakistan, Bangladesh and Nigeria). This means that UN forces are often poorly trained, and also a waste of money.

Cons

[1] Most of the UN's work is, rightly, not intervention in ongoing conflicts, but peacekeeping after they have been resolved. If the UN becomes a permanent antagonist in global conflicts, its ability to negotiate peaceful settlements is hugely undermined.

[2] This force will not go anywhere. Assuming it is controlled by the UN Security Council, as it must be logically, Russia and China, not to mention the USA, will be highly reticent about sending it into battle. As such, it is a pointless gesture.

[3] The UN's current work is indeed mainly in peacekeeping, but that is not what a standing army would do. Rather, intervention to prevent invasions is precisely the kind of work that conventional forces, trained for battle, do best. Moreover, most armies are increasingly being trained for precisely the kind of missions the Proposition team describe.

[4] Such a force would be riddled with practical difficulties. What language would it use? Where would it be based? Would it recruit directly? Who would fund it? Such co-ordination is very difficult; for that reason, it will be ineffectual.

Possible motions

This House would give the UN a standing army.
This House believes the UN needs a rapid reaction force.

Related topics

United Nations, failure of the
Non-UN-sanctioned military intervention
National service, (re)introduction of
Armaments, limitations on conventional
Sanctions, use of

United States of Europe

This links closely to the earlier debate about expansion of the European Union, but instead focuses on what the EU itself should do. While in many respects, the EU already resembles a single state (with its own currency and central bank, an apex [supreme] court and reams of legislation on the minutiae of central government), in others, it remains a union of independent, sovereign member states (each with their own military, fiscal policies and public services). This debate is about whether the EU should follow the US model and devolve much greater power to a central government, while allowing individual member states to retain small areas of autonomy.

Pros

[1] As the EU is already a common trade area and (largely) has a common currency, there are many problems that arise that can only be managed by a central government. As the Eurozone crisis has shown, when countries like Greece are allowed to spend without limits, but the whole of Europe has a stake in preventing their economic collapse, they spend far too much; this is only solvable by having a strong central government that prevents these collective action problems from arising.

[2] Even in the USA, there is no longer one shared language – some US schools now teach in Spanish as a first language for example. The United States of Europe would similarly have several languages. Switzerland and Canada are other examples of countries with successful federal governments, but no single shared language. There is no need for alarmism. As the example of the USA in particular shows, federalism is quite compatible with cultural pluralism and the retention of different national and ethnic traditions.

[3] A federal Europe offers fascinating possibilities for multilevel governance; for instance, it is arguable that where the EU

Cons

[1] There is no need for a federal model to prevent these problems. Indeed, if the EU's Stability and Growth Pact had been adequately enforced, this problem would never have arisen. Rather, the EU can impose harsh sanctions on those breaking its common rules in certain areas, while leaving those matters that only concern what happens within national borders to member states.

[2] The EU is not a logical political or cultural unit. Unlike the USA, it does not even have a shared language. Each of the nation states of Europe has its own particular culture, language, legal precedents, constitution, customs and traditions. It is not an appropriate candidate for federalisation. Entry into a United States of Europe would mean the 'normalisation' of each country so that it lost its historic traditions and institutions. That is bad for those countries, but also means that the EU will be hard to govern, as there will be no communal bonds binding the people together.

[3] The EU is, in essence, a relentlessly centralising organisation; it accrues power to Brussels, rather than devolving it anywhere else. Moreover, such power will be

felt unable to legislate for the whole of Europe, it would instead devolve powers to regional or local government, which might be a far more appropriate decision-making body with better information and more accountability.

highly unaccountable, because normal electoral mechanisms will not effectively control it; when there are no existing pan-European political parties, and no leader can speak the language of everyone under their jurisdiction, issues will inevitably be very poorly understood.

Possible motions
This House would federalise Europe.
This House welcomes the United States of Europe.

Related topics
European Union, expansion of the
Euro, abolition of the
Should Britain leave the EU?

SECTION D

Economics

Bonuses, banning of

This debate will inevitably tend to focus on bankers, because their bonuses tend to cause such uproar in the media, but bonuses are also a very common way of remunerating all sorts of executives. Many states have taken steps to limit bonuses, both in state-owned banks (especially the UK) and private sector ones too (e.g. Switzerland). Bonuses can come in cash or shares; the latter can be less desirable to CEOs especially, as they are often prevented from selling them for a limited period. Inevitably, steps might be taken to evade such limits.

Pros

[1] Bonuses are an unjust reward frequently given for not really creating any genuine value. Often, they have become totally divorced from performance, and are given even in years where companies make huge losses. Some contracts even contain 'guaranteed' bonuses, which misses the point of them completely; they should be special rewards, not 'par for the course'.

[2] Bonuses skew the incentives of those who are dependent on them, encouraging them to take absurd risks. This is because they require the banker not just to perform well, but to outperform his/her colleagues; this means that s/he might gamble on dangerous products that may not be in the company's interests; investment in sub-prime mortgages is the prime example of this.

[3] Bonuses encourage a focus on the short term. As they are calculated at the end of each financial year, the goal is to earn as much money as possible in that time; as such, there is a total disregard for investments which may not mature for a number of years, and also no qualms about assets that might rise slowly for five years and then crash catastrophically. No one gets their bonus in previous years taken back, so such investments are still winners for the bankers.

Cons

[1] Bonuses do represent a genuine and deserved reward. It is a misconception that they are especially generous payments for exceptional success; rather, they are just a form of performance-related pay. While they are paid in loss-making years, that is because particular individuals or teams have generated income for a business; they are not to blame for the firm's entire performance.

[2] Bonuses align incentives perfectly with the firm's overall goals. Companies should take risks, and that is healthy. Indeed, paying only a flat salary is much more problematic, because workers have no incentive to do more than the basic requirements of their job. Moreover, as this policy requires firms to increase base salaries, they will suffer major cash-flow problems, as they will now have much higher base costs even when not making profits.

[3] Only badly designed bonuses create a focus on the short term. But with 'clawbacks' or bonuses paid based on long-term performance of an investment, executives are encouraged to look into the future. This is particularly so where compensation is in the form of shares, as then personal wealth is directly linked to the company's value.

[4] It is not at all easy to get round a ban on bonuses; financial regulators are highly 'savvy', and can spot and punish attempts at circumventing the ban.

[4] Such a ban is laughably easy to evade. Firms will simply rename bonuses, or come up with more creative ways of paying them; for instance, the use of company cars or jets, or 'gifts' of high-value objects like works of art. Moreover, base salaries could simply be linked to past years' performance, which has exactly the same effect.

Possible motions

This House would ban bonuses.
This House believes that bankers do not deserve what they get.

Related topics

Capitalism v. socialism
Salary capping, mandatory
Failing companies, bailing out

Child labour can be justified

Child labour is often a taboo; in the words of the International Labour Organization (ILO), what it does to victims is 'deprive them of the chance to be children'. However, it has also been exceptionally common throughout history; until the twentieth century, even in Western Europe, most children worked, albeit part-time. This debate has two strands; first, whether even at its best, child labour could be justified; and second, whether given the said reality that many children who 'labour' are in fact slaves, measures ought to be taken against it. It can be an analysis debate about whether child labour is right, an individual choice debate about buying goods produced with child labour, or a policy debate about legalisation. For the most part, the focus is on the developing world.

Pros

[1] There is no principled barrier to children going out to work; the ages of 16 or 18 are arbitrary limits, and many children are ready for work before this. The refusal to use child labour is based on an overly sentimental idea of childhood, rather than on a realisation that the culturally accepted age of adulthood varies hugely by country; if anything, preventing children from working is cultural imperialism.

[2] In many developing countries, education systems are minimal, and are certainly

Cons

[1] We are all entitled to a period of life where we are free from the stresses and strains of 'real' life, and have the chance to grow and personally develop. Children do not have the strength or stamina to do full-time work; these are objective facts, and not cross-cultural variations.

[2] It is a caricature to paint developing countries as lacking education systems; most do, and progress is rapid. Between 2000 and 2008, the enrolment rate in primary education globally rose from 80

not free or affordable for most people. Here, the alternative to child labour is not education; rather, it is an empty, pointless existence, which would be made better if children could start getting good work habits and skills.

[3] In many cases, child labour is the only route out of poverty for families. Where there is a lack of state benefits, if the primary bread-winner becomes ill or dies, then children may need to go out to work to support their families. Alternatively, when wages are simply too low, it may take more than parents working to support a large family. Children may also be needed to help their families with agricultural work.

[4] The legalisation of child labour would bring it out of the criminal underworld in which it presently operates, and improve it. It is inevitable that desperate children and families will want to engage in child labour, and so it is better to stop it being a black-market activity in which children are used in dangerous mining activities, as in the Democratic Republic of the Congo.

per cent to 89 per cent, and this is the one of the United Nations Millennium Development Goals that has been broadly successful. If child labour is encouraged, more parents will take their children out of school to work, undermining this progress.

[3] Child labour is not a viable or helpful route out of poverty. First, because it pays very poorly, it rarely offers much to families anyway. Second, it hurts children's long-term financial prospects, because educated children will earn more. Third, it may act as a smokescreen for a failure to provide adequate foreign aid to alleviate this poverty.

[4] Child labour is very hard to regulate, and child workers are easy to use, because they cannot speak out. This means that child labour will always be closely associated with slavery, abuse and the use of children for dangerous work. Legalisation would not have stopped recent labour abuses, but does increase the group of children who can be abused.

Possible motions

This House would buy goods made with child labour.

This House believes child labour is morally acceptable.

This House supports child labour.

Related topics

Fairtrade, we should not support

Welfare state

Mandatory retirement age

Smacking, remove parents' right to

Euro, abolition of the

At the time of writing, in 2013, the euro is on a precipice, with the Greek financial crisis threatening its very existence. It is currently used in 17 EU member states and five further countries that have unilaterally adopted it. Interest rates are set by the European Central Bank (ECB), which aims to keep inflation at or below 2 per cent, but its mandate has now generally broadened to other crisis prevention measures. The euro is also the model for the proposed African and Gulf area single currencies.

Pros

[1] The fundamental problem with the EU is that monetary union without fiscal union is unsustainable. Because they share a currency, the other member states cannot allow a highly indebted economy like Greece or Portugal to crash. But they also have no means of preventing Greece from running up unsustainably high levels of public debt. So there will always be members who take advantage of this to overspend.

[2] The benefits of the Eurozone are fairly minimal. As long as the EU retains the free movement of goods, the barriers created by having different currencies are fairly minimal. They simply require conversion and careful hedging of currency risk.

[3] A single interest rate for an area as large and diverse as the Eurozone is simply impossible to set correctly. At any given time, there will be some economies growing faster that need inflation strictly controlled, and others that need growth boosted; these two goals are contradictory. Moreover, in countries with high home ownership, raising interest rates has a much bigger impact (as mortgages become more expensive). The rates set will tend to reflect France and Germany's priorities, rather than being a fair reflection of need.

Cons

[1] The answer to the lack of a fiscal union is not abolition of the monetary one, but either to go all the way and accept full fiscal union, with the ECB collecting taxes centrally and then redistributing them to the states for spending; or to impose tighter sanctions for states which breach the Stability and Growth Pact, the EU's existing fiscal control mechanism.

[2] The Eurozone increases cross-border trade by reducing the costs related to having separate currencies. For instance, tourists are more willing to spend if they can readily identify how much things are worth, and businesses will invest more in other countries where there is no risk that currency fluctuations will devalue their investments.

[3] The setting of a single interest rate is undoubtedly challenging, but that does not render it impossible. Indeed, it simply represents a compromise between different interests. Moreover, by allowing smaller states to 'borrow' the credibility of experienced central bankers from larger states, markets gain greater confidence in the promise of low inflation and stability in smaller states.

[4] There is always a downside to currency revaluations. Member states will experi-

[4] Abolishing the euro will allow exchange rates to settle at a level which is far better for international trade. Major exporters like Germany will see their exchange rates rise, making imports cheaper; while Greece will be able to reap the benefits of a fall in its interest rates by increased tourism and exports.

ence rapid shocks as the costs of their imports rise; that is particularly problematic for a country like Greece, where people are already very poor, as their cost of living shoots up.

Possible motions

This House believes that the euro has had its day.

This House would abolish the euro.

This House believes that one currency means more problems.

Related topics

United States of Europe

European Union, expansion of the

Regional trade blocs over global free trade

Failing companies, bailing out

The global financial crisis and subsequent economic downturn have greatly increased the number of private companies threatened with bankruptcy. In many cases, governments have responded by bailing out those companies. Bailouts can take many forms: they can be conditional on firms following certain policies or restructuring their operations; or they may involve the government taking a share in the ownership of the company; or they may take the form of injections of cash or the provision of loans repayable at low interest over long periods. It is hard to cover this range of variations, so debates should focus on the principle of governments providing money to keep companies afloat. Most of the prominent examples are from finance; Bear Stearns, Fannie Mae and Freddie Mac, and AIG in the USA, Northern Rock in the UK and the Anglo Irish Bank in Ireland. Prominent non-financial cases include the rescue of Chrysler and General Motors by the American government in 2008, Parmalat in Italy in 2003, and the rescue in 2010 of Dubai World, Dubai's state-owned investment company, by fellow emirate Abu Dhabi.

Pros

[1] Large numbers of people are often dependent on these companies for their jobs. In the short run, these jobs will not be created again elsewhere; rather, they will be non-existent, jeopardising the futures of these employees and imposing the burden of caring for them on the state. In the long run, older employees may find themselves unable to retrain or gain employment in another industry, meaning that financial collapse simply condemns them to an early retirement. As the company cannot afford to pay its debts, these people's pensions are also often lost.

[2] Many other firms are also dependent on a company on the brink of collapse. They may have money invested in it, as in banking, or require its goods and services, such as parts it manufactures that go into producing a car. These firms will be exposed to enormous losses and reduced productivity if they are no longer able to rely on the collapsed company. This can send shockwaves reverberating through the whole economy; many analysts agree that the decision not to bail out Lehman Brothers in 2008 severely worsened the global financial crisis.

[3] Sometimes these firms are in trouble because of bad management or a flawed business model, but often the trigger of their collapse is merely short-term factors in the market, such as rumours of financial weakness (as happened to Northern Rock) or a temporary fall in demand in a key market. Bailing out these companies allows them to survive these short-term shocks and emerge stronger. If the company rises in value later on, the government recovers its money anyway by taking shares in exchange for the bailout.

Cons

[1] Bailouts are often enormously expensive; the UK's public debt nearly doubled as a result of the 2008 bank bailouts. This is not just a standard cost/benefit argument; rather, the point is that bailouts have the effect of worsening the very economic indicators they are supposed to improve, because they reduce confidence in a country's ability to pay back its debts. Ireland's experience here is especially instructive; having nationalised its failing banks, it finds itself in 2013 having to restructure its national debt for fear of defaulting, endangering not one bank but the whole national economy.

[2] Often, these firms need to be allowed to fail, because their weak profits reflect the fact that there is no demand for their goods and services any more, or that they simply cannot compete with other firms doing the same thing. For instance, the US auto industry bailouts simply protected an industry which no longer has the capacity to produce equally good cars at the same costs as Japan and China. Such industries should be allowed to fail, so that the process of 'creative destruction' can reallocate their employees and capital to more profitable industries.

[3] The idea that some companies are 'too big to fail' creates a dangerous mix of incentives for their management and shareholders; there is less incentive to cut costs, and a large incentive to take dangerous risks for the possibility of profit, knowing that a bailout will be forthcoming if those risks fail. This ultimately leads more and more firms to fail, and so radically increases taxpayer costs.

[4] Spending money on bailouts is an unfair way of distributing it. It simply

[4] Governments have a choice in these situations between letting the firm fail altogether and using taxpayers' money to gain influence over them. Conditional bailouts allow them to force firms to pursue policies which are good for the economy, such as extending cheap loans to small businesses or reducing the number of homes they repossess.

[5] Some firms are of particular strategic importance, regardless of their economic viability. For instance, governments may need to maintain defence corporations (the US government has bailed out Lockheed Martin in the past) so that they can guarantee arms supplies, and they may bail out a national airline or important cultural firm for reasons of national pride. In these instances, profit making is not the only criterion we should use to determine whether a firm succeeds.

preserves the profits of already rich shareholders and the salaries of CEOs, using tax money taken from ordinary people. The state is often careless about taking adequate shares in the firms it bails out, so that it gets nothing in return when companies recover. Bailout money should instead be spent on giving tax breaks and benefits to people on more modest incomes.

[5] Finally, many firms in need of bailouts have been involved in criminal, or at least morally dubious, activities, for which they should not be rewarded. Parmalat (an Italian food company) went bankrupt in 2003 in large part because its shareholders and managers had been engaged in elaborate fraud schemes; and Northern Rock (a UK building society that was nationalised by the UK government in 2008) was in particular danger because it had many of its assets in complex, tax-avoiding foreign trusts. The state should not encourage and reward this behaviour.

Possible motions

This House would never bail out failing private industry.

This House would let the banks fail.

This House believes that the USA should not have let Lehman Brothers collapse.

This House would refuse to socialise losses and privatise profits.

Related topics

Bonuses, banning of

Salary capping, mandatory

Capitalism v. socialism

Fairtrade, we should not support

Fairtrade is a movement that is undoubtedly noble in motive, namely to help farmers in the developing world receive a fair price for their goods. However, economists are deeply divided as to whether the specific prescriptions of fair trade are effective in alleviating poverty; or whether, conversely, they do more harm than good. This debate is rarely so prescriptive as to involve banning fair trade outright, but can take the form either of a policy (such as limiting its labelling) or individual choice (not buying its products). Fairtrade products are many and varied, including chocolate, coffee, wine and fruit, and also come from many different countries. So a more nuanced approach that pays attention to differences between Fairtrade products may be called for.

Pros

[1] There is considerable doubt about the economic merits of Fairtrade, and it may simply be 'too soon to tell' whether or not it is beneficial. But given that, it is certainly not the most efficient form of charity we can give (and that is what Fairtrade is, given that it involves paying more for a product in order to help the poor). So we should donate our money elsewhere, and Fairtrade charities certainly should not benefit from the false moral high ground that their name gives them.

[2] Fairtrade requires farms to be run as co-operatives; it requires those who work on them to have some prior assets, which means that the very poorest are left out. This is particularly problematic, as they now have fewer potential employers in their area, and so their wages are driven down.

[3] Fairtrade is used by Western companies and supermarkets as a means of price discrimination; that is, they make its products more expensive, and also trade them as luxury goods, while keeping a non-Fairtrade range. This simply allows them to reduce consumer welfare, without

Cons

[1] While there may be doubt about Fairtrade, the assumption that we should choose alternative forms of charity makes little sense. Most people do not think in this way; they have no time to consider the efficiency of charities, but might spend a few extra pennies when given a choice in the supermarket.

[2] Joining a Fairtrade co-operative is incredibly cheap. In Rwanda, for instance, it costs about US$0.60 per head. That is not beyond anybody's reach. Once in the co-operative, workers reap the benefits of a share of profits, labour rights and minimum wages, which are all hugely beneficial.

[3] It is unacceptable for firms to hijack moral consumerism for their own ends, but we should legislate against that, not do away with Fairtrade altogether; as it grows as a movement, so will scrutiny of it, which will prevent these practices.

[4] Minimum wages will have little, if any impact, in this context, where wages are tiny relative to huge farm profits. Moreover, even if they do, a small number being unemployed in a context where

in fact paying more to those who produce the goods.

[4] By demanding a minimum wage, Fairtrade creates a category of workers who are employable when paid a wage below the full-time minimum, but not at or above it; this is because it is not profitable to employ them at the full-time minimum wage. When the minimum wage is introduced, therefore, they lose their jobs. While the data on minimum wages in advanced economies are mixed, that is because these economies are fast-growing so jobs may not actually be lost. That is not the case here.

Fairtrade provides large amounts of employment is an acceptable cost.

Possible motions
This House would boycott Fairtrade.
This House would not allow Fairtrade labelling.
This House believes that Fairtrade is no such thing.

Related topics
Capitalism v. socialism
Sanctions, use of
Child labour can be justified

Inheritance tax at 100 per cent

Most advanced industrial economies level some form of tax on inherited wealth, although it is usually only charged above a certain threshold, and certainly is not close to 100 per cent of the total assets considered. However, some states (Australia, Israel, some US jurisdictions) have abolished it and others have scaled it back. Importantly, inheritance tax (IHT) does not require anyone to lose anything they had before; it is impossible for someone to be made *worse off* by inheriting a taxed bequest. There is also generally an exemption for small items of sentimental value. Related debates include substantially raising inheritance tax or scrapping it altogether.

Pros

[1] People do not deserve the wealth they inherit; they had nothing to do with the creation of their parents' assets, and it is an arbitrary consequence of their birth. So there can be no complaint about taking it away from them.

[2] People do not have a right to dispose of their income however they wish; we already impose taxes on income and assets because we acknowledge that people have been dependent on what the state and society provided them with to make their

Cons

[1] It is not possible to say that just because people have not earned wealth themselves, they have no entitlement to it. The nuclear family is a fundamental social unit, and it is a basic human instinct to want to keep assets within it. In some ways, families are extensions of ourselves, and thus their assets are also our own.

[2] People have a right to dispose of their income in the way they wish, so that even if the recipients of an inheritance do not 'deserve' it, they should still receive it. We

money. So there is no absolute right to gift money to others.

[3] Often, inherited wealth simply sits idle, because those who possess it simply have more money than they can spend. A 100 per cent inheritance tax would transfer this money to people who would actually spend it, so providing the economy with a valuable boost.

[4] Windfalls of inherited wealth that people acquire around the time when their parents die (generally middle age) exacerbate inequalities; for instance, they allow people to get onto the housing ladder, converting rent into equity, or send their children to private schools. This means that social inequality is perpetuated further.

should respect the wishes of the dead, and it is wrong that when parents have worked hard to earn money, their children's entitlement to it should be ignored. That is especially so because they have already paid tax on this wealth; they should not be taxed on it again.

[3] Rather than inhibiting the economy, large inheritances serve a vital function in increasing investment, because the rich do not leave their wealth idle, but put it into private equity funds which then spend it trying to help promising businesses. Without these funds, global business would find it much harder to raise any capital.

[4] Rather than being an unfair benefit, injections of capital in middle age simply help families get by before they have real assets to speak of. When they have children, their expenses often go up far more than their salaries. Inheritances simply allow them to live moderately comfortable lives.

Possible motions

This House supports a 100 per cent inheritance tax.

This House believes that all of the dead's property should go to the state.

This House would stop double taxation of inheritance assets.

Related topics

Capitalism v. socialism

Utilitarianism

Salary capping, mandatory

Social contract, existence of the

Regional trade blocs over global free trade

In spite of the growth of the World Trade Organization, which now has over 150 members committed to liberalising international trade, pure global free trade is a far-off prospect. Meanwhile, regional trade blocs (groups of countries which offer each other greater trading benefits) are growing fast. The EU is the most prominent, but there are many others, including NAFTA (North America), ASEAN (Southeast Asia),

Mercosur (much of Latin America) and ECOWAS (Economic Community of West African States). These vary in their extent; for instance, the EU is fully integrated, extending totally free movement of labour and capital to its members, while NAFTA is more limited and focuses on reducing goods tariffs.

Pros

[1] Regional trading blocs are perhaps a stop-gap to global free trade, but given the complexity and intricacy of global trading relations, true global free trade is still far off, so we are better off accepting and channelling energy into regional blocs, as these provide more immediate economic benefits.

[2] Given the enormous disparities between economies in terms of productive capacity and sophistication, exposing all countries to unbridled free trade will simply crush poorer countries, as Western and Chinese businesses rush into their markets and outprice them. Regional free trade offers a compromise between the need for expanding markets and the need for protection.

[3] Free trade cannot be unfettered completely, but requires institutions to promote it and occasionally limit it. These determine when countries are allowed limited protectionism to protect vital national interests (culture, public health or national security), but the WTO's Dispute Settlement Body has primarily proved to be a tool of Western nations with expensive lawyers, allowing Western farm subsidies to continue, while forcing a Western concept of 'liberalisation' on the poor. By contrast, the European Court of Justice has instituted genuine free trade, and only allowed very occasional limits on it.

[4] Free trade does not occur in a vacuum; it requires a complex architecture of

Cons

[1] Rather than representing a step en route to total free trade, the setting up of regional blocs entrenches the regional system. Regional blocs tend to put up large external tariffs on goods from outside the region, and so actually reduce the likelihood of global free trade and undermine the WTO's objectives.

[2] Free trade is not going to happen overnight. It is, of necessity, a gradual process of barrier reduction. States can retain transitional protectionist measures as they grow, preventing the shock caused by foreign entry into their markets, while ultimately moving towards free trade.

[3] There are problems with the WTO Dispute Settlement Body mechanism, but these can be fixed; for instance, by having a more representative panel of experts sitting in judgement. Creating free trade in a narrow set of countries, even if it is more 'complete', ultimately has less of a net impact.

[4] Such managing institutions are far from necessary. Much harmonisation occurs simply because of the free market system, while competition rules are an unnecessary addition to the basic process of allowing goods to move freely.

associated institutions to manage it effectively, including common regulations on health and safety, and harmonised competition laws. The whole world is simply on much too grand a scale for such institutions, which can, by contrast, be more effective at the regional level.

Possible motions

This House prefers the WTO to the EU and NAFTA.

This House believes that regional trade blocs are better than global free trade.

Related topics

Capitalism v. socialism

Fairtrade, we should not support

Failing companies, bailing out

European Union, expansion of the

United States of Europe

Euro, abolition of the

Salary capping, mandatory

This debate is not unlike the debate about limiting bonuses, but salary caps have a less direct impact on incentive structures for executives, so this debate is more about the morality of earnings. Pay for CEOs has risen particularly rapidly in recent years, and certainly much faster than average earnings. To put it in context, the average American CEO earns US$9.7 million a year, or 3,489 years of salary for the average worker.

Pros

[1] Salaries should reflect what people are actually worth, but these salaries simply cannot. It is just not possible that, in any meaningful sense, a CEO is worth 3,500 times more than an ordinary worker. This pay must be brought under control, because it goes against basic principles of equality.

[2] Salary rises constitute a 'collective action' problem. Corporations do not really think that their CEOs are worth as much as they pay them, but the need for 'big name' corporate leaders means that they compete to pay more. A cap stops that spiral.

Cons

[1] Salaries do reflect the profit making of their recipients. Someone who is very good at banking genuinely produces millions of dollars in value. That is the nature of the whole underlying economic structure, not salaries themselves.

[2] This is not a 'collective action' problem; it is competition. If firms genuinely do not value their employees that much, then they can let them go and get someone less expensive. That is how a free market in labour works.

[3] Nothing about this policy redistributes wealth to those doing socially valuable jobs. Money not earned by top CEOs

[3] Pay has lost any sense of contact with the moral worth of the job being done. It is a disgrace that bankers and footballers earn millions, while teachers and nurses struggle to make ends meet. When placed in stark comparison like this, we can see that those salaries cannot be justified.

[4] Keeping salaries closer together would encourage the sense that 'we're all in this together'. It would improve social cohesion, and so reduce crime and improve community spirit. It is the symbolism of high-earning individuals that makes people think that the social system does not help them.

simply goes into corporate profits, which in turn go to investors; those are not people who really deserve it, but those who already have large fortunes (often not self-made ones) to invest.

[4] Salaries are not the main source of wealth for the super-rich. They earn their money from investments or companies they own; salary caps may reduce the number of very wealthy CEOs, but do nothing about über-wealthy oligarchs or property magnates, who are the real symbols of the failure of capitalism.

Possible motions

This House would cap executive salaries.

This House believes that the best paid employee in a company should earn no more than 10 times the wage of the lowest paid employee.

Related topics

Failing companies, bailing out

Bonuses, banning of

Utilitarianism

Capitalism v. socialism

Marxism

Inheritance tax at 100 per cent

State pensions, ending provision of

Like the future of healthcare and unemployment benefits, this issue is made particularly topical by the rapidly escalating costs to developed countries of old-age entitlements (pensions and free medical care). As life expectancy increases, the average age of the population is growing, and in the twenty-first century, many more retired citizens will be supported by many fewer taxpayers. It has been said that a society can be judged by how it looks after its oldest members, but can a state sustain a universal pension scheme or should we be made (or left to choose) to invest in private pension schemes or investments to secure our own future?

Pros

[1] Although civilised societies should provide for their citizens in old age, it does not follow that governments must be involved. Private pension schemes could ensure that everyone planned for and funded his or her own retirement income, reducing the burden on the state and its taxpayers.

[2] Government bureaucracies seldom provide services as efficiently as their private counterparts. A better system would be to force citizens to invest in pension plans, but with considerable freedom as to how this is done. This system is successful in Chile, and personal and corporate pension schemes are still in existence everywhere. The skill of investment managers to guarantee returns is likely to provide higher pensions than the government can.

[3] Private pension schemes are not subject to political interference. This is a risk with state pensions, especially since older people are more likely to vote than the young, and can therefore elect governments that will pay generous pensions while squandering resources for the future. This is especially true in the USA where cuts to Medicaid and Medicare are seen as political suicide, since a president doing so risks losing the retired vote.

[4] Privatising pensions ends the 'dependency culture' and gives responsibility back to the individual, who should learn to live with his or her own economic choices and the consequences. Some may choose to invest in pensions, others in their children's education in the expectation that they will repay the gift. It should be a personal choice, and lazy spendthrifts should not benefit from an equal state pension.

Cons

[1] It is society's duty to care for its elder citizens, and it is the government's duty to ensure that those who cannot look after themselves are catered for. Many people do not earn so much that they would, or could, contribute voluntarily to a pension scheme; a state-controlled scheme is the only way to ensure they do not become penniless upon retirement.

[2] The problems of government control which exist in nationalised industries are not true of the welfare state – pensions, healthcare, education and so on – since the free market is a poor way of guaranteeing these goods.

[3] Governments can at least monitor state pension funds and guard against fraud. The exploitation of the Mirror Group pension fund by Robert Maxwell, discovered after his death in 1991, showed how vulnerable private funds can be to dishonest businesspeople. Political interference is a strong possibility anyway; in 1997, the Labour government in the UK removed tax advantages from private pension schemes. Governments also have the onus to intervene to prevent private schemes from 'going bust'; this unwritten guarantee encourages private firms to speculate recklessly (e.g. the savings and loan industry in the USA in the early 1980s, or Asian banks in the 1990s).

[4] This is a remarkably heartless attitude that would leave those who do not invest wisely, leave investment too late or cannot afford to invest in the first place without the safety net of government support. Self-sufficient individuals can (and do) invest in private pension schemes over and above the National Insurance system,

[5] Whether or not a state pension scheme is desirable, it is simply not affordable. With an increasingly ageing population, it is a ticking time bomb which threatens to jeopardise countries' economic stability. As many countries are going through austerity measures, it is only fair that the elderly feel their share of the pain too.

Possible motions

This House would privatise the pension system.
This House would put an end to handouts to the retired.

Related topics

Capitalism v. socialism
Welfare state
Mandatory retirement age

giving them all the freedom they need to create a comfortable retirement.

[5] The main problem facing governments is not the meagre amount given in state pensions but the generous pension schemes of public sector workers. These are being addressed by many countries as part of their austerity measures. There has to be some delay in changes to pensions as individuals have to be given enough notice to make their own provision.

SECTION E

Social, moral and religious

Abortion on demand

Abortion was always considered sinful, and was criminalised in Britain and most states of the USA in the nineteenth century. Backstreet abortions became a usual way to limit the size of families. In Britain, the 1967 Abortion Act legalised abortion when it was advised by a doctor on medical grounds. In the USA, the *Roe* v. *Wade* case of 1973 in the Supreme Court set down the principle that in the first three months, abortion is to be allowed; and in the second trimester, it is to be allowed if it is required in the interests of maternal health. In neither country is 'abortion on demand' – abortions undertaken principally as a form of birth-control at the wish of the pregnant woman – officially allowed, but doctors (especially those in private clinics) will happily certify that carrying the pregnancy to term would cause severe mental distress to the woman. In many Catholic countries, abortion is still illegal.

Pros

[1] It is a woman's right to decide, in conjunction with the father when appropriate, whether she wishes to have a baby. It is her body and she ultimately should control what happens to it. It is people, not fertilised eggs or foetuses, that have 'rights'.

[2] If abortion is not allowed on demand, women will go to 'backstreet abortionists' where lack of expertise and unsterile conditions can be a serious risk to health. Such backstreet abortions result in an estimated 68,000 deaths per year, according to recent World Health Organization (WHO) figures.

[3] There is no definitive answer as to when a foetus becomes a person in its own right, but up to 24–28 weeks, the foetus is so undeveloped that it is not reasonable to consider it a person and to accord it rights.

[4] In many areas of the world where overpopulation and chronic food shortage are perennial problems, abortion helps prevent bringing children into the world

Cons

[1] The right to do as we wish to our bodies must be curtailed by the rights of others to be free from harm. In many instances, the right to do as we wish to our body is overruled; for example, drug laws exist to guard against making a person a danger to others by altering their mind with drugs. In this case, the mother's rights are overruled by the right to life of the unborn child.

[2] One could argue against banning *anything* on the grounds that people will carry on doing it on the black market. Abortion is morally wrong and banning it will reduce the number of abortions that occur.

[3] A foetus can survive if born prematurely from as early as 20 weeks, and this boundary is being made earlier all the time by improved incubator technology. Given that we cannot be sure at what point a foetus is a person or can feel pain, we should err on the side of caution and consider the foetus a person from conception or shortly afterwards. Abortion, therefore, is murder.

who would probably know only deprivation, illness, starvation and early death.

[5] In an increasingly secular and scientific world, the religious views of some people about the infusion of a foetus with a soul by God at conception, for example, should not be imposed upon the rest of society.

[6] Many young girls who become pregnant would have their future, their education, their family relationships and their career ruined by the birth of a child. Others are pregnant as the result of rape or incest and would have their suffering multiplied indefinitely by carrying the child to term. We cannot put the alleged 'rights' of a dividing cluster of cells ahead of such concrete harm to a person.

[7] We allow contraception. Abortion is, in effect, no different – the prevention of the development of a potential human being. In the case of the 'morning after pill', the analogy is even closer. If we allow these measures, then we should also allow abortion.

Possible motions
This House would put the mother first.
This House believes that the unborn child has no rights.
This House believes that a woman's body is her temple.

Related topics
Population control
Euthanasia, legalisation of
Surrogate mothers, payment of
Sex education
Contraception for under-age girls

[4] We can address overpopulation in the developing world with other measures such as increased availability of contraception as well as economic and technical aid programmes.

[5] Human life is sacred, as is recognised by the billions of adherents of the main world religions. God creates each individual at conception and so abortion is murder, and an act against the will of God that destroys God's work.

[6] Young people should be encouraged to have a more responsible attitude to sex and pregnancy, and should deal with the consequences of their actions whatever they may be. There are even schools now specifically for teenage mothers and their babies to attend. In cases of rape or incest, either the child can immediately be put up for adoption, or exceptions could be made just in these distressing instances.

[7] Barrier methods of contraception (condom, cap) are qualitatively different from abortion in that no fertilised egg ever exists to be destroyed. Other methods (coil, 'morning after' pill) that are logically equivalent to abortion should not be allowed.

Affirmative action

There are many minority (and sometimes majority) groups which have suffered historical injustices, and are now under-represented in higher education, business and politics; e.g. women, certain ethnic minorities or castes, and those with disabilities. Are laws protecting equal opportunities enough to address this issue or is affirmative action (AA), or positive discrimination as it is known in the UK, needed to redress the balance and create a level playing field? There are a number of systems of AA including quotas, loaded short lists, additional points or prioritisation. A debate may look at one model or argue the issue in principle. There are many smaller debates within the theme which look at one group or one industry, but this case gives an overview.

Pros

[1] There has been unfair historical discrimination which has led to under-representation today; for example, in the USA women were late in getting equal rights and the black community were discriminated against in law until the 1960s. Even today, for every dollar earned by men in the USA, women earn 74 cents; African-American women earn 63 cents. This is also true of the black population of South Africa after apartheid and the lower castes in India after centuries of oppression. This under-representation must be addressed; equality is a human right and should not just be words on the statute book, but should be seen to happen in practice. Men, and the majority ethnic community in many countries, have an unfair advantage which skews this equality and AA redresses that.

[2] Under-representation is bad in practice as well as in principle. Countries are damaged by not having access to the brightest talent from the largest pool. They also benefit from a greater level of diversity; e.g. representation in parliaments is improved by having more women; and confidence in the police is created

Cons

[1] Affirmative action is wrong in principle. Meritocracy is the only fair system and all discrimination must be outlawed. It is unjust to punish today's white men for the historical injustices committed by others. It is also unfair as it does not give help based on need; it is saying that, for example, in the USA, a rich black man deserves more help than a poor white man, and therefore is still defining people by their race or gender rather than their needs or talents.

[2] Affirmative action can damage the development of a country; for example, South Africa is a country that needs to develop economically for the well-being of all its people (black unemployment is very high), but its priority is AA which means that it is putting less qualified people into jobs and thereby jeopardising development. This is also true with the Policy of Reservation in India which increases the brain drain from that country. This helps neither majorities nor minorities.

[3] Affirmative action is unnecessary because countries evolve organically towards equality. Countries accord pro-

through a mix of races/religions – e.g. in Northern Ireland.

[3] Countries that now have equal opportunity laws, but no AA still see under-representation (e.g. black under-representation in universities in the USA, after AA was outlawed; Wales only produced equal representation for women in their Assembly through AA). This is because equal opportunities legislation does not create a culture of change. Affirmative action is the only effective way to address the issue of equality.

[4] Affirmative action only needs to be a short-term measure as it creates a real change which then renders it unnecessary. It does this in four ways. First, self-perpetuation (e.g. women value other women, so a female CEO is less likely to be sexist when hiring and promoting). Second, AA creates role models who raise aspirations and inspire others. Third, AA leads to a change of culture; e.g. women make the workplace more women-friendly. An example of this is that women in parliament in Sweden have introduced better maternity rights. Fourth, AA encourages a breakdown of prejudice both in the workplace and in society as a whole, because when people work together, they learn to value each other, which has beneficial consequences.

tection from discrimination in the law to women and minorities. The first people from these communities then begin to succeed and this then cascades through society. It is a natural process and does not need interference. All countries at present are at a different stage of this process; e.g. Sweden already does not need AA for its women, whereas the Roma in Slovakia are currently under-represented, but are beginning to campaign for their rights in a way that indicates their evolution is starting.

[4] Affirmative action impedes the removal of prejudice rather than causing it to progress. It does this in four ways. First, resentment against minorities increases prejudice, which leads to more discrimination in the long term. Second, AA encourages a culture of mediocrity by saying that a certain race/gender cannot get there on its own. Third, AA backfires: e.g. drop-out rates for black students in the USA at the time when they had AA was triple that of white students. Fourth, AA robs individuals who would have been successful anyway of their achievement and says they only made it because of the policy.

Possible motions

This House would use affirmative action to redress historical injustices.

This House would support quotas for women in parliament.

This House would use positive discrimination to widen diversity in universities.

Related topics

Slavery, reparations for

Political correctness

Homosexuals, ordination of

Alcohol, prohibition of

This debate looks at whether the government should intervene to stop the social and health problems related to alcohol, or whether people should be allowed to make their own decisions in relation to drinking. A Proposition team may want to think about the enforcement and penalties attached to the policy as most people are familiar with the failure of Prohibition in the USA.

Pros

[1] Statistics show undeniably that alcohol plays a role in many crimes. In the UK, it is a factor in 65 per cent of murders, 40 per cent of cases of domestic violence, and a third of all cases of child abuse; the Association of Chief Police Officers puts the proportion of violent crime that is alcohol-related at about 70 per cent. Studies state that 80 per cent of people treated in accident and emergency departments are there because of alcohol use, with 10 people killed through drink-driving every week and thousands permanently scarred every year in drunken fights. Drinking while pregnant harms an unborn baby. The government must intervene in response to these horrifying statistics by banning alcohol consumption.

[2] As well as posing a risk to others, alcohol also harms the user, increasing the likelihood of liver failure, some forms of cancer and involvement in accidents. Alcohol is also linked to high blood pressure, strokes and heart disease. Alcohol abuse can also have serious psychological effects. It is a common misconception that alcohol is not physiologically addictive, but regular use can result in a physical dependence, with all the problems that implies. As an addict cannot truly be said to be exercising 'free choice', the state has an even stronger right to intervene.

Cons

[1] Alcohol is a factor in crime and can cause social problems. However, the vast majority of those who consume alcohol do so responsibly – for them, drinking is a harmless and pleasurable activity, which adds to their enjoyment of social events. Alcohol *abuse* should be tackled; to penalise the majority for the actions of a minority is not the solution. Prohibition would be a ham-fisted and overly simplistic way to deal with a complex issue.

[2] While the state has the right to act against citizens when their actions are causing harm to others – as it does at the moment when drinking leads to violence or public nuisance – it does not have the right to interfere in their private lives. Drinking may carry a health risk for the individual, yet so do many legal activities, including most forms of sport; moreover, alcohol differs from most illegal drugs, because responsible usage in moderation is neither addictive nor harmful (indeed, some medical research implies that it can do you good).

[3] Alcohol cannot be treated in the same way as other drugs. After thousands of years, drink plays an important role in our social lives, and even in religion; many of our social structures have been built up around it. Many businesses would collapse with an alcohol ban. As Prohibition in

[3] As alcohol is a harmful and addictive drug, our treatment of it should be the same as our treatment of cocaine or heroin. Moreover, alcohol is for many addicts the first drug on the path to ever harder drugs. Removing this first link in the chain may be an important step to solving the drug problem altogether.

[4] A great deal of money and effort is directed towards solving the problems caused by drink. Surely it would be wiser to focus efforts on eradicating the root cause of these problems?

[5] Many countries, especially in Northern Europe, are seeing binge drinking on the increase, with a particular rise in young people and women drinking specifically to get drunk. This is leading to a situation where town centres are taken over on Friday and Saturday nights by drunken revelry and anti-social behaviour. When they sober up, intoxicated drinkers regret their actions, which can include casual, unprotected sex. Sexually transmitted disease (STDs) and teenage pregnancy rates could be slashed by banning alcohol.

America (1920–33) demonstrated, any such legislation cannot work – instead, it drives ordinary citizens into the hands of criminals, and encourages experimentation with other drugs.

[4] To say that alcohol is the root cause of many social ills is a dangerous over-simplification – rather, it is the *result of* those ills. Throughout history, it has been convenient for politicians and moralists to blame drink for 'corrupting' citizens. From the time of Hogarth's *Gin Lane* through to Victorian England, it was seen as one of the most significant dangers facing society, yet this was simply to ignore the fundamental injustices that drove the poor and the desperate to alcoholism. It is these that we must tackle.

[5] There are other ways of reducing binge drinking without banning alcohol outright for everyone, which would be a serious infringement on liberty. Increasing the price of alcohol, raising the drinking age, limiting the measures of alcohol served and restricting licensing hours could all be used to tackle problem drinking.

Possible motions
This House would ban all alcoholic drinks.
This House believes that alcohol is a scourge on society.

Related topics
Protective legislation v. individual freedom
Drugs, legalisation of
Smoking, banning of
Organ donation: priority for healthy lifestyle

Animal experimentation and vivisection, banning of

Human treatment of animals can be a highly emotive subject. A dolphin trapped and killed in a trawler net, a rat deliberately mutated by genetic engineering, a red deer hunted to the point of terrified exhaustion and shot, a rabbit with eyes and skin blistered from chemical and cosmetic tests, a captive lion robotically pacing its tiny cage at the circus or zoo – all of these are distressing images that arise in the context of debates about the human treatment of animals. But what are the arguments behind these emotional appeals? The Australian philosopher Peter Singer was one of the first, in the 1970s, to argue that animals have rights and that they should be treated with the respect due to a human animal. This is still a contentious claim, but one that more and more people seem to accept. The arguments on 'animal rights' in Section A consider whether animals have rights, and whether, if they do, we should be doing more to recognise and respect those rights. We currently use animals from bacteria to primates in many different ways – for food, clothing, entertainment in circuses and zoos, medical experiments, biotechnology (e.g. using bacteria to synthesise human hormones) and cosmetic testing; in sports such as greyhound racing and horse racing, and even as objects of 'field sports' such as fishing, shooting, foxhunting and hare-coursing. Some would argue that all of these uses of animals are wrong and that they should never be used as a means to a human end. Others would take the opposite view that it is right and natural for us to use other species for our own benefit, and that this is indeed the key to our continuing evolutionary success. This debate and the other debates on animals weigh up the pros and cons of our treatment of animals in various contexts. A debate on animal experimentation could be on cosmetic testing only or on medical testing. The arguments here focus on medical testing.

Pros

[1] Vivisection involves the exploitation and torturing of innocent animals to benefit humans, and this is wrong on principle. Mice are bred to be susceptible to skin cancer, exposed to high levels of radiation and allowed to die. Rats are genetically engineered to grow full-size human ears on their backs, and baboons are deliberately infected with the HIV virus. No economic or medical gain can justify such cruel and cynical exploitation of our animal cousins. More advanced mammals – especially primates (monkeys and apes) – have complex nervous systems like ours and are similarly susceptible to pain and fear.

Cons

[1] On principle, it is right and natural that we humans study, use and exploit the natural environment for our own benefit. That is the way that our species has come to thrive and prosper and it is right that we should continue to do so through experimentation on and exploitation of both vegetable and animal resources. Animals are not people and do not have 'rights', and anthropomorphic sentimentality should not get in the way of scientific and medical progress.

[2] Experimentation on animals saves lives. Animal experimentation and research have historically produced innumerable medical

[2] The successes, necessity and efficiency of animal research have been greatly exaggerated. In fact, vivisection is wasteful, inefficient and often unsuccessful, as well as being cruel. In the USA alone, an estimated 50–60 million animals are killed annually in the name of scientific research, but with highly unreliable results. Half of the drugs given approval in the USA by the FDA (Food and Drug Administration) between 1976 and 1985, all of which had been tested on animals, produced side-effects in humans serious enough to cause them to be taken off the market or re-labelled with warnings; the Thalidomide disaster in the late 1950s and early 1960s is another such case. This is because vivisection is flawed as a scientific method. One species (e.g. rats, rabbits or dogs) cannot serve as a reliable experimental model for another (humans); penicillin is fatal to guinea pigs, for example.

[3] There are more humane and more efficient alternatives to vivisection. For example, in the 'Entex test', vegetable proteins extracted from the jack bean mimic the cornea's reaction to foreign matter and so can be used in the place of live rabbits to test for the eye irritancy of products. Tissue and cell cultures can be grown in the laboratory from stem cells or single cells from humans or animals – these can be used for tests in the place of live animals. Computer simulations of diseases and drug treatments can also be used in the place of vivisection. These technologies are improving all the time.

[4] Scientists are put in danger when they are asked to work in laboratories where animal testing occurs. The Animal Liberation Front claimed responsibility for fire-bombing labs and attacking researchers'

and scientific breakthroughs that could not have been made in any other ways; experiments on cows were instrumental in developing the vaccine that eliminated smallpox worldwide; experiments on dogs in the 1920s led to the discovery of insulin for the treatment of diabetics; genetic experimentation on mice and primates is currently helping to develop gene therapy for cystic fibrosis. Animals from mice to primates to humans share the same essential biology and physiology (with analogous organs, nervous systems, immune systems and hormones).

[3] There are no alternatives to animals for research into complex immunological, neurological and genetic diseases. Computer simulations are only applicable to simple conditions of which we have full understanding. In more complex cases, our lack of understanding of the diseases (e.g. AIDS, cancer, muscular dystrophy) means we must experiment either on animals or on humans. People cannot be expected to volunteer as guinea pigs for untested drugs at all stages of their development.

[4] Scientists and laboratories can and should be protected, but we should not compromise the development of lifesaving drugs because of the threats and intimidation of terrorist groups.

homes and cars in 2006. It is not acceptable to ask civilians to expose themselves to this risk and make themselves a target.

Possible motions

This House would ban all animal testing.

This House would put science ahead of animal welfare.

This House believes that no cosmetic products should be tested on animals.

Related topics

Animal rights

Blood sports, abolition of

Vegetarianism

Zoos, abolition of

Drugs, legalisation of

The legalisation of drugs has long been an important issue, but in recent years, it has taken on a global dimension. 'Plan Colombia', a scheme to encourage lawful enterprises in Colombia, has largely defeated the drug cartels in that country, but at the same time Mexico has collapsed into lawlessness at the hands of gangs. As well as the general debate about legalising all drugs, debates may arise about legalising specific drugs, or about more creative policies such as the legalisation of drugs within certain areas.

Pros

[1] The role of legislation is to protect society from harm, but not to protect people from themselves. We do not legislate against fatty foods or lack of exercise, both of which have serious health implications. The individual's freedom is paramount unless serious harm is done by a particular act. Taking soft drugs does not harm anybody else and has only minimal negative effects on the person taking them – it is a 'victimless crime'. As such, it should not be a crime at all.

[2] Individuals should be left to choose their own lifestyle and priorities. If that includes using drugs for pleasure and relaxation, then that is a perfectly valid decision.

Cons

[1] It is right that governments should legislate in a way that overrides personal freedom to protect people from themselves as well as from each other. That is why bare-knuckle boxing is banned and seatbelts are compulsory in some countries (e.g. Britain). These are ways in which personal freedom is overridden by legislation designed to protect personal safety. Soft drugs are harmful; cannabis smoke (as well as the tobacco with which it is often mixed) is carcinogenic, and prolonged cannabis smoking has been shown to cause brain damage and significant loss of motivation and short-term memory. Amphetamines interfere with the nervous system in a potentially damaging way.

[3] The law is currently inconsistent. Cannabis and speed have comparable physical and mental effects to those of alcohol and tobacco, which are legal drugs. If anything, alcohol and tobacco have more seriously damaging effects. Tobacco-related diseases kill millions each year, and alcohol is responsible for deaths on the road, civil disorder and domestic violence on a huge scale. Cannabis and speed make people 'spaced out' or hyper-active, respectively, for short periods in social situations and are relatively harm-less. If alcohol and tobacco are legal, then soft drugs should be too.

[4] Legalisation allows for the creation of regulated environments in which drugs can be sold and taken; this has manifold benefits. First, it means that the state can monitor what goes into drugs, so that they are not 'cut' with more harmful substances (such as, for instance, crushed glass which dealers often mix with cocaine). Second, it means that drug addiction can be treated as a medical rather than a legal issue, and so addicts can get better help and support; needle exchanges for heroin users, for instance, can be very helpful. Third, it allows the state to make tax revenue from drugs, to recoup the costs of any social damage that is done.

[5] Legalising drugs breaks the power of drug cartels that are destroying states around the world. Gangs have become so powerful in Mexico that they effectively have overrun law enforcement and large swathes of local government, forming their own private militias; they are funded and sustained in this by their monopoly on supply lines of drugs into the USA, which can only pass through criminal gangs because drugs are illegal.

Drug-takers also put others at risk by taking mind-altering substances that can lead to unpredictable and dangerous behaviour.

[2] The government should provide moral leadership as well as legislating to pro-tect the health of the individual and the safety of others. The drug-using lifestyle is a shallow, hedonistic, apathetic, inward-looking, uncreative form of escapism. Governments should legislate and speak out against drugs to discourage young people from this lifestyle and encourage them to engage in healthier and more creative pastimes.

[3] The effects of soft drugs may be 'comparable' with those of alcohol and tobacco, but there are important differ-ences. Cannabis and speed are mind-altering in a way that alcohol and tobacco are not. The fact that harmful and dan-gerous substances (tobacco and alcohol) are already, regrettably, socially entrenched is not a good reason to allow two more such substances to become more widely used and socially acceptable.

[4] Regulation can control for certain effects of drugs, but ultimately it cannot side-step the central problem, which is that drugs are harmful. Rather than being facilitated in their addictions, individuals should be discouraged from ever using drugs, and the state should do whatever it can to stop them getting involved, especi-ally as softer drugs can act as a 'gateway' to harder ones, exposing young people to the huge harm of a heroin or crack addiction.

[5] Even if illegality helps to explain the power of drug gangs, there is no evidence that legalisation would in fact help to weaken them. Now that they have such

power, there is no reason to believe that they will give it up without a fight. Moreover, legalising drugs prevents both national governments and the international community taking a strong law enforcement stance against drug gangs, because they no longer have a mandate to punish them unless they can catch them doing other illegal activities.

Possible motions

This House would legalise all drugs.

This House believes that drug taking is a matter of individual choice.

This House believes that the solution to Mexico's drug problem is legalisation.

Related topics

Protective legislation v. individual freedom

Alcohol, prohibition of

Smoking, banning of

Euthanasia, legalisation of

The term 'euthanasia', coming from the ancient Greek words meaning 'good death', is used to refer to voluntary rather than compulsory euthanasia. Voluntary euthanasia is when an individual asks to be given a lethal injection to put them out of pain and end his or her life. If a patient is helped to end his/her own life, then this is referred to as assisted suicide, and the arguments for or against are almost identical. Compulsory euthanasia – killing those who are terminally ill or who are above a certain age regardless of their wishes – is everywhere regarded as murder. In the Netherlands, voluntary euthanasia has been legal since 1983 and other countries have followed by legalising euthanasia or assisted suicide including Switzerland, Belgium and Luxembourg.

Pros

[1] People should be allowed to request a 'mercy killing' to end their suffering. Victims of cancer, AIDS or motor-neurone disease may know, in the later stages of their illness, that the only prospect for the short remainder of their life is more physical degeneration and acute suffering. They should be allowed to die with dignity with the help of, for example, a lethal injection or an overdose of morphine from a doctor.

[2] Someone may wish to write a 'living will' stating that if they ever become a

Cons

[1] However much a patient is suffering, it is the role of a physician, as expressed in the Hippocratic Oath that all doctors have to take, to cure disease and restore patients to health, not to kill them. Doctors should not be forced to compromise their professional oath, nor be put under the great moral pressure of deciding when to advise a patient that euthanasia might be the best option. With the highly effective painkillers now available, there is never any need even for the terminally ill to suffer great pain. Use of painkillers, not euthanasia, is the answer to painful terminal illness.

'vegetable' or are in a persistent vegetative state (PVS) as the result of an accident, they do not wish life support to be continued. We should respect the wishes of such people rather than extend their lifespan, when quality of life has completely deteriorated.

[3] At present, doctors are sometimes allowed, in effect, to carry out euthanasia on the grounds that the amount of painkillers they had to use to alleviate the patient's suffering in fact turned out to be fatal. Instances of this 'double effect' of a drug are not currently considered wrong, and allowing euthanasia is only an extension of this principle.

[4] Just as the right to vote includes the right to abstain, and the right to free speech includes the right to be silent, the right to life should be seen to include the right to choose to die. It is 'my body, my life, my choice'. Not allowing those who are too physically ill to commit suicide to do so with help amounts to discrimination against people with severe disabilities, since it is not illegal for others to commit suicide. Euthanasia, or 'doctor-assisted suicide', should therefore also be allowed.

[6] Euthanasia also spares the loved ones of a patient the needless agony of watching them slowly degenerate and die in great pain, and gives them the comfort of knowing that they carried out the patient's last wishes. In many cases, a death through euthanasia can provide a pain-free and loving goodbye.

[2] People have been known to recover from comas and PVS after considerable periods, and some 'terminally ill' patients make miraculous recoveries. Allowing euthanasia would risk killing people who could otherwise have had years more life. With euthanasia, as with capital punishment, the price of a mistake is too high. A patient in a coma or PVS may have changed their mind subsequent to writing their 'living will', but not altered the document. In such cases, the loved ones would be authorising the killing of someone against their wishes and ruling out the possibility of their recovery or cure.

[3] There is a qualitative difference between seeking to reduce someone's pain and their dying as a secondary effect, and deliberately killing them. Doctors should not be allowed or required to kill their patients.

[4] There is no such thing as a 'right to die'. Suicide is always wrong, and is only legal because the act is seen as one of mental illness and is treated as such. If somebody is considered a suicide risk, then they are committed to a psychiatric unit; if a medic is called to someone who has attempted suicide, then they do all they can to revive that person. One should not respect anybody's right to end their own life. While it is true that suicide is not illegal, *assisting* suicide is. Allowing such a practice will immediately open up grave dangers of abuse by unscrupulous doctors and relatives who would like to see a certain patient 'out of the way' for the purposes of inheritance or freeing up scarce medical resources.

[6] Patients could feel under pressure to opt for euthanasia so as not to be a burden

Possible motions

This House would legalise voluntary euthanasia.
This House believes in the right to die.
This House would assist suicide.

Related topics

Protective legislation v. individual freedom
Abortion on demand
Organs, legal sale of

to their family. If it is an option, is it not selfish not to take it? It is better to provide palliative care and counselling to help patient and family manage their natural time together.

Gay marriage, legalising of

A bill was passed through the House of Commons to legalise gay marriage in February 2013, but it remains a controversial topic in the UK and around the world. Many countries have now legalised it including the Netherlands, Spain and Canada, and it is legal in nine US states. Supporters of gay marriage see it as an important factor in equal rights, whereas its opponents see marriage as an inherently heterosexual union. A Proposition team may want to consider whether it would force religious institutions to marry gay couples, or whether it simply wants the union to be legally recognised where it is performed voluntarily by religious leaders or in civil ceremonies.

Pros

[1] To complete the worldwide movement towards equal rights for homosexuals in society, we should allow homosexual couples the right to a public legal and religious recognition of their lifelong loving commitment to one another. Homosexuals, as equal members of society, should have equal access to both civil and religious forms of marriage.

[2] Whatever its historical roots, marriage is clearly not just for the purpose of reproduction. Infertile heterosexual couples are allowed to marry; therefore, homosexual couples should be allowed to marry. Homosexual couples, like heterosexual couples, may wish to marry as a prelude to adopting or fostering children, and this should be encouraged as part of a modern

Cons

[1] The equality of homosexuals with other members of society is achieved by decriminalising homosexual activity and allowing equal opportunities to homosexuals in terms of education and employment rights. Supporting gay rights does *not* mean ignoring the obvious differences between homosexuals and heterosexuals. Marriage is historically and logically a heterosexual institution, the extension of which to homosexual couples would be meaningless and perhaps even a misrepresentation of their distinct identity.

[2] Marriage is primarily an institution to allow for the creation of children in a stable family environment. Homosexual couples can never produce a family and to allow them to marry is to overlook the

understanding of the family and of family values.

[3] Society has always been able to adapt religious teachings and develop interpretations of religious principles proper to each new era. Religions should respond positively to the role that homosexual couples can play in communities. Those sectors of religious communities that condemn homosexuality outright will simply find themselves increasingly marginalised as society progresses. Those homosexuals who wish to marry may choose, in any case, to reject the homophobic religious traditions and marry in a civil ceremony.

[4] Many societies give certain financial advantages to married couples – e.g. tax allowances. To deny these advantages to committed homosexual couples is an unjustifiable case of discrimination on the grounds of sexual orientation.

[5] It is circular to argue that homosexuals are not parents and so are not candidates for financial rewards open to parents. If homosexuals were routinely allowed to adopt and foster children, then it would be appropriate to reward and encourage stable homosexual family homes with financial incentives. What we want to see is a reinvention of 'family values' in which homosexuals can marry, be parents, and receive the same rights and benefits as their heterosexual counterparts.

history and meaning of marriage. We can endorse their love for one another without pretending that they are just like a heterosexual couple. Furthermore, their relationships, not being child-producing, do not *need* the same permanence for the sake of children that a marriage provides.

[3] Marriage is primarily a religious institution and all the main religions condemn homosexuality. It would be hypocritical of the Jewish and Christian communities to endorse homosexual marriage when their sacred scriptures condemn homosexuality.

[4] The financial advantages offered to married couples are not to encourage marriage for its own sake, but to encourage the creation of traditional family units. Child-support payments and tax relief on mortgages serve the same purpose – to encourage the creation of stable family homes. It is this that society seeks to encourage, not sexual unions *per se*.

[5] Homosexuals, by definition, will not produce children, and so are not appropriate candidates for financial incentives to home-making and the maintenance of family values.

Possible motions
This House would legalise gay marriage,
This House celebrates homosexual home-makers.
This House demands new family values.
This House believes that marriage should only be a union between a man and a woman.

Related topics
God, existence of
Homosexuals, ordination of
Homosexuals, outing of
Marriage
Polygamy, legalisation of

God, existence of

It is commonly held in educated Western culture that religious belief is irrational and unsubstantiated. But can all the great geniuses of Christianity and other religions throughout the ages have simply been mistaken, not to mention the billions of religious believers worldwide today? Some twentieth-century theologians, such as Paul Tillich, have redefined God as 'the ground of being', in an attempt to get away from simplistic and anthropomorphic conceptions of God as a very powerful person, or even as an old man with a long beard. Does this idea of God make any sense? Can traditional conceptions of a personal, intelligent, benevolent Creator God be rejuvenated? Or is all talk of God rendered meaningless in a modern scientific world?

Pros

[1] The universe is governed by natural laws and forces that seem to be the product of an intelligent mind. That mind is God, who created the universe. This fact of the universe's dependence on God is expressed in the Genesis myth of the Jewish and Christian traditions, and in other myths around the world.

[2] Unlike other animals, we are moral beings with consciences. This is because we were created by God, who is a moral being who set down the moral as well as the natural law.

[3] Around 40 per cent of people in Britain report having had a 'religious experience' of some kind in which they were aware of a power greater than themselves or of a supernatural personal being. People have had such experiences throughout history of the 'numinous', the 'sublime' and the divine. It is arrogant to think that we can write off all these experiences as being entirely mistaken.

[4] The fact that there are saints in the world capable of supreme charity, devotion and healing (such as the late Mother Teresa of Calcutta) reveals that there is a

Cons

[1] We do not need God to explain natural laws and forces – they would simply have to exist for us to be here at all and for there to be a universe. The fact that we find laws and forces should not, therefore, be a source of surprise. The universe being a 'brute fact' that we cannot explain is a more intellectually honest answer than inventing a supernatural Creator.

[2] Moral rules are created by human communities so that people can live harmoniously with one another. They vary from culture to culture and are merely human constructions. It is a mistake to take moral feelings – the result of the moral rules set down by a group of people – to be the result of the existence of something supernatural.

[3] Such feelings and experiences can be explained in terms of natural psychological needs and of brain processes. It is no coincidence that Christians, but not Buddhists, have religious visions of Christ or of the Virgin Mary. These experiences are the product of religious teaching and often also of sensory deprivation: use of drugs, sleep deprivation, fasting, medita-

source of ultimate love to which humans have access (God) and which can triumph over human evil and selfishness. Evil in the world is a result of human disobedience to God, as symbolised in the story of the Fall of Adam and Eve from their original state of innocence. Natural suffering, such as famine, is a sign that the world may be disobedient, but it is also free. God's love and forgiveness could make no sense in a world without freedom for humanity and for nature.

[5] The universe, like everything else, must have a meaning, purpose and destiny. It is God who provides and guarantees that meaning and purpose to the universe and to individual people. The universe and humanity can be redeemed in the end by the love of God. There is objective meaning and redemption above individual human lives – there is a greater cosmic process of which we can have intimations through belief in God.

Possible motions

This House believes that God is not dead.
This House believes that God created the world.
This House believes in God.

Related topics

Churches in politics
Disestablishment of the Church of England
Homosexuals, ordination of
Religious teaching in schools

tion or other deliberately mind-altering practices.

[4] Human beings are so selfish and, often, evil in their dealings with nature and each other, that it is impossible to believe that a loving God exists. Why would a loving God allow the sexual abuse of children, the starvation of innocents in Africa or the Nazi Holocaust? On top of the evil perpetrated by humans there is the suffering of animals in nature and that of people in natural disasters such as famines, earthquakes and floods. The natural world as much as the human world reveals indifference and evil as much as goodness or divinity.

[5] The universe is ultimately meaningless. We have limited mental powers and there is no rational way for us to find meaning in the 'brute fact' of the universe's existence. Also, the strong link made by modern brain science between what used to be called the 'soul' and the brain makes it impossible that we could exist in any form after our death.

Holocaust denial, criminalisation of

In spite of the obvious and incontrovertible evidence that the Holocaust was one of the most horrific events in human history, there remains a small number of radical neo-Nazi politicians, historians and their supporters who seek to deny that the Holocaust took place. It cannot be stressed enough that this is *not* a debate about that question, but about whether denying the Holocaust ought to be illegal. That is already the position in 17 European countries (most notably, Germany and France), and the EU has called for others to follow suit. In recent years, the view has also become popular in the Middle East as part of a political narrative about Israel, and has been prominently expressed by former Iranian president Mahmoud Ahmadinejad.

Pros

[1] The Holocaust is not up for debate; it happened, and the evidence is incontrovertible. Where such a historical fact is so well established, no useful purpose can be served by allowing people to say that it did not happen; all this does is cloud the historical record. In particular, any attempts to generate historical debate about the issue must be based on fabrication, lies, or the wilful distorting of evidence.

[2] The denial of the Holocaust causes great pain to Jewish people and those close to them. For them, it is important that there be public recognition of the horrors that were perpetrated against them because of their race, and Holocaust denial undermines that. It is not distant from their lives or unimportant, either because many of them will have been alive during the Holocaust, or they know someone, perhaps an elderly relative, who was in a concentration camp. Moreover, because anti-Semitism is present in society today, Holocaust denial is a constant reminder of the peril of hatred and violence.

[3] Holocaust denial is often a 'dog-whistle' for other very pernicious views,

Cons

[1] While it cannot be disputed that the Holocaust took place, this does not mean there is no room for an important and useful historical debate about the precise manner in which it happened, the precise numbers of dead, etc.; the recent discovery that the number of Jewish ghettos across Europe was much higher than previously believed, for instance, is a good example of how we are still learning lessons about the Holocaust. Banning 'denial' might have a chilling effect on the willingness to question the various orthodoxies about the Holocaust.

[2] No one has a right not to be offended. Without wishing to trivialise the psychological harm caused by Holocaust denial, the state cannot protect people against it; there are simply too many forms of psychological harm, all different and hard to measure, that the state cannot involve itself. If it were to do so, then all potentially offensive speech acts would have to come within the ambit of the state's criminal legislation, which would be an unfair restriction on freedom of speech.

[3] While being racist is unpleasant, it is not illegal; we do not ban racist political

such as anti-Semitism, racism and homo-phobia. We should not allow people to use this as a recruiting tool towards racist political parties, which are often dangerous and violent; by banning Holocaust denial, we remove an important signalling mechanism for those groups.

[4] As their views depend so strongly on fabrication, lies and rhetoric, Holocaust deniers cannot usefully be drawn into an open public debate; they simply repeat their lies, without engaging with the other view. In consequence, they will not be defeated by more discussion; instead, they must be banned.

parties, and we should not seek to do so, because there is a democratic right to free political association; while we may find these views distasteful, that is the price we pay for living in a democracy.

[4] As always with radical and false views, the best way to defeat them is to challenge them in public. As they have no foundation, they will not be able to provide supporting facts, and their views will quickly crumble. When, in 1996, David Irving sued Deborah Lipstadt of Penguin Books for libel when she accused him of academic dishonesty, he overwhelmingly lost the case. These ridiculous views are then rightly subject to ridicule, and defeated.

Possible motions

This House would ban Holocaust denial.
This House believes that Holocaust denial is not
    an acceptable cost of free speech.
This House would never allow the denial of
    mass human rights abuses.

Related topics

Censorship by the state
Extremist political parties, banning of

Homosexuals, ordination of

The first decade of the twenty-first century has seen a heated debate within the Anglican Church about whether it should allow the ordination of openly gay clergy and bishops. The Church of England, the Episcopal Church in the USA and the Anglican Church of Canada have accepted some gay clergy and, in 2004, Gene Robinson became the first openly gay minister to be made a bishop (the Bishop of New Hampshire in the Episcopal Church). However, the Anglican Communion worldwide is split on this issue, and in 2008, there was a boycott of the Lambeth Conference, such was the strength of the schism. Those opposed believe that homosexuality is against Christian teaching and have declared themselves in a state of 'impaired communion' with their liberal counterparts. The arguments here focus on the Anglican Church, but can be easily adapted to apply to other faiths.

Pros

[1] One of the merits of the Christian religion has always been its ability to adapt its principles of love and inclusion to societal values as they evolve. It is now clear, scientifically and sociologically, that homosexuals are not 'deviant' or 'diseased', but equal, normal members of human society. There is no reason why they, any more than women, should be excluded from serving God and society as Christian ministers. Homosexuals and heterosexuals alike are sometimes guilty of the misuse of their God-given sexuality in abusive and unloving ways. However, it is not right to bar all homosexuals from ordination any more than it would be right to bar all heterosexuals from ordination on the grounds of the misconduct of which some are guilty.

[2] The Bible (especially the Old Testament) contains many regulations (e.g. regarding diet, cleanliness, clothing, circumcision, etc.) that Christians do not feel obliged to follow. The biblical opposition to homosexuality should be treated by Christians like these other forgotten 'purity rules'. In biblical times, homosexuality was not socially integrated and maybe existed in unstable situations detached from love and open to abuse. That is no longer the case, so the view should be rethought. Jesus himself, the central figure of authority in the Bible for Christians, never made any statement against homosexuality.

[3] Many parts of the Christian community are happy for their ministers to have sex purely for recreation – i.e. married ministers using contraception. It is therefore illogical to deny homosexuals the right to ordination on the grounds that they have non-reproductive sex. If

Cons

[1] The strength of the Christian religion rests on its ability to stand up for unchanging moral standards in a changing and morally degenerating world. Homosexuality is a misuse of natural gifts from God, a rejection of His design, and even if it is socially tolerated, it cannot be an acceptable way of life for a Christian minister who must stand as a moral example to the members of the church and provide a role model of Christian living. The existence of a 'gay gene' does not make homosexuality morally right any more than other biological predispositions (e.g. to aggression, alcoholism or promiscuity) make their outcomes morally right. The analogy with the ordination of women does not hold either: people have no control over their gender, but they do have control over their sexual behaviour.

[2] The Bible, the authority on which Christianity is based, condemns homosexuality. If Jesus had wished to see the age-old Jewish condemnation of homosexuality overturned, he could have taught his disciples accordingly. In other cases (e.g. rules about the Sabbath), Jesus was prepared to challenge the orthodox view. However, he did not do so in this case. Therefore, we must assume that he was happy with the Old Testament view. The condemnation of homosexuality is repeated in the New Testament in St Paul's Letter to the Romans.

[3] It is also clear from the Bible that sex is intended to produce children. The Bible condemns 'fornication', which is the use of sex for pleasure rather than procreation. All homosexual sex falls into this category and those who practise it cannot be role models for the Christian community.

celibacy is required, then it can be practised by those of any sexual orientation.

[4] The argument that homosexual sex is wrong because it is outside the sacrament of marriage is circular. It should only remain outside the sacrament of marriage if it can be established on *other* grounds that homosexuality is wrong.

[5] Since heterosexual ministers who condone homosexual love within their congregation are not (generally) sacked, it is illogical to sack celibate homosexuals for holding the same view.

[6] A large minority of the Christian community is homosexual. These gay men and lesbians need spiritual direction as much as heterosexual Christians do. It is right that there should be a significant minority of homosexual Christian ministers who can truly empathise with the needs of this portion of the Church.

[7] The Church risks rendering itself irrelevant and out of date if it does not reflect modern views. Church attendance is falling in many Western countries and part of that is due to the illiberal stances that the Church takes, which put off young people. Allowing gay ministers would resonate with the young who have grown up expecting equal rights.

[4] Sex is also something that should take place only within marriage. Marriage is a sacrament of union between a man and a woman for procreation. So again, homosexual sex is necessarily outside the 'proper' Christian life.

[5] Even non-practising homosexuals are unacceptable as Christian ministers since they condone a form of sex rejected by the Bible and Christianity as against the natural purpose given to sex by God.

[6] Homosexuals should indeed be given spiritual guidance by Christian ministers, but simple affirmation of homosexuality is not the Christian answer. Lesbians and gay men need to be encouraged by ministers to overcome their urges and to live in a truly Christian way. The simple existence of homosexuality is not an argument for ordaining homosexuals. The clergy are there to lead and guide, not as a representative microcosm of society.

[7] Many people are attracted to the Church precisely because of its opposition to our increasingly permissive society. Even if some people are deterred, the Church is not a commercial organisation that should change its policies in order to attract more customers; it must uphold the scripture and do its best to spread its message.

Possible motions
This House would ordain homosexuals.
This House believes that the road to God is not necessarily straight.
This House calls for a representative clergy.

Related topics
Gay marriage, legalising of
God, existence of
Homosexuals, outing of
Churches in politics

Homosexuals, outing of

If the media know that a public figure is gay but they have not come out of their own accord, should their privacy be respected or should they be 'outed'? Is there a duty to be out, or should people be able to hide their sexuality if they wish? This debate is not about a law, but rather about the principle.

Pros

[1] Prejudice against homosexuality is linked to the fact that gays are seen as a tiny minority in society. In fact, it is estimated that as many as 10 per cent of people are gay. If this were known by the general public, it would greatly reduce the existing prejudice and discriminatory behaviour. Therefore, 'outing', or the naming of gay individuals who are currently 'in the closet', is in the long run a valuable weapon against bias. This is particularly true in the case of gay celebrities who can serve as role models.

[2] Many closet homosexuals are in fact hypocrites, maintaining heterosexual lifestyles and even campaigning against gay rights (two members of John Major's Cabinet in the UK in the 1990s who were widely believed to be gay by the media, but never exposed, voted against an equal age of consent). It is doubly important that they be outed.

[3] It is true that many people do not know what is good for them. Because of the traditional prejudice against homosexuality, 'coming out' can be a terrifying experience that gays resist through fear of rejection, condemning themselves to a lifetime of secrecy, unhappiness and lack of fulfilment. Society is more embracing than ever and coming out will usually improve one's quality of life, with very little backlash. John Amaechi, the NBA

Cons

[1] There are quite enough gay celebrities to fight the cause already – most of whom have come out voluntarily – and society is changing to embrace homosexuality even without widespread outing. Declaration of sexuality is one of the most important decisions in life and must be made by the individual concerned. Even if outing were to help the fight against discrimination, each individual case must be the choice of the person concerned, not anyone else's.

[2] It is society's fault, not that of politicians or bishops or sports stars, that people are forced to cloak themselves in heterosexuality for the sake of their careers. There are many constituencies where an openly gay political candidate would stand no chance of success. Until society accepts gay men and women in all walks of life, those with ambition are faced with a stark choice – admit their homosexuality and give up their chance of being a politician, a vicar, or so on, or pretend otherwise. This may be hypocritical, but we can understand why it is done.

[3] The consequences of outing can be terrible. Coming out frequently entails rejection by family and friends and the destruction of careers. It can lead to a complete change of lifestyle and requires careful and meditative preparation. To out someone who is not prepared can lead to nervous breakdowns or even suicide.

basketball player waited until he retired to come out and later said that he had 'underestimated America' as the response had been much better than he had feared. Outing can therefore be beneficial for individuals, even if they would not choose it at first.

Many public figures have indeed given up their careers or killed themselves to avoid being outed.

Possible motions
This House would 'out' gay celebrities.
This House would name them but not shame them.
This House believes that staying in is the new coming out.

Related topics
Gay marriage, legalising of
Homosexuals, ordination of
Privacy of public figures

Immigration, limitation of

This debate looks at the harms and the benefits of immigration and is a very emotive subject in many countries. Levels of immigration vary greatly from country to country and the models used differ vastly, so the clearest debates will probably focus on one country or will look at the principle that immigration does more harm than good. It may make more sense within a particular jurisdiction to debate relaxing the immigration laws.

These arguments are focused on economic migration with an assumption that a country will fulfil its duty to take asylum seekers.

Pros

[1] High levels of immigration damage the cohesiveness of communities. Current citizens feel that their culture and way of life is under threat. Different languages, dress and religion emphasise the 'otherness' of immigrants and lead to divided communities. This in turn increases crime and anti-social behaviour and decreases civic participation and volunteering, as people feel as if they have less of a stake in their country.

[2] Immigrants pose an economic threat to existent citizens. Skilled immigrants

Cons

[1] Immigration leads to vibrant communities where different cultures rub up against each other and make everyone's lives fuller. Areas such as cuisine and the arts benefit hugely from the 'melting pot' which immigration produces, which is why cities such as London and New York are so exciting.

[2] Immigration leads to the economic growth of a country and all citizens share the benefits of this. Many Western countries have ageing populations and need

coming from abroad reduce the need to invest in domestic training in professions such as medicine and engineering. In both skilled and unskilled work, there is a risk of wage deflation as immigrants undercut domestic workers. In times of unemployment, immigrants may take jobs which would otherwise go to citizens.

[3] High levels of immigration put a strain on the infrastructure of the host nation. Housing and schools can suffer in particular. In areas of high immigration, there is often a shortage of school places, and the schools have to work harder to accommodate many different languages within the school population.

[4] The perception of immigration can be worse than the reality, but this still leads to resentment and less fulfilled citizens with high levels of prejudice. Many people believe that immigrants have taken their jobs, their places on housing waiting lists or their child's school place. Others blame immigrants for crime and feel unsafe in their neighbourhood. Whether or not this is true, the perception in itself leads to unhappiness.

[5] Immigration is damaging to the home countries that lose their talent abroad. Brain drain is particularly serious in areas such as medicine, education and science and technology where those trained individuals could have made a real difference to the development of their nation had they stayed.

[6] Immigrants themselves do not always find the better lives they dreamed of. They may find that language barriers or unrecognised qualifications mean that they have to take lower-status work than they had expected, or they may not be

young immigrants to balance out their demographics. Often immigrants are doing work which others do not wish to do, or they may be filling skills gaps within a country. Everybody should be grateful to the doctors and teachers who immigrate to their countries and keep their services running.

[3] If the country's economy is growing due to immigration, then the government should be able to invest in its infrastructure, building more schools, hospitals and houses and therefore promoting more growth; it is a virtuous cycle. Immigrants pay taxes which fund the services they use.

[4] We need to tackle prejudice, rather than immigration itself. Political parties should not target immigration for easy votes and the media should be responsible in their coverage of the issue. If the government focuses on improving public services, keeping employment levels high and the streets safe, then people will not need a scapegoat. Many citizens are themselves the descendants of immigrants and are now fully integrated and accepted. There is no reason why perceptions should not be altered.

[5] Many countries rely on the income which is generated abroad by those who emigrate. Somebody who is working as a cleaner in the West may be able to support their extended family by sending their wages home. The exchange of ideas which immigration promotes can also lead to increasing pressure for better human rights and a more democratic society.

[6] Immigrants can make their own decisions about whether they benefit from immigration and if they decide they do not, then they are free to leave. Most do

able to find work at all. They may be forced into illegal labour where they are badly treated or end up on the streets. Even immigrants who do find work may be unhappy due to the unwelcoming response of the country and the problems with balancing two cultures.

not as they find in their new home a better standard of living, more freedom, more opportunities and ways to support their families.

Possible motions

This House would shut the door to immigrants.

This House believes that affluent nations should accept significantly more immigrants.

This House believes that immigration does more harm than good.

Related topics

Should Britain leave the EU?

Welfare state

Mandatory retirement age

Currently it is illegal to enforce a mandatory retirement age in many countries including Canada, the UK and Australia, on grounds of age discrimination. But should public sector employers be given a mandatory retirement age, perhaps of 65 or 70? Should that be extended to private companies as well? The debate could be held for all public sector workers or it could either be narrowed to some professions such as the judiciary, or expanded to cover private companies. It could open up into the world of the self-employed, or the freelance artistic community, although such a requirement would be much harder to enforce.

Pros

[1] Although many judges, surgeons or entrepreneurs will be able to work effectively after the age of 65, many will become less and less competent, lucid and reliable as the effects of old age set in. The impairment of judgement or skill may be slow and gradual, or dramatic. But without a mandatory retirement age, there is no easy way to oblige someone whose faculties are impaired to stop working – even when it might be endangering life or causing miscarriages of justice. A mandatory retirement age of 65 for all would

Cons

[1] This is a repressive and draconian measure and a complete over-reaction, especially in a world with an ever-increasing proportion of people over 65. There may be some who become incompetent as they get older, but they must be dealt with on an individual basis – using existing mechanisms to prevent them from practising medicine, law or commerce on the grounds of their incompetence. The huge majority whose faculties are not impaired should be allowed to continue working for as long as they are able to.

guarantee that this does not happen, and would put an end to the making of crucial constitutional and judicial decisions by senile, out-of-touch judges and politicians.

[2] In the world of the arts, musicians, writers, actors and composers continue to work way past the normal retirement age. This prevents young talented performers and writers from breaking into the field. A mandatory retirement age would prevent those over 65 from taking paid jobs (book deals, film roles, positions in orchestras) and hence open up the field for young talent to come through. Mandatory retirement would thus encourage meritocracy in the arts as well as in business. Older artists could continue to do creative work on an unpaid basis, and should be encouraged to work for charities and teach younger artists, perhaps from underprivileged backgrounds, on a voluntary basis in their retirement.

[3] Mandatory retirement should not be seen negatively. Too many people these days are dominated by their careers and the world of work. As more and more people live beyond retirement age by two decades, this period of life should be free from the stress and strain of work. It provides a time for people to pursue creative and educational interests, and also to give something back to the community with charitable work. Those who are 'workaholics' need a mandatory retirement age to give them the spur to develop other sides of themselves and broaden their lives.

[4] Looking at employment as a whole, we still suffer a problem of unacceptable youth unemployment levels. A mandatory retirement age will free up more working

Mandatory retirement would unnecessarily and unjustly curtail many careers and pointlessly deprive the community of the wealth of experience and ability that older lawyers, doctors and businesspeople have accumulated. Most judges, for example, are over 60, because they require a huge amount of experience to be able to do the job.

[2] Many composers (e.g. Sir Michael Tippett who continued to work past his ninetieth birthday), actors (e.g. Sir John Gielgud who won an Oscar at the age of 77; Jessica Tandy who won an Oscar for her role in *Driving Miss Daisy* at the age of 82), poets (e.g. Sir John Betjeman who became Poet Laureate at the age of 66) and writers (e.g. the phenomenally successful popular novelist Catherine Cookson who only started writing in her forties and produced huge amounts of work from her sixties to her early nineties) produce their best work after the age of 65. Younger performers and writers will get their chance, and there is already much media exposure for 'prodigies' and young stars, especially in the film and music industries. If anything, an effort needs to be made to give older artists more exposure in a world dominated by the young.

[3] People must not be treated like children. This legislation would be an extreme measure characteristic of an overbearing 'nanny state'. We must let individuals decide for themselves whether they wish to devote their entire life to their job or prefer to follow other pursuits. Some people may need to keep working for financial reasons, if for example, they have not paid off their mortgages or they are still supporting children.

opportunities that can be offered to the young jobless – those who are more likely to be supporting families, buying houses and so on.

Possible motions

This House calls for a mandatory retirement age.

This House would put youth before experience.

Related topics

Term limits for politicians

State pensions, ending provision of

[4] Such a law would be disastrous economically. The rapidly ageing population in Western countries – where people are living longer and longer – means that a greater proportion of the population are drawing pensions and a smaller proportion are working to provide the money. A mandatory retirement age would only make this worse. There is also evidence to suggest that people's health and mental faculties can decline quickly after retirement, and so this measure could increase the number of years that pensioners require medical care.

Marriage

Frank Sinatra once sang that 'love and marriage go together like a horse and carriage'. Did this view die with Sinatra in 1998 or is it still a defensible one? Is there something special about marriage that differentiates it from the ever more popular arrangement of cohabitation? Does marriage provide children with a more stable family home, or is the marital status of their parents (or parent) immaterial?

Pros

[1] Marriage is the foundation of the stable family unit within which children can have the best possible start to life. Studies repeatedly show that children who grow up with married parents are the best adjusted and most successful. Therefore, for the sake of their children, prospective parents have a duty to marry in order to provide the real security and trust that children need. A couple who are not married will never be able to offer the same psychologically crucial promise of security to each other or to their children.

[2] It is important that marriage is valued in order to uphold a healthy and rational view of what loving relationships are

Cons

[1] Parents do not need to be married in order to provide a stable home life for their children. It is the quality of the relationship that matters, not whether a marriage licence has been signed. If parents fight or a relationship ends, it will affect the children regardless of whether their parents are married.

[2] Marriage is an unnecessary curb on freedom and happiness. True love in all its intensity does not actually last a lifetime, and it is unreasonable to sentence oneself to a lifetime of enforced fidelity to someone with whom the spark has gone. Especially now that we are living longer and longer, lifetime commitment is

about. Loving relationships are about working together for mutual respect and support over a long period – not just about 'falling in love', sex and romance, which are relatively superficial ends. It is interesting to note that arranged marriages have a high success rate – perhaps because they do not give couples false and superficial expectations of total sexual and romantic compatibility.

[3] The fact that marriages fail does not mean that we should give up trying. Social and legal institutions such as marriage, the Church, the criminal justice system and so on exist to provide ideal models to which to aspire, often with success. We should not abandon the ideal of truly loving couples providing stable homes for their children.

[4] Although marriage does hold a spiritual dimension for many religious people, it is relevant in a secular society as a civic institution as well. Couples who cohabit are not making a public and legally recognised lifetime commitment to each other. The decision to marry represents a step forward in the relationship, the wedding allows a celebration of the couple, and the marriage itself allows both parties to feel secure in the long term. In addition, many legal and financial rights that a spouse enjoys are not granted to cohabiting couples, and so marriage acts as the state's recognition of the relationship.

[5] Marriage has evolved to match social changes. In Western culture, there are now very few arranged marriages and there are no dowries for daughters, so both men and women are free to follow where love takes them. A modern version of the Christian vows can be taken or a couple can write their own and women do not

unrealistic and unnecessary. Therefore, we should not make promises we cannot keep, but instead acknowledge that even long-term relationships can end when the love is lost or one partner falls in love with somebody else. What meaning does a marriage have if the 'till death do us part' vow is so easily broken?

[3] In the face of the very high divorce rate (up to 42 per cent in the UK) in today's world, we should rethink our approach to relationships and parenting. People get married knowing that they can change their mind whenever they want and this has undermined marriage. It is time to admit that marriage does not work in today's society and to look at alternatives. It is often the rigid and unrealistic constraints of traditional marriage itself that make a relationship stifling and unbearable.

[4] Marriage was originally a religious concept and it makes sense if your faith still prohibits sex outside marriage. However, today when couples live and sleep together for years before they marry, what is the point of the ceremony? They return, after the wedding ceremony, to exactly the same life as they had before. For some, their wedding is the first time they have visited a church for years, thereby starting their union in an act of hypocrisy. The state should accord the same rights to cohabiting couples.

[5] Marriage is an inherently sexist and homophobic institution. Women are 'given away' as if they were a possession and take their husband's name as if their identity is unimportant. In the traditional marriage vows they pledge to 'obey' their husbands. These views are outdated in today's world of gender equality. Although

have to take their husband's surname. A vote to legalise gay marriage in the UK was passed in the House of Commons in 2013, but many other countries got there first, including the Netherlands, Canada, Sweden, Spain, as did nine US states. This shows that marriage continues to adapt to stay relevant.

[6] Many people enjoy planning and throwing a huge wedding and see it as one of the happiest days of their lives. People are free to spend their money how they wish and this is a way which brings joy to the couple and their families and friends. However, it is possible to spend almost no money on a wedding and the fashions for celebrations change over time. A dislike of ostentatious weddings should not be seen as a reason to oppose the institution of marriage.

this is changing in some countries, most of the world and most organised religions oppose gay marriage, which creates discrimination within society.

[6] Marriage, for many, has become more about the wedding than the life that follows. There is huge pressure on young people and their families to throw 'fairy tale' occasions which perhaps they cannot afford. In the USA in 2012, the average cost of a wedding was over US$26,000. In the UK in 2008, the figure was higher, at over £20,000. This leaves young couples crippled with debt at a time when they are finding it harder than ever to get a foot on the housing ladder.

Possible motions
This House would get married for the sake of the children.

This House believes that marriage is an outdated institution.

This House believes that the state should incentivise marriage.

Related topics
Gay marriage, legalising of

Polygamy, legalisation of

Surrogate mothers, payment of

National identity cards

The arguments below assume a motion on the introduction of compulsory identity cards. A debate on voluntary identity cards is possible, and the last set of points addresses this. A Proposition team can clarify the debate by defining what information would be held on the card, whether it would be compulsory, and if so, what the penalties would be for failing to have one. Many countries including Belgium, Germany, South Korea and Pakistan issue compulsory ID cards. Others such as Italy, Japan and Canada have systems of voluntary ID cards while the UK, Denmark and Australia among others have no national schemes.

Pros

[1] Many forms of crime depend upon individuals claiming to be someone else (e.g. benefit fraud, tax evasion, dealing in stolen goods, terrorism, gaol-breaking, illegal immigration, or lying to the police after another crime). Without ID cards there is no form of standard identification for domestic use that is widely accepted. Different forms of identification are demanded for different activities. If a country had one official and standard form of ID, verification by the police would be easier and many crimes would be avoided. With the increased terrorist threat in the world, ID cards have become a matter of national security.

[2] Many European states require identity cards, yet they are hardly authoritarian police states. When they are abroad, tourists willingly carry a passport, while at home almost all drivers carry a driving licence. Carrying identification causes no problem to innocent people; it is only criminals who would resist. Encouraging police harassment is a negligible risk; the circumstances under which ID cards would be demanded could be carefully regulated.

[3] National identity cards are useful not only for society, but also for the holder. There are many daily transactions where identification is required; currently we are forced to carry a large number of separate cards. In the USA and the UK where driving licences bear photos, they are used as identification for a wide variety of purposes (proving the owner is old enough to drink, guaranteeing cheques, etc.). Modern smart-card technology would allow one small card to encode a huge range of information, including

Cons

[1] Identity cards represent a major intrusion by the government into the privacy of the individual, and would greatly increase state control. In order to be effective, card carrying would have to be compulsory (as with a road tax disc), and failure to produce the card would be a crime. This would use up valuable police and court time.

[2] Countries such as the UK, Australia and Denmark value their liberties highly and are wary of any attempts to undermine them, which is why they have resisted ID cards. National identity cards would allow a considerable degree of police harassment in the name of enforcing the policy, probably targeted at minority groups who are already more likely to be stopped on suspicion of motoring and other offences. This harassment is a particular problem in France with the immigrant population. Relations between minority groups and police would only grow worse.

[3] With separate cards we have a choice about whether and when to carry them, and which ones to take out with us. Smart-card technology is so advanced as to be dangerous; we would have no idea what information was contained on our ID cards that could be read by others, and no choice about how much information to declare. Employers and the police could discriminate against us on the basis of hidden facts that we should have the right to keep hidden. The cost of introducing millions of smart cards and vast numbers of card-reading machines would be enormous. Theft of the cards would become major business, and the police are always technologically less advanced than the

photographic images, retina and finger-print records, signature, passport, driving licence, criminal record, bank and credit details, health records and even employee and library/club membership details.

[4] Given that most people currently carry all their multiple forms of identification in the same wallet or handbag, the problems of losing a single card are unlikely to be worse in practice. The chance of being impersonated is less if photo, retina and fingerprint details cannot be detached from the card; at the moment, a thief could discard all forms of photo ID, but keep, for example, a credit card and forge the signature. In addition, the majority of identity theft now occurs through the Internet rather than through the stealing of cards.

[5] Identity cards could be made volun-tary, producing many of the benefits of compulsory cards while avoiding most of the issues of civil liberty.

Possible motions

This House would introduce a national identity card.
This House would remain anonymous.
This House would scrap compulsory ID card schemes.

Related topics

Protective legislation v. individual freedom
Zero tolerance

criminals, as credit card fraud and online financial crime suggest.

[4] The chance of losing all your forms of identification in one go is high and immensely inconvenient – your entire identity would be erased until a new one could be obtained, which would presum-ably be a strict and lengthy process. If criminals did obtain card-reading tech-nology, they could have access to all parts of your life via a stolen card and identity theft would become much easier.

[5] Voluntary schemes are likely to be the thin end of the wedge, soliciting public support before proposals to make cards compulsory are tabled. In any case, unfair suspicion would naturally fall on those who chose not to carry them – an infringement on civil liberties. Courts might take 'not carrying a card' into account with the same scepticism with which the right to silence is treated. Voluntary in theory would become com-pulsory in practice if banks, rail com-panies, airlines and so on demanded cards to be shown as part of transactions.

National service, (re-)introduction of

The Proposition team needs to define what it means by 'national service'. In post-war Britain, in several continental European countries and in Israel today, national service means military service with one of the armed forces. This is a valid debate, but other forms of national service could be considered: public service on environmental projects, working with the homeless, people with disabilities, those who are underprivileged, and so on. A choice between the two could be offered. Other issues should be considered: at what age should it be compulsory (pre- or post-university, or should there be a choice)? How long should it last? Should it be for men and women, as it is in Israel, or for men only as in countries such as Turkey and Singapore? Most of the key arguments, however, remain the same whichever model is chosen: do the benefits of national service to the individual and society justify the compulsion? Germany, Italy and France have all abandoned national service in recent years, but other countries are debating its reintroduction.

Pros

[1] It is the right of the state to call upon its citizens to serve it in times of need, and democratic governments in particular have a mandate for such action. National service is often used in times of war. Conscription on a permanent basis would keep a 'standing army' ready and trained for times of emergency as well as catering for other eventualities.

[2] National service promotes a clear sense of nationhood, integrating individuals from diverse groups and fostering a respect for different cultural and regional traditions. Over a generation, this will help to create a more cohesive yet tolerant society, more committed to public life. We can compare older generations in the USA and the UK with their more feckless successors, and look to the states of Switzerland and Israel where national service provides valuable social cohesion.

[3] National service also provides the young with valuable experience, teaching self-discipline, a sense of purpose and

Cons

[1] There would need to be a 'clear and present danger' to the nation to justify military conscription; people's liberty cannot be removed 'just in case'. The military does not wish to see the reintroduction of conscription, as it would dilute the professionalism of a standing army, and many of its best instructors would waste time training recruits who do not wish to be there. The nature of warfare has changed and most conflicts no longer require large numbers of troops, but rather streamlined, well-equipped and well-trained forces.

[2] National service could easily be used for propaganda, not celebrating differences but seeking to eradicate them; the armed forces do not have a strong reputation for political correctness. Compulsory patriotism is questionable and may be misused by politicians.

[3] Compulsory service is likely to be resented, undermining any possible benefits. An elaborate bureaucracy would be

important skills (e.g. driving, IT, administration and personnel management), along with a wider sense of responsibility to the community. It also develops physical fitness and it can be a start to work as a mechanic, electrician, paramedic, chef and many other careers.

[4] National service would provide a way to tackle social problems, from the environment to urban deprivation and major disaster relief.

[5] National service would be a civic duty equivalent to jury service and paying taxes, and the loss of liberty would be justified as such. Conscripts would be repaying their debt to the society which offers them largely free education and (in many countries) welfare benefits throughout their lives. The safety of a nation is something that everybody benefits from and so everybody should contribute to it.

[6] National service would give everyone a stake in the military. Decision makers and the electorate as a whole will all have served and will all have family members in service. This will give a great understanding of the realities of military pressures. Troops would only be sent into a war zone where necessary and for the right reasons because of the heightened public involvement.

Possible motions

This House supports national service.
This House would bring back the draft.

Related topics

Pacifism
United Nations standing army
Social contract, existence of the

needed to prevent candidates evading call-up, which would often be easier for the prosperous middle class than for working-class families – as in the USA at the time of the Vietnam War. The scheme would cost vast sums even without this bureaucracy. If personal development is the aim, then the money would be better invested in training schemes and apprenticeships.

[4] As with any form of forced labour (e.g. slavery or workfare), leaving such projects to national service recruits will simply ensure they are done badly, with little enthusiasm. Many people are currently paid to undertake the kind of work that non-military national service would involve; their jobs and salaries would be at risk. It might also discourage volunteering; if the state provides a workforce for such projects, there is no incentive for anyone else to help. A better alternative would be to incentivise a voluntary national service plan, perhaps with lower tuition fees at university for those involved.

[5] It is wrong in principle to compel adults to work against their will. It is worse still to compel them to risk their lives in the armed forces. Eighteen year olds may wish to be studying at university, volunteering abroad or may already be parents themselves. They should be allowed the freedom of choice to follow their own path. Taxpayers already contribute to the welfare state; there is no need to make them pay this debt twice.

[6] A national service may actually lead to a country getting involved in more conflicts, as it will need to justify the conscription, will not find its troops are overstretched and will need something to do with all its conscripts.

Political correctness

Political correctness is a movement that originated in the USA in the 1980s. Its aim is to promote liberal and egalitarian attitudes especially through modifications to language and behaviour. In Britain, the main initial reaction to political correctness was one of derision, especially based on extreme examples of 'PC' talk. However, some examples of political correctness, such as the use of 'she' and 'her' rather than 'he' and 'his' as the default personal pronoun (e.g. 'the reader is asked to use *her* imagination') have become widespread and accepted. The central question in this debate is whether modifying language and behaviour at the everyday level can really have a large-scale impact on equality and social justice. As always, address the principles and beware of playing 'example tennis'.

Pros

[1] Political correctness is concerned with social justice. It is paying attention in detail to language and behaviour in order to rid it of ingrained prejudice, discrimination or oppression. It aims in particular to combat racism, sexism, homophobia and discrimination on the grounds of physical appearance or handicap. The great value of political correctness is that it recognises the need to challenge attitudes and behaviours from the bottom up – starting with the very language that has embodied prejudice and discrimination over the years. Political correctness has successfully argued for using something other than just 'he' as the default personal pronoun, for the use of 'chair' or 'chairperson' instead of 'chairman', and for 'Ms' instead of 'Miss' and 'Mrs' (to abolish the discrimination between men and women, with the latter, unlike the former, being defined by their marital status).

[2] Political correctness recognises the important role of language in shaping attitudes and behaviours. If it is socially acceptable to call people 'fat', 'ugly', 'stupid', 'short', 'spastic', 'bent', 'bitch',

Cons

[1] Political correctness may be well intentioned, but it has no important consequences. The real battle ground for social justice should not be incidental uses of language, but real attitudes in the workplace and in society at large. It is implausible and patronising to suggest that people cannot understand that 'man' just means 'all people' or that they really use it in a way that implies men are superior to women. Political correctness is a distraction from real issues of discrimination.

[2] It is absurd to believe that political correctness is to be thanked for drawing our attention to discrimination and abuse. The movements campaigning for women's rights, black rights and gay rights all predate political correctness. Political correctness reveals an unhealthy and patronising obsession with so-called 'rights' and discrimination. Adults can cope with being teased about their height, weight, age or IQ without the need for the verbal witchhunt of political correctness. More serious issues of discrimination are dealt with by the law.

'Paki' and so on in derogatory ways, then attitudes will not change. It is right to challenge such name-calling and discrimination wherever it is found. We have political correctness to thank for alerting us to this hurtful behaviour and making us watch the way we think, speak and act.

[3] It is easy for opponents to pick out silly examples where political correctness has been taken to extremes. The existence of such examples does not mean that the whole movement should be abolished.

[4] It is up to the groups in question to find their own names. However, it is still right to challenge the use of names that have been part, in the past, of discriminatory ways of thinking and talking – that was the original reason for challenging the uses of 'black' and 'white'. It may be that terms such as 'black', 'queer' or even 'bitch' can be 'reclaimed' by a group and used positively. But there will always be a difference between someone choosing to use the word 'queer' to describe themselves, and being labelled with these terms by others. Political correctness is not committed to any particular new names, but seeks to challenge the unthinking use of old discriminatory ones.

[5] People need to keep up with changing language in order to avoid causing offence. However, if somebody uses insensitive language but is otherwise tolerant, they should be corrected rather than judged.

[3] Political correctness is too often taken to extremes. A London teacher forbade her class to see the film of *Romeo and Juliet* because it did not provide gay role models. A teacher in America suspended a six-year-old boy from school for kissing a girl – this, it was claimed, was sexual harassment.

[4] Political correctness is often self-defeating in that it creates exclusive, patronising or just silly names for groups that it believes are being discriminated against. Using the term 'African American', it could be argued, implies that black Africans in America are not 'real' Americans. Calling someone 'differently abled' rather than 'disabled' is patronising. Calling a bald person 'follically challenged' is just silly.

[5] The existence of politically correct language leads to people who are not in the know with the latest ever-changing vocabulary being wrongly labelled as racist or sexist. People who had been told to say 'black' rather than 'coloured' are then attacked for doing so. People should be judged for their actions and attitudes rather than having linguistic traps set for them.

Possible motions

This House would be politically correct.

This House believes political correctness has reduced discrimination.

This House believes that political correctness will bring social justice.

Related topics

Censorship by the state

Pornography

Extremist political parties, banning of

Polygamy, legalisation of

Polygamy is the practice of marrying more than one person at the same time. It is illegal in much of the world today, but it is recognised in various Islamic countries including Saudi Arabia and some African countries. The Church of Jesus Christ of Latter-day Saints officially ended the practice of polygamy (or plural marriages) in Mormonism in 1890, but splinter groups still practise it today and many people associate polygamy with the Mormon community.

Pros

[1] The government should respect freedom of choice. Nobody is forced into polygamy or harmed by its existence, and so the government should stay out of marriage and not interfere in people's private lives. This is particularly true if polygamy is part of one's religious practices, as with some branches of Islam. In this case, there would need to be a very strong harm to justify limiting religious freedoms and no such harm exists.

[2] Polygamy is a valid lifestyle choice. A marriage between three or four people may work very well. If someone falls in love again, it does not have to end a marriage – a larger, stable union can be created. It allows for roles to be shared out and takes the pressure off our busy modern lifestyles. For example, there could be two incomes in the family in addition to a full-time homemaker, which could improve everybody's quality of life.

[3] Who says a marriage has to be between two people? That is an inflexible view. Many countries have moved away from the Christian definition of marriage being between one man and one woman by allowing gay marriage. This provides a precedent for a more flexible and modern approach to marriage. In addition, the Bible and the Qur'an both include

Cons

[1] It is hard to confirm the consent of all parties in a polygamous relationship, especially the original wife. Because of this, we cannot be sure that we would be protecting freedom of choice rather than allowing a man to force polygamy on an unwilling wife. If the woman does not believe in divorce or has no resources, she may feel trapped and unable to object. In this case, the woman would be harmed.

[2] Women in polygamous relationships are likely to be less happy. This view of marriage is often misogynistic and supports the idea that it is the man's needs that are important and women must serve him. In all societies where polygamy is practised (Islamic, Mormon, African) it is the man who takes multiple wives rather than the reverse. This concentrates all the power with the man and perpetuates outdated patriarchal structures in place of equal unions.

[3] Marriage by its nature is 'two becomes one'. Marriage is a religious concept and most religions are offended by polygamy, which they see as institutionalised infidelity. If polygamy is condoned, it dilutes the very idea of marriage. People can choose informal alternative lifestyles, but marriage as an institution should protect the security and equality of a union of two.

examples of polygamous relationships, so the 'union of two' is a cultural practice rather than a scriptural rule.

[4] If the government recognised polygamy, then all parties involved would acquire legal rights; otherwise, some people will be vulnerable. Where polygamy is practised outside the law, a second wife has no financial recourse in the case of a divorce or death. It is not illegal for a married man also to have a mistress and there can be no disadvantage in allowing this relationship to be legally recognised. Adultery is not preferable to polygamy.

[4] It is very difficult to provide rights for multiple parties in a marriage. Who, for example, is next of kin? Imagine a situation where a decision had to be made whether or not to switch off a life-support machine: how could a law protect everybody's rights here? In reality, one wife would have to be given precedent, which would undermine the role of any other wives.

Possible motions
This House would legalise polygamy.
This House believes that in marriage, 'two's company – three's a crowd'.

Related topics
Marriage
Gay marriage, legalising of

Population control

Unlimited population growth cannot be a good thing; Thomas Malthus pointed out 200 years ago that the human capacity for reproduction could disastrously overtake the resources available to mankind. The debate now is whether we are heading for a 'Malthusian' disaster, and whether measures to avoid it should be 'soft' (education of women, economic growth) or 'hard' (promotion of free contraceptives, abortion, penalties for large families, etc.). A Proposition team that ducks the second type and sticks only to soft measures does not deserve to win this debate. The classic example of a successful population control regime is that in China, the 'one-child policy'; in recent years, however, this has been relaxed, questioning its relevance for the modern age.

Pros

[1] Malthus argued that human reproductive potential was geometric (1–2–4–8–16, etc.) while growth in resources was only arithmetic (1–2–3–4–5, etc.). Eventually a disparity between the two will end in crisis, such as war over resources, famine, malnutrition, epidemic disease and environmental devastation.

Cons

[1] Malthus predicted a major population crisis in the mid-nineteenth century, but none came. In the 1970s, the neo-Malthusian book *The Limits to Growth* by Donella Meadows predicted further catastrophe, also erroneously. Most disasters are caused by ideological or ethnic rivalry, poor government management of

POPULATION CONTROL   145

Such tragedies are clearly identifiable today and are sure to become worse unless steps are taken to limit population growth. We owe it to future generations to give them a chance of existence free from malnutrition, poverty and so on.

[2] There are, of course, other global problems, but population control still needs addressing; problems of inequality are often exacerbated by those of overpopulation. Human prosperity and happiness and the environment are all affected.

[3] Many different means exist to restrict population, but it is not necessary to compel individuals to undergo vasectomies, abortions, contraceptive injections, and so on. Instead, governments can apply economic pressure on those with large families, as in China where second and subsequent children disqualify families from a range of state benefits. Contraception can be distributed widely and cheaply (often a big issue in Africa), and educational programmes can enthusiastically promote the advantages of small families. Moreover, governments can do more to provide better provision for parents in old age, which will reduce the incentive for people to have lots of children to support them when they retire.

[4] Restricting population growth has other spin-offs, particularly the empowerment of women, who can be given control of reproduction. This allows them to pursue education and job opportunities, as well as better health and longer life expectancy. The spread of sexually transmitted diseases is contained when condoms are more widely used.

[5] The reason that sons are more highly valued is that they go out to work, whereas

resources (famine) or greed (which causes much environmental devastation, such as the Bangladeshi floods). It is difficult to prove any link between natural disasters and overpopulation.

[2] The real problem is not rapid population growth, but inequitable distribution of resources between a rich Northern hemisphere and a much poorer South. More urgent priorities that need to be addressed are different and fairer trade and development policies. An end to EU agricultural protectionism would greatly aid Africa, for example, while the large quantities of meat eaten in richer countries currently require a much less productive use of agricultural land than if our diets were more vegetarian.

[3] Attempts to limit population growth have ignored basic human rights, with state intervention (e.g. China, with its one-child policy) or attacking deeply held religious beliefs (Catholicism and Islam) through promoting contraception and therefore, by implication, relaxed sexual morality. Such measures are often deeply unpopular within societies on which they are imposed, and only totalitarian governments (such as China) are able to implement them. The state has no right to interfere with people's family lives.

[4] If our aim is the empowerment of women, then legislating against families of more than one child, for example, seems entirely counterproductive. Such a measure radically reduces the control of women over their reproductive life. It is certainly a good idea to increase the availability of condoms and provide education on safe sex and STDs, but that does not mean that we should make contraception (or sterilisation, or one-child families)

daughters are baby-making machines. Population control measures will increase women's economic value by freeing them from a life of child rearing to go to work. In turn, this will lessen the preference for male offspring.

compulsory. This would be an unacceptable constraint on personal freedom.

[5] In societies that value male children more than female children, this would lead to selective abortions and the abandonment of baby girls, as parents will want to make sure that their one child is a boy.

Possible motions
This House would introduce one-child policies across the developing world.
This House would tie aid to population control.
This House believes that Malthus was right.

Related topics
Abortion on demand
Euthanasia, legalisation of
Marriage
Sex education
Contraception for under-age girls

Pornography

Pornography laws vary from country to country. The Internet has changed the nature of the debate as anyone with a computer now has unlimited access to a vast world of online pornography. It is harder to regulate both the production and the viewing of pornography in this area, so is it time to accept it as a healthy part of our sexuality? It is assumed in this debate that anything that is illegal in reality should also be in pornography, so child pornography, rape, bestiality, etc. are outside the scope of the debate and the Proposition team should clarify that.

Pros

[1] We aspire to live in states free of censorship. Censorship is only to be used as a last resort to protect groups which might be put in danger by certain material. So, for example, many states have legislation against incitement to racial hatred. This is a form of censorship. But in the case of pornography, this does not apply, since no one is harmed by the photographing or filming of consenting

Cons

[1] Young men and women are lured into debasing and objectifying themselves by the economic power of pornographers. Banning pornography would protect against this exploitation and against the objectifying attitudes that pornography engenders. It is naïve to say that pornography is harmless.

[2] The availability of pornography, even if it is properly restricted to those over 18 or

adults for publication to other adults for their sexual pleasure.

[2] Pornography legitimately explores the realms of sexual fantasy, which is a rich aspect of human experience that it is prudish, oppressive and ignorant to deny. Admittedly, it is desirable that the availability of pornography should be restricted to adults only, but for them there should be no restrictions. Pornography is used by many couples as a way to spice up their sex life, and hence even acts as a way to strengthen and stabilise marriages and relationships. It is not true that all of the images available are misogynistic; many show women in empowered positions.

[3] Pornography can be part of a wide spectrum of approaches to sex and entertainment that are available. There is no need to ban it. Some people may be turned on by less explicit films and novels, but that does not mean there is no place at all for pornography for those who enjoy its direct approach.

[4] A clear distinction needs to be made between pornography made and used by consenting adults and pornography involving children. The latter is always unacceptable and should be attacked with the full force of the law. However, the people involved in popular adult magazines such as *Playboy* and adult TV stations are not in any way connected with child pornography.

[5] Sexual abuse and rape will exist with or without pornography. Pornography does not cause these crimes, even if some of the perpetrators may like pornography.

[6] The use of potentially suggestive pictures of attractive men and women to sell newspapers, magazines and other products

over 21, sends a message of social consent to the objectifying of women in particular. It encourages young men to see women as sex objects. From an early age, young men, through access to pornography, see women in crude sexual poses rather than seeing them just as fellow humans. Such attitudes are insidious and lead to disrespect and discrimination in the workplace and elsewhere.

[3] Elements of human sexuality can be explored in music, poetry, literature, theatre and films in more subtle, interesting and erotic ways. Pornography is trash in comparison – simply bad photography and bad writing of the most superficial kind.

[4] The more that pornography is tolerated, the more it will spread, and the more cases of abuse and exploitation will occur. There is already a disturbing increase in cases of child pornography, which is the result of a lax attitude to pornography in the past. It is not possible to tell from an image whether a girl is over 18 or whether she has freely consented to be filmed or photographed.

[5] Many rapists and sexual abusers are pornography fanatics. It seems likely that pornography fosters obsessive, unbalanced and violent sexual attitudes. We should ban and seek to wipe out pornography with the same strength as is currently applied to the war on drugs.

[6] Pornography is infiltrating every aspect of the media, from music videos and underwear advertisements to 'lifestyle' magazines and tabloid newspapers. Some urgent action needs to be taken to counteract this cultural trend. It is disingenuous to suggest that pictures of men and

is not an instance of pornography, but a normal and acceptable part of our consumerist culture.

[7] The Internet has allowed people to enjoy pornography in their own homes privately without having to visit sex shops or clubs. The vast amount of pornography available has meant that people can explore their sexuality and find material that caters to their taste. It has also meant that trying to ban pornography is almost impossible, as access is so easy.

[8] The more types of pornography that are legally recognised, the more those involved in the production can be protected. Illegal pornography is a shady world, but a regulated industry could ensure proper pay and working conditions for its workers.

women are used equally to sell products. It is almost exclusively pictures of the half-naked bodies of *women* that are used, and these pornographic images continue progressively to undermine respect for women as individual human beings.

[7] The Internet has magnified the problems with pornography. People from a younger age than ever before are accessing more pornography, and the material is becoming more graphic. Young boys who grow up with a diet of online pornography have warped expectations of sex and an unhealthy perception of women. Adults are also finding that they are lured into more extreme pornography than they would have accessed before the advent of the Internet, and that ease of use means they spend more time indulging. When anyone can download pornography onto their computers or phone with one click, it is very difficult to regulate things such as whether the user is underage and whether the material has been produced consensually. An outright ban with the criminalisation of production and use is the only effective option.

Possible motions

This House would legalise all adult pornography.

This House believes pornography is harmless fun.

This House believes pornography saves marriages.

This House would ban extreme pornography.

Related topics

Censorship by the state

Marriage

Prostitution, legalisation of

Sex education

Protective legislation v. individual freedom

Prostitution, legalisation of

The actual act of prostitution – exchanging sex for money – is legal in many countries, although other practices associated with it are not. In Britain, for example, solicitation (i.e. negotiating with potential customers), advertising, 'curb-crawling' or running brothels (where two or more prostitutes work) are all illegal, while prostitution itself is not. In the USA, it is a misdemeanour, except in parts of Nevada. But that is not to say that Britain encourages prostitution – the act is legal because it happens behind closed doors and any law against it is unenforceable. This debate is therefore about the principle of tolerating open prostitution. A Proposition team may want to clarify whether they would legalise all practices related to prostitution, or whether they would have a more regulated system such as licensed brothels.

Pros

[1] It is an adult's right to do with his or her body as he or she chooses, and this must include having sex with a consenting partner. The exchange of money does not invalidate the right to have sex. If two individuals have no moral problem with selling sex, they should be left alone to do it. Athletes, construction workers, models and actors all sell their bodies in a way and we have no problem with that. People can buy drinks, presents and even houses for people that they wish to have sex with. Why is the giving of cash so different?

[2] Prostitution is a method whereby people who want sexual relations can easily have them. There are many people who are too busy, too unattractive, too shy or too lazy for the considerable effort of starting and maintaining a successful relationship. Some want variety or the fulfilment of specific fantasies. Unless it can be proved that prostitution is immoral in an absolute sense, then clearly it performs a valuable and popular function.

[3] Whatever moral position is taken, it is clear that legalising prostitution would bring the many benefits of open regula-

Cons

[1] There is no parallel between the use of bodies by actors or builders and by prostitutes. The latter do not have the choice whether to sell their body or not; it is a male-dominated world and many young women are locked into a life of dependency on customers and pimps. Consensual sex implies that both partners approach the act from an equal footing, with the same opportunities; this is clearly not the case with prostitution.

[2] The sale of sex debases an activity that is fulfilled only in loving relationships. In particular it encourages infidelity by offering an easy opportunity for conscience-free, extra-marital sex. The loving relationship is an ideal that should be encouraged, and people who are less attractive or too shy should be made to see that they can have such a relationship, rather than being relegated to a lifetime of visiting prostitutes.

[3] At the moment, the spread of STDs among prostitutes is very low. They are well versed in spotting symptoms in customers, and insist on the use of condoms just as dentists use rubber gloves. Also, the

tion. In particular, the spread of sexually transmitted diseases (STDs) demands that all prostitutes should be issued with licences, regularly renewed on the completion of a negative test for disease.

[4] Many prostitutes are forced into the profession because they have no skills or opportunities for other careers. Once involved in the black market, they are abused by pimps, are susceptible to drugs and other crime, and at the mercy of violent customers, with no legal rights of redress. Bringing prostitution into the open allows these men and women to pursue a career safely, outside the black market, with none of its dangers.

[5] The stigma attached to prostitution as it stands is immense, and a woman with one conviction becomes unemployable and is trapped into a life of crime. This stigma would recede with legalisation, as it did in France until the Second World War, when it was common and tolerated for girls to work in brothels for a few years, saving up for marriage dowries.

[6] As has happened with New York's sex stores and strip clubs in the late1990s, the legalisation of brothels would allow their location to be dictated by local authorities. They could be situated in industrial areas, away from residences and from each other, thereby avoiding the existing problem of illegal establishments spilling out into residential areas .

sort of customer who might break the law in visiting prostitutes now is unlikely to be conscientious about demanding recently renewed licences.

[4] Prostitutes are forced into the black market because they are usually homeless and need the rewards that crime can offer. Legalised prostitution, in the free market, will inevitably lead to a drop in prices and profits due to competition. Prostitutes – and especially pimps – will merely move on to other criminal methods for lucrative profit: drugs, child prostitution, theft and so on.

[5] There should be stigma attached to a crime. We might as well legalise robbery to avoid endangering the future employment prospects of burglars.

[6] The location of brothels can already be dictated by authorities: namely, by shutting them down. The only reason why areas such as King's Cross and Soho in London, for example, are full of them is because they have traditionally been ignored by a police force content to keep them under supervision. Far more concerted efforts could be made against the prostitution industry, and the fact that they have not been made is not an argument for legalisation.

Possible motions
This House would lift all restrictions on prostitution.
This House believes that sex is sacred.

Related topics
Protective legislation v. individual freedom
Pornography
Zero tolerance

Right to strike for public sector workers

This debate focuses on employees such as teachers, doctors and nurses, transport workers, etc. who are working within the public sector. It may or may not include emergency service workers depending on the definition. It does not usually cover the armed forces. In many countries, trades unions in these areas are very strong and workers use striking as a bargaining tool for better pay and working conditions. Is this an important protection of workers' rights against their powerful government employer, or is it anti-democratic to hold the government to ransom in this way when it has been elected?

Pros

[1] The right to strike is a key part of a fair society, as it shifts some power from the employer to the employee. Without it, the employer – in this case, the government – can do what it likes to its employees and they have no redress.

[2] The right to strike is particularly important in the public sector, as there is no, or little, competition between employers, so employees cannot easily find work elsewhere. For example, if you are a teacher in a country with very few private schools, then the government is not competing to hire you and you cannot leave for an alternative employer. Without the right to strike therefore, you are forced to put up with any changes to your contract.

[3] A general election is not the place to decide on the details of nurses' pay or immigration officers' working hours. The country elects a government, but is not giving it a direct mandate on every detail of working conditions for its employees.

[4] A strike allows workers to raise awareness of their plight and therefore informs the electorate on the government's actions which they can take into account when they vote.

[5] Strikes are not always about more money for workers. Sometimes they are

Cons

[1] The government is not like any other employer. It is the representative of the people, voted for by the people and governing in the interests of the people. It is not motivated by profit or greed. There is no need to have this check on its power.

[2] Public services are usually essential and it is irresponsible to interrupt them through strike action. A teachers' strike threatens a child's education; a nurses' strike jeopardises a patient's life. People who go into these industries should not cause suffering to the people they look after.

[3] The government has a mandate for its actions from the electorate. If the people do not like its actions, the government is accountable at the next election. It is anti-democratic if a party has been voted in on an agenda of austerity to hijack this and demand pay rises that the country has rejected at the ballot box.

[4] The country often does not support strikes and the general public often loses sympathy for the workers. The strikes cause great inconvenience to the country, which the public resents, and they can lead to a loss of trust and respect for the strikers, as it seems that they are risking services for their own financial gain.

complaining about policies that will affect the quality of service that the public will get. For example, nurses may be striking over job losses that they believe will affect patients' safety.

Possible motions

This House would remove the right to strike from public sector workers.

This House believes that everyone should have the right to strike.

Related topics

Capitalism v. socialism

Civil disobedience

Democracy

Salary capping, mandatory

Fairtrade, we should not support

[5] Most strikes are a simple form of blackmail; the public will suffer unless the strikers' pay and/or working conditions are improved. This is selfish, as when the government is also the employer, the extra money has to come from the taxpayer and therefore strikers may be making the whole country worse off.

Slavery, reparations for

This issue could be set in many countries where there is a history of a slave trade. It is often set in the USA where the descendants of many slaves live and where there is a strong lobby for more recognition and justice for this community. It could also be run country to country (e.g. that Britain should pay reparations to Jamaica; or the West should pay reparations to Africa). It may need to be established exactly who is to pay the reparations (countries or companies, for example) and who will receive them, and how much they will be; or it may be possible to have the debate as a principle.

Pros

[1] There is a real economic harm to descendants of slaves due to discrimination caused (both in terms of wealth not passed down through families, and now the lower earning power of, for example, African Americans).

[2] There has been a real economic gain to the country and to individual descendants of slave owners, as money that came from cotton, sugar, etc. was made on the back of slave labour.

Cons

[1] There are no slaves alive to whom reparations can be paid, and it is not appropriate to pay descendants (perhaps great-grandchildren) who have never had any contact with slavery and have not suffered as a result of it. A country's duty should be to make sure that all sections of the community have equal opportunities and are free from discrimination. If this is not the case, then resources should be directed towards solving this problem at a

[3] There is a justice in transferring the wealth – both in terms of the unpaid wages and also in terms of a penalty for the moral crime which was committed and for which nobody has paid.

[4] There is a strong symbolism in the act which shows that society has a deep regret that slavery happened and helps us to move forward. This could help to address current continuing racial divides.

[5] There are precedents: in the 1980s, the USA paid reparations to survivors of Japanese American internment during the Second World War; the German government paid reparations to victims of the Holocaust and their families. The question of who pays and who receives money could be decided by an independent commission. In most cases, clear lineage can be established.

Possible motions

This House supports reparations for slavery.
This House believes that the US government should pay reparations for slavery.

Related topics

Marxism
Child labour can be justified
Affirmative action

community level, not giving money to individuals.

[2] There are no slave owners or traders alive to pay these reparations. Nobody alive was involved or supports the use of slaves, so there would be no justice in punishing the innocent. It is impossible to calculate how much a country gained from slavery, but all of that wealth should now benefit all of its citizens equally. It is also very complex because of changing colonial powers: should the USA pay, or France and Britain?

[3] The slave owners of the time were breaking no law. Society has now moved on and moral and legal positions have changed, but it is not fair to enact a retrospective punishment when people were acting within the law.

[4] The reparations could actually inflame racism. A white majority would resent being punished for a crime they took no part in and this may harm race relations.

Smacking, remove parents' right to

A useful tool in child-rearing or an outdated act of barbarism? Smacking continues to be controversial. It is banned outright in some countries such as New Zealand and much of Europe. Others restrict it to certain ages (in Canada, it is illegal to smack a child under the age of 3 or over the age of 11). Many countries, including the UK, define and legalise 'reasonable chastisement', but place limits such as forbidding smacking to the head or with an object. In the UK, if there is a bruise or cut after smacking, the perpetrator can be imprisoned for up to five years.

Pros

[1] The use of force is barbaric and it is made more, not less, acceptable if it is used against a defenceless child. Even if no long-lasting physical damage is inflicted, there are emotional side-effects to being hit that will remain.

[2] There are many other methods that should instead be used to teach good behaviour: verbal correction, 'grounding', withholding of pocket money and so on. It is not morally justified to cause pain to others, even in a parent–child relationship.

[3] Parental use of force teaches children that violence can be acceptable. Too many criminals, bullies and children with other behavioural disorders have been beaten as part of their upbringing for the link not to be accepted. Parents are not necessarily trustworthy and many abuse the right of chastisement. Others may simply misjudge the level of force they use in the heat of the moment and cause serious injury to their child.

[4] By introducing fear and intimidation into the parent–child relationship, you undermine trust and therefore other forms of positive discipline such as praise and encouragement. If a child has high self-esteem and self-confidence, they are more likely willingly to follow their parents' rules and meet their expectations.

Cons

[1] 'Spare the rod and spoil the child.' A short, sharp expression of force, such as a smack or a spanking – which inflicts no serious or lasting damage – is an extremely effective method of discipline. It is espoused by many childcare experts.

[2] There are sometimes no effective alternatives, especially in children's formative years, before they have developed faculties of reason and fair play to which parents can (try to) appeal. Children need to be taught the difference between right and wrong. A smack can quickly communicate that boundaries have been crossed and parental authority can be established.

[3] It is possible for the law to distinguish between 'reasonable chastisement' and child abuse and the latter must be punished. However, the existence of bad parents does not mean that the majority of good parents should be denied the right to raise their children as they see fit. The number of parents who have used smacking to produce well-raised children testifies to the usefulness of the punishment.

[4] Spanking and smacking should be seen as part of a wider strategy of child-rearing. They should be used only selectively, for acts of wilful disobedience and misbehaviour, and only after milder forms of discipline (removal of privileges, addition of chores) have failed. Encouragement and praise should be given for good behaviour.

Possible motions
This House would ban smacking.
This House would allow parents to physically punish their children.

Related topics
Capital punishment
Parents, responsibility for the criminal acts of their children

Smoking, banning of

This is fundamentally another debate about whether the government should intervene to protect individuals from themselves. Many Western governments have now passed legislation to discourage smoking, including banning tobacco advertising, banning smoking in public places, raising the minimum age for smoking, significantly raising taxes on tobacco and covering cigarette packets in graphic health warnings. Are these measures enough or do they go too far? Or do we still need to stop all smoking in private as well?

Pros

[1] Smoking tobacco is proven to cause emphysema, chronic bronchitis, heart disease and cancer of the mouth, throat, oesophagus and lungs. Half of the teenagers currently smoking will die from disease caused by tobacco if they continue to smoke, 25 per cent before they are 70. The nicotine in tobacco makes it extremely addictive. It is the responsibility of the state to protect citizens from themselves, which is why bare-knuckle boxing and heroin are banned.

[2] In recent years, more and more evidence has emerged of the effects of cigarette smoke on non-smokers – 'passive smoking'. Like drink-driving, it greatly increases the risk of serious harm to oneself and to others. Growing up in a smoking household can seriously affect your health. Banning smoking in public places helps those who work in the service industries, but what about the children and spouses of smokers who are confined in cars and houses breathing in second-hand smoke all day? They must be protected.

[3] At present, millions of law-abiding citizens smoke, but 70 per cent of them say they want to give up. The banning of tobacco would be a severe but effective way of ensuring that these people *did* stop

Cons

[1] Tobacco does indeed increase the risk of contracting certain diseases, but the banning of smoking would be an unacceptable encroachment on individual freedom. We allow adults to choose how much fat to eat, how much exercise to take, or how much alcohol to drink. All these decisions have far-reaching health implications, but we do not ban cream cakes, laziness or beer. Individuals must be left to decide for themselves if they want to take the risk of smoking, rather than being dictated to by a 'nanny state'.

[2] Passive smoking has been a problem in the past, but this can be effectively addressed by the banning of smoking in public places. We should also be aware that the massive air pollution caused by motor vehicles poses a significantly greater threat to everyone's health than do the relatively insignificant 'emissions' of cigarettes.

[3] We must allow people to make their own decisions unless certain and immediate dangers are involved (as with heroin, say, but not tobacco). People can become addicted to coffee, jogging, shopping and many other things. It is up to them to kick the habit if they want to and are able to. Banning tobacco would immediately create a culture of millions of addicted

smoking. These people are not the sort to get involved in underground drugs activities and so would simply stop smoking. Banning smoking is a form of 'tough love'.

[4] Unlike some other drugs, tobacco has *no* positive effects. Alcohol can make people relaxed and sociable and uninhibited in a positive way. Cigarettes give the illusion of relieving tension simply because of the relief of nicotine withdrawal; in fact, smokers are the most tense, fidgety and anxious of all. Tobacco is particularly expensive and used more by the poor than the rich. It is not hard to use all of your government benefits on smoking. The present measure of ever-increasing taxes on cigarettes does not make people stop smoking, but just makes them poorer, more unhappy and more dependent on the drug.

[5] The economic cost of smoking to a country's health service comes to hundreds of millions of pounds each year. Millions of working hours are lost annually to industry and commerce as a result of smoking-related illness. Those who smoke 20 cigarettes a day or more have twice as much time off work due to illness as do non-smokers. This is an unacceptable economic cost for something with no benefits.

criminals, forming a black market as did Prohibition in 1920s America.

[4] Smoking is relaxing. Even if the effect is the result of nicotine withdrawal or is mainly psychological, it does not alter the fact that for many people, smoking is a genuine pleasure on which they choose to spend their money. It is true that to increase tobacco duty imposes a tax on the poor, which is why the duty should be reduced rather than increased – but that is not an argument for banning smoking. Banning smoking in some parts of public meeting places and forms of public transport is as far as the anti-smoking movement should reasonably go.

[5] In the UK, revenue from duty and VAT on cigarettes exceeds the cost to the National Health Service by more than 10 to 1. Working hours are lost through many different sorts of self-indulgence.

Possible motions
This House would ban smoking.
This House believes tobacco is a hard drug.

Related topics
Protective legislation v. individual freedom
Drugs, legalisation of
Alcohol, prohibition of

Veil, prohibition of the

In 2011, France and Belgium banned the wearing of veils which cover the face, including the niqab. Some Muslim-majority countries also restrict the wearing of the veil and Turkey has banned it outright since 1997. These countries say that they are protecting secularism and/or promoting women's rights, but opponents see it as a gross infringement of civil liberties and an attack on religious freedoms. A Proposition team should consider explaining what their punishment would be in the definition.

Pros

[1] The veil is a symbol of the repression of women and allowing it damages all women in society, whether or not they are wearing it themselves. It is particularly damaging to Muslim women as it creates a stereotype of 'the submissive Muslim woman', which can lead to discrimination.

[2] While some women freely choose the veil, many do not and need protection from being forced to do so. Some of those who do choose to wear the veil do so only because of cultural indoctrination. A liberal society needs to provide freedom from this.

[3] Women wearing the veil cannot participate fully in society and so it harms assimilation. The veil can be an obstacle to education, work and communication. It has been described as a 'walking prison'.

[4] When France introduced a ban on the veil, it did so with a penalty of a fine. In Belgium, it can be punished with a seven-day jail sentence. Most people, however, do not wish to break the law and will comply with the legislation.

Possible motions

This House would ban the wearing of the veil.
This House believes that women should not be allowed to wear the burka in public.

Related topics

Protective legislation v. individual freedom
Immigration, limitation of

Cons

[1] A liberal society should be tolerant of religious and cultural practices where there is no clear harm to the individual involved. It is important to respect religious freedoms. Women who do not wear the veil are not affected by those who do. Women who show a lot of flesh can also create negative views of women, but nobody is proposing that we ban the mini-skirt.

[2] We should not restrict individual choice. Many women do choose to wear the veil and find it liberating rather than restricting. Displaying skin is not an objective good. This policy is particularly harmful as it limits only women's freedoms and therefore is sexist. Many Muslim women have come to Western countries fleeing persecution – they should not face more persecution here.

[3] The veil in and of itself need be no barrier. Women in Arab countries participate at all civic levels, while wearing the veil. Maybe it is the Western societies that need to shed their prejudice. Besides, assimilation is not necessarily the goal. People should not have to 'blend in', but should be allowed to retain their identity.

[4] If this proposal is enforced, the women who have not chosen the veil themselves will be forced to stay inside and therefore enjoy less freedom, so the policy is counterproductive. The enforcement of punishment for disobeying this law (e.g. forcible removal of the veil, imprisonment) is problematic in all its forms.

Women fighting on the front line

The status of women in the armed forces varies from country to country. In 2013, the USA lifted its ban on women fighting in combat infantry units, joining Israel, Norway

and Canada among others. But many countries including the UK, Russia and India still
have a ban.

Pros

[1] Equality is at stake here. No woman
who wants to fight for her country, and
passes the necessary physical and mental
tests, should be prevented from doing so
because of her gender. Women have
proved themselves in all walks of life,
despite prejudices to the contrary. This last
bastion of sexism must be removed.

[2] Women have proved themselves
capable of this type of work; they fight on
the front line in the German, Australian
and Canadian armies, they do similar
frontline jobs in the emergency services
and they serve on naval ships on the front
line. Including them on the front line does
not compromise the efficacy of the army.

[3] Having women on the front line
produces a more balanced force and
reflects all the other parts of the armed
services. It also provides a wider pool of
recruits to pick from, which should ultimately improve quality. An overly 'gung
ho', testosterone-driven approach can lead
to poor behaviour and the presence of
women may actually help this.

Cons

[1] The armed forces must put quality
before equality. When people are risking
their lives, we cannot ask them to compromise their security for the sake of a
social crusade. Women's rights are not set
back by this as there are many routes to a
successful career in the forces. This reflects
the 'equal but different' principle which
also means that sports teams can be all one
gender.

[2] Women cannot match the physical
strength and endurance of men, and their
psychological and hormonal profile is not
well matched to the aggressive demands of
close combat. It is possible that some
women may pass a theoretical test, but that
does not mean that they will stand up to
the conditions of real combat.

[3] Having women on the front line will
compromise the 'band of brothers' spirit.
Men treat women differently; this could
manifest itself as the men wanting to
protect the women and therefore making
bad combat decisions, or it could also lead
to resentment and bullying of the tiny
number of women who passed the physical test and found themselves in a unit.
Romantic attachments could also undermine the team.

Possible motions

This House would allow women to fight on the
front line.

This House supports a ban on women in the
infantry.

Related topics

Affirmative action

Pacifism

National service, (re)introduction of

SECTION F

Culture, education and sport

Arts funding by the state, abolition of

Many countries subsidise the arts to some degree. The French, for example, subsidise their film industry; the Indian government gives money to dance, music and drama; and the British government, through the Arts Council, has supported arts projects, some of which have invited controversy. In contrast, the USA gives very little support to artists, but does fund free access to national art galleries. The arguments vary slightly in the debate, depending on whether you are talking about giving the money towards the creation or the consumption of the arts, but most definitions will cover both.

Pros

[1] The role of the state in the modern world is not to prescribe the means of expression of its citizens. Funding of the arts by the state amounts to such prescription – money will always go to one favoured art form (often traditional figurative painting and sculpture) rather than others (e.g. more conceptual art forms). To avoid having a pernicious influence over artistic expression and development, state funding of the arts should be abolished. The ideal of art is individual expression – this is incompatible with state (or arguably, *any*) patronage.

[2] We have learned from the past (especially in communist regimes) that funding of artistic projects (including the composition of music) all too easily slides into the realm of propaganda. Art should be free to criticise the government.

[3] There are many more important things for which public money is needed – obvious examples include books and equipment for schools, new drugs and technologies for hospitals, social security payments for single parents and the unemployed. Every spare penny should be channelled into these areas. Public spending should be on necessities, not luxuries. Art is of no material use to the

Cons

[1] If the state does not provide carefully administered funding for the arts, then only the independently wealthy or those given patronage by the rich will be able to practise as artists – this is unacceptably elitist and haphazard. Art has been associated with patronage of various forms from classical times onwards. Just as religion has always found a compromise with secular authorities, so the 'pure' artist will always find a compromise between the ideal of individual expression and the economic realities of life as an artist. Only the state can fund the arts in a responsible way, appointing committees of artistic experts to make responsible, relatively impartial and up-to-date decisions about which art forms and artists are funded.

[2] We can, indeed, learn from history. What we learn is that arts funding must be given without any strings attached – that artistic freedom must always be guaranteed rather than the state dictating to the artist. Mistakes of past regimes do not mean that state funding of the arts must be scrapped, any more than the fact that democratic processes have been abused by autocratic regimes means that democracy should be scrapped.

nation and so is not a proper object of public expenditure. It would be better to lower taxes and let people choose to spend the extra money in their pockets on whatever art form they wish, be it visual art or anything else.

[4] If there is no demand for works of art, then why are they being produced? It is simply a form of pointless self-indulgence by artists. The state has no business subsidising plays, paintings or concertos for which there is no demand. Artists should compete in the free market like everyone else trying to sell a product. If there are too many artists for the limited demand, then some artists (actors, painters, musicians) should simply retrain, as did, for example, coal miners in the 1980s when their usefulness was exhausted.

[5] In some countries, the arts are indirectly funded by unemployment payments to young musicians and artists who claim dole payments and do not seek work, but simply want to develop their artistic talents. But there is no reason why such people should not organise their time to include part-time work as well as time for their artistic development. It is illogical to assume that artistic talent must go hand in hand with a chaotic, self-indulgent and undisciplined lifestyle.

[3] It is very simplistic to see benefit only in material goods such as textbooks and medicines. Civilised societies need moral and mental education and healing as much as they require educational and medical equipment. Artists (poets, painters, actors, comedians, sculptors, musicians, film-makers) provide unique moral insights and function as irreplaceable critics of society and politics (a cross between academics and jesters). A society without arts would be soulless and blind. Investing in a thriving arts scene can ultimately repay dividends as tourists visit cultural attractions and the economy benefits.

[4] There are some areas where we should not let the market dictate policy and spending. Public transport and health services, for example, should be kept in state ownership to ensure that they are run not according to supply-and-demand alone, but on a moral basis, so that non-profit-making activities – e.g. train services to remote areas, or expensive treatments for rare medical conditions – are not scrapped. Arts funding is a similar case. The state should fund the arts to ensure that they are not sacrificed on the altar of heartless free market capitalism. Capitalists may be philistines, but that does not mean that the whole of society should be made culturally illiterate by abolishing state funding of the arts. The market will follow 'safe' artistic options, whereas art needs the freedom to take risks and to be ahead of the curve rather than follow public opinion. Many artists we celebrate today would not have flourished if they had relied on the market of their day rather than patronage.

[5] Young artists need the time to develop their talents which would be restrained by

Possible motions

This House would abolish state funding of the arts.

This House believes that the arts are of no material benefit to society.

Related topics

Capitalism v. socialism

BBC, privatisation of

Cultural treasures, returning of

Indigenous languages, protection of

Music lyrics, censorship of

a typical 9-to-5 job. The artistic temperament is not compatible with such a routine. It is perfectly acceptable for such gifted young people to live on state benefits while developing their unique talents.

Beauty contests, banning of

Beauty contests and pageants exist across the world, with the largest and most famous example being Miss World. There are also many local, national and niche contests and a large community of teen, child and even baby beauty pageants. A debate can be had about all beauty contests, and there is also an interesting debate to be had concerning other events which include children.

Pros

[1] The existence of beauty pageants is bad for women because of its contribution to the pressure to conform to one idealised view of beauty. Pageant queens are almost always slim and busty. Caucasian women are usually deeply tanned; Asian women are often lighter skinned than average. Labelling and celebrating this as 'beauty' leads to a feeling of inadequacy in many women. It adds to the increasing trends for cosmetic surgery, sun beds and eating disorders, as women find that they cannot be happy as themselves. Society should celebrate healthier values such as 'beauty is in the eye of the beholder' and 'beauty is only skin deep'.

[2] Beauty pageants are also bad for women because of the perceptions of

Cons

[1] Beauty pageants reflect the ideals of beauty in society, they do not create it. Women are bombarded by images of beauty all the time and the pressure that exists comes from the media and their peers.

[2] Both men and women can be judged on many criteria and in many spheres. There are competitions which, for example, judge women's writing (the Women's Prize for Fiction), there are lists such as the Forbes list of the most powerful women, and there are many women's sporting events. Beauty pageants celebrate one aspect, the physical, but they are balanced by many other views of women. It is as valid to judge the physical as it is to judge other attributes. This is also true of men, as

women that they propagate in society. In the twenty-first century, women in much of the world have achieved legally protected gender equality and wish to be taken seriously in business and politics. Deciding on who should be Miss World by asking contestants to parade around in swimsuits while men judge their legs, creates a perception that women are valued in the bedroom and not the boardroom – that they are defined by their looks and not their intellect or personality. This is a damaging message to send to society and young girls and boys in particular.

[3] Beauty pageants are demeaning and can be dangerous for the participants. Where is the dignity in being assessed like a prize animal? The pressure on contestants is huge and there is a high risk of eating disorders. In contests involving young girls, contestants may have been forced into the pageants by pushy parents.

[4] Beauty pageants are culturally insensitive. While many Western women are offended by the swimsuit parade, the reaction in other parts of the world can be more extreme. In 2002, Miss World had to leave Nigeria because of the riots it sparked. There is also an element of cultural imperialism as, although women from around the world do win the title, the ideals of beauty that they conform to were formed in the West.

[5] Beauty pageants are unique in celebrating beauty alone and also in quantifying and judging it. Modelling is about the clothes; music stars and actresses are celebrated for their creative skills. These industries do not try to define beauty and, in fact, many alternative-looking women

male equivalents such as Mr Universe exist alongside many other ways of rating masculine talents.

[3] Nobody is forced into entering a beauty pageant. The contestants should be allowed the freedom of choice to compete. Many women enjoy beauty pageants and the preparation for them and see them as fun. No third parties are harmed, and so the government should not intervene to limit liberty in this way. In the case of minors, parents should have the responsibility to make the choice along with their children, as they are trusted to make much bigger decisions.

[4] No country is forced into entering Miss World or holding local pageants, but many do so and are proud of the women who represent them. Tolerance and inclusivity are promoted through the contest as women of different races, religions and nationalities stand together equally. Women from across the globe have won Miss World, promoting the idea that beauty can come in different shapes and colours.

[5] It is unfair to target beauty pageants in this way. Advertising, modelling, music videos and film are showing increasingly provocative images of 'perfect' women. Magazines airbrush their photos; beauty queens are real women. Dancers in music videos are sexualised in their swimsuits; beauty queens are demure.

[6] Beauty queens are good role models who use their titles to promote good work. Many are ambassadors for good causes and raise large sums for charity. Contestants are interviewed and they show a wide variety of interests, levels of education and personality, illustrating that they are more than 'just a pretty face'.

are successful. That is why beauty pageants are particularly pernicious.

[6] Beauty queens are poor role models. It is true that many of them are educated, successful and have lots of hobbies and great personalities. So why are they allowing themselves to be objectified in this way?

Possible motions
This House would cancel Miss World.
This House would ban beauty pageants.
This House believes that beauty should not be judged.
This House would ban child beauty pageants.

Related topics
Size zero models, banning of
Cosmetic surgery, banning of
Pornography
Prostitution, legalisation of

Blood sports, abolition of

There are different examples of blood sports in different cultures; cockfighting is illegal in most Western countries now, but is popular in much of Asia and Latin America; some parts of Spain still enjoy bullfighting. In the UK, foxhunting was banned in 2004, but the legislation is not rigorously enforced, and in 2013, hunts still take place up and down the country; Pakistan recently banned dogfighting, but it is still popular in rural areas. A debate may focus on one of these sports or look at banning them collectively. Not all of the arguments work for all of the sports – the issues around bullfighting and hunting, for example, overlap but are different, so be sure to pick your arguments accordingly. See also the introduction to the debate on 'Animal experimentation and vivisection, banning of' (Section E) and the entry on 'Animal rights' (Section A) for a general summary of animal rights debates.

Pros

[1] There is a continuum between humans and the rest of the animal kingdom. Animals such as birds, hares, foxes and deer can, like us, experience stress, fear, exhaustion and pain. As conscious beings, we should accord these animals rights and not inflict suffering and death on them for the sake of our entertainment. The infliction of unnecessary suffering on domestic and captive animals is already a criminal offence – this offence should be extended to cover all animals.

Cons

[1] Humans are both at the top of the food chain and of the evolutionary tree, and as such, may use animals to their own ends, while preferably minimising their suffering. Blood sports exist as a way to derive community enjoyment from the hunting of animals that would be killed anyway. The opposition to blood sports is largely based on anthropomorphic sentimentality and squeamishness. People have always had to kill animals to feed and protect themselves. In the modern metropolitan

[2] In the case of hunting, it is defended on the grounds that it is legitimate pest control or legitimate hunting for food. Claims that hunting is a form of 'pest control' are usually bogus. Foxes, for example, are particularly inefficient predators, accounting for only a tiny percentage of livestock lost each year. Foxes were imported into Britain specifically to be hunted, when deer populations waned early in the twentieth century, and fox hunts still deliberately nurture fox populations. Foxes are not eaten. Hunting with hounds – killing the quarry only after hours of terror and exhaustion – is not an effective way to kill hares, foxes or deer. Shooting is more humane and efficient, if they really need to be killed to protect livestock or reduce populations. Game birds are bred specifically to be shot. These practices are a particularly stark example of the abuse of humanity's position as 'stewards' of the natural world.

[3] Nobody has a right to continue with cultural practices which are harmful (to humans, animals or society as a whole). Cultures must evolve to conform to society's values. Public executions and freak shows were once culturally significant. They have gone, and blood sports must go the same way.

[4] Public opinion has moved against blood sports and there are lobbies in many parts of the world to outlaw practices where they still go on. They are seen as outdated and barbaric and they do not fit in with our views of a civilized society in the twenty-first century.

[5] There are alternatives to blood sports that could maintain employment for those involved in the industry and maintain the pursuit as a hobby, but without the cruelty

supermarket age, people have the luxury of distancing themselves from the actual business of doing so.

[2] Blood sports often kill animals that are destructive of animals raised for food. The huge majority of farmers agree that foxes are pests that attack their livestock. Shooting, poisoning and trapping – the alternatives to hunting with hounds – are not more humane. All these methods potentially leave animals to die a slow and painful death (most farmers are not trained marksmen – a shot is more likely to wound a fox than kill it, leaving it to starve through its inability to hunt). The death of an animal caught by hunting hounds is over in a second or two. Other blood sports kill animals that can be eaten – pheasants, grouse, deer, hares and fish – some of which are also a pest to agriculture and forestry (e.g. hares, deer). And it is hardly logical to complain about the shooting of birds that were bred to be shot. As it is, they have a perfectly natural life ended instantaneously when they are shot. If it were not for blood sports, these birds would never have had a life at all – they would not have been born.

[3] Some blood sports are culturally important, such as bullfighting in Spain. In these cases, the cultural rights of humans must be put before the dubious rights of animals.

[4] There is still a lot of support for blood sports such as bullfighting, which is seen as an important part of Spain's cultural heritage. Many of those who oppose hunting have never been hunting themselves and are city-dwellers. They live a life detached from the realities of rural life and farming, and hence can afford to take an idealistic stance on 'animal rights'. In rural

to animals. Examples of this are 'drag-hunting' where an artificial trail is laid and followed by hounds, or shooting at targets on a range.

[6] Bans send out a clear message that animal cruelty is unacceptable, and over time the activity will decrease. More effort could be put into enforcement with harsher penalties. If the government is failing in enforcement, why would it be any more effective in regulation?

Possible motions

This House believes that the unspeakable should leave the inedible alone.

This House believes that blood sports are legalised barbarism.

This House would ban bullfighting.

This House would re-legalise foxhunting.

Related topics

Animal experimentation and vivisection, banning of

Animal rights

Vegetarianism

Zoos, abolition of

communities, there is very little support for a ban.

[5] The banning of blood sports would undermine the rural economy, since hunting provides jobs for many and protects agricultural land. As explained above, there is no need for an alternative such as drag-hunting, since blood sports are not gratuitous entertainment, but the carrying out of legitimate and necessary killing of pests or game in an enjoyable fashion.

[6] It has proved impossible to enforce bans on blood sports. Dogfighting is still popular, though illegal, in Pakistan; nobody knows how many illegal cock-fights take place globally; and in Britain, it is believed that groups have found ways around the foxhunting ban and escaped prosecution. These ineffective bans undermine the government and it would be better to work to regulate conditions for animals involved in the sport.

Boxing, banning of

Boxing is a combat sport where two people fight by throwing punches with gloved hands. It originated in Ancient Greece and is an Olympic sport. It is a popular sport in many countries today, but it has many opponents who believe that it is barbaric and that the harm done to the boxers themselves and to society as a whole merits a ban. The arguments in this debate broadly apply to other contact sports (or 'collision' sports in some terminology) such as some martial arts or rugby.

Pros

[1] Boxing should be banned in order to protect individuals from serious physical injury and death. Boxers have died from injuries they have received in the ring (e.g. the Cuban boxer Benny Paret in the 1960s). Many others have received debilitating, non-fatal injuries. Young people are introduced to these sports at an impressionable age when they may not be old enough to make decisions based on all the relevant facts – there is also great peer pressure to be 'hard' and take part in boxing, and a promise of huge fame and riches if you are successful. A ban is the only way to ensure that young people in particular are protected from the dangers involved.

[2] Unlike football, cricket, skiing or swimming, in which there may be some *incidental* injuries from accidents or (in football) illegal tackles, in boxing, injuries result from the central activity of the sport. The whole point is to knock one's opponent unconscious which can mean temporarily detaching the brain from the inside of the skull. Both the British Medical Association and the American Medical Association have repeatedly called for a ban on boxing. Such forms of 'sport' are uncivilised and unacceptably dangerous, resulting in paralysis, brain damage and death for many unfortunate participants.

[3] The idolisation of boxers gives young people role models who are revered simply for their brute force and ability to injure other people. The 'fighting talk' that the boxers engage in before a big fight where they threaten and insult each other magnifies this. Such role models can only have a negative effect and perpetuate the

Cons

[1] It should be up to individuals to decide whether or not to take part in boxing. We let people decide for themselves whether to drive cars or smoke cigarettes – both, proportionately, far more dangerous. In general, we should let people decide for themselves what risks to take unless there is a good reason not to – for example, heroin taking, which is excessively and universally harmful and destructive and highly addictive.

[2] In fact, there are relatively few deaths from contact sports compared with deaths from incidents of drowning in long-distance swimming and in sailing, for example. There are risks inherent in all sports. Cricket balls on the head, sliding football tackles, skiing accidents, crashes in 'Formula One' racing are all inherent risks of those pursuits, not in some way incidental, in the same way that accidents in boxing are an inherent risk. The distinction between inherently and incidentally dangerous activities is a spurious one. There is always a referee in the boxing ring, who can maximise safety for the boxers. If boxing matches went underground, they would probably be more brutal.

[3] Boxers can actually be very positive role models: they offer an example of success achieved through hard work and discipline. Many boxers, such as Frank Bruno, have done wonderful service to charities, and others are very articulate – for example, Chris Eubank. Muhammad Ali has been an inspiration to generations both as a boxer and as a man. Many boxers come from working-class backgrounds and go on to become household names in professional boxing or to represent their

trend towards increased violence and aggression among young people. Rather, we should revere sportsmen who display merits that we value in society.

[4] Violence as entertainment is uncivilised and has a brutalising effect on society. If crowds are encouraged to cheer on fighters in a ring, then they will also cheer on fighters in the school yard or in a bar, or seek to be cheered on themselves. Boxing muddies the message that violence is unacceptable. Seeing a boxer's nose broken or a fighter knocked unconscious desensitises our responses to violence and normalises something that needs to shock.

Possible motions

This House would abolish contact sports.
This House would ban boxing.

Related topics

Protective legislation v. individual freedom
Violent video games, banning of
Music lyrics, censorship of
Performance-enhancing drugs in sport

country in the Olympics. This can be aspirational and offer a way out of poverty to deprived young people.

[4] It is simplistic to believe that admiration for boxers leads to violent behaviour. People find all sorts of scapegoats for the incidence of violent behaviour – television, films, video games, sports – but in fact, violence endures no matter what forms of sport and entertainment prevail. In the nineteenth century, bare-knuckle boxing, a more brutal sport than modern boxing, was immensely popular, but it does not seem that teenagers were more violent then than they are now. Boxing could actually help to make our streets safer by providing a structured outlet for aggression. There are many inner-city programmes that teach boxing to teenage boys to get them away from gangs and into gyms.

Co-education

In some countries, state education is almost entirely co-educational. Other countries, like the UK, have a more diverse variety of schools, with church schools and many private schools choosing to educate girls and boys separately. Is the opposite sex a distraction from a good education or is segregation unnatural? A definition in this debate may need to specify an age range as some countries have single-sex schools only from 7, 11 or 13 and some mix genders only from 16.

Pros

[1] It is only natural to teach boys and girls together, for social and economic reasons. University, the workplace, families are co-ed. Segregation during their teenage years does not prepare young people to work and live alongside each other in the future. Co-education gives girls and boys an easy confidence and understanding when dealing with the opposite sex.

[2] Both boys and girls benefit from being with each other. The presence of girls usually leads to better behaviour among boys who would otherwise enjoy an 'oppressively male' atmosphere with its associated traits: arrogance, crudity and juvenile behaviour. Teenage girls mature faster than their male counterparts and so are good influences on them. An all-female atmosphere can lead to bitchiness and can create an atmosphere of high pressure with more issues such as eating disorders and self-harming being reported. It may be that the presence of boys diffuses some of this pressure.

[3] Competition between the sexes is greater than between same-sex rivals, and this competition can lead to higher standards of academic achievement, especially among boys. A classroom environment is enriched by diversity and the different views that boys and girls bring, leading to a more well-rounded education. If single-sex schools often outperform co-ed schools academically, this could be because they are usually private, grammar or religious schools which may have fewer discipline problems and a better work ethos.

[4] The system of single-sex schools arose from the chauvinistic society of the past,

Cons

[1] It is more natural for the sexes to be taught apart, especially in the formative years between 7 and 15 when children prefer the company of their own sex. In the Caribbean, many single-sex schools are based on the belief that gendered responses from children confirm the natural differences between the sexes.

[2] Confidence is a product of maturity and children can be just as shy in co-educational schools as in mixed schools. In fact, co-education can lead to behaviour that is extremely detrimental to education: boys are led to show off and even sexually harass girls, while both are distracted by each other. The teenage pregnancy rate is increasing in co-educational schools. Girls may be less likely to speak up in class as they do not want to appear clever or 'geeky' in front of the boys.

[3] Competition should be discouraged and students should not be used as pawns to provoke each other into working harder; it is the teacher's job to inspire them, and they should not be motivated by rivalry. Academic achievement is in fact generally higher in single-sex schools, and studies have shown that girls in particular perform better in a single-sex environment. Some education theorists believe that girls and boys tend to display different learning styles, which means that teachers in single-sex schools can tailor their approaches more effectively.

[4] Children of a certain age shy away from the opposite gender and prefer many activities characteristic of their sex. It is only natural that they should be taught during this period by same-sex teachers. While men and women should have equal

where men held all major positions in society and were accordingly given a better education. It then moved on to different curricula, with girls learning to sew while boys concentrated on science. It is now recognised that the sexes have equal rights: of employment, of social benefit and of education. The best way to ensure that this equality happens in practice is by educating the sexes together. The fact that single-sex schools tend to have a majority of teachers of that sex – especially in the higher positions such as that of head teacher – means that women teachers are discriminated against in boys' schools, and vice versa, and that young people lack strong role models of the opposite sex.

[5] It is possible to separate out girls and boys for classes such as sports and sex education, if it is deemed appropriate, but schools may decide that everyone benefits from staying together across the whole curriculum. It is easy to provide separate facilities and uniform where necessary, so these need not present barriers. In fact, the practical problems of having two of everything in separate schools are larger.

rights, this is not the same as saying they are identical. In fact, girls in particular are more likely to pursue typically 'male' subjects, such as sciences and mathematics, in an all-female environment where there is no stigma. Single-sex schools may therefore lead to greater gender equality in society by producing top female engineers and scientists.

[5] There are also a number of subjects that cannot be taught in the presence of both sexes, or should not be taught in the same way: sex education, women's issues, etc. Sports are also gender-specific. In a co-educational school, you also need separate facilities such as changing rooms and WCs, and there are issues about which staff can go where and deal with which problems.

Possible motions

This House would educate boys and girls together.

This House would send their children to single-sex schools.

Related topics

Examinations, abolition of

Sex education

Affirmative action

Cultural treasures, returning of

It is difficult to define a cultural treasure, but the Proposition team must have a go, and perhaps nominate a body that will make specific decisions. Treasures can be defined as including relics, documents, artefacts, etc. The British are most under pressure to return many treasures held in the British Museum and so the arguments highlight them and high-profile treasures such as the Parthenon (or Elgin) Marbles from Greece, the Rosetta Stone and artefacts from the Tomb of Tutankhamun from Egypt, and the Benin Bronzes from Nigeria. Other countries, however, can also be included; for example, there are Korean treasures, taken during the Korean War, in the Smithsonian in Washington, DC.

Pros

[1] Cultural treasures leave their country in morally dubious circumstances and therefore should be returned. The majority of artefacts were taken during the Age of Empire, when the European powers believed that they could help themselves to whatever they wanted. Other treasures were stolen or bought from those who had no right to sell them.

[2] At present, the country keeping the cultural treasures is benefiting from them instead of the country of origin and this is unfair. The main benefit is that their population can easily access artefacts – for example, a school trip to the British Museum to see the Rosetta Stone – whereas an Egyptian child would have to be very rich to fly to England to see it. The masses are therefore denied access to their cultural heritage.

[3] The country also benefits from the tourism. Many visitors are attracted to London to see the British Museum and its artefacts such as the Parthenon Marbles. Those tourists then spend money in British restaurants, hotels and shops, thereby benefiting the economy. This money should rightfully be going to the poorer countries from which the objects were stolen. It is a continuation of the practice of getting rich from imperialism. Scholars also locate themselves near the artefacts, so universities are able to attract the top academics and further their reputations.

[4] It is important to have good diplomatic relations with countries around the world and absurd to jeopardise these to play 'finders keepers'. An example of this is the good relations needed with Greece over the arrest in 2001 of British citizens for spying when they took photos of Greek

Cons

[1] This policy is very difficult to apply in practice. First, how do you define a cultural treasure – who would decide and where do you draw the line? Second, what happens when there are diverse claims (e.g. the Mona Lisa – painted by an Italian, but important to French culture for hundreds of years)? Third, what happens when that culture does not exist anymore (e.g. Incas, Ancient Egyptians, Aztecs, etc.)? Fourth, do authorities still return the treasure if there was a legitimate sale? Fifth, what if an item of cultural significance is not country-based; for example, an important Muslim artefact or an important example of an architectural or artistic school? Finally, would one return treasures to politically unstable regimes?

[2] Cultural treasures belong to the world. Great works of art, artefacts from ancient civilisation or items of political significance are relevant and significant to all of humanity. The fact that it was sculpted on your doorstep does not make it most relevant to you – especially when the civilisations have changed (as with Greece and Italy). Ancient Greece and Rome set up all of Western civilisation – the treasures are not more significant to modern-day Greece and Italy than they are to Britain or France.

[3] Because cultural treasures belong to the world, we should have the best access for the world. Cities such as London are a huge draw for tourists, so many people from around the world can see and enjoy the treasures while on a visit. Such cities also have the infrastructure to support these tourists and their viewing, and London is safe in a way that countries like Egypt and Ethiopia are not.

planes. The consequently poor relationship with Greece meant that British citizens suffered.

[5] Artefacts in a case in the British Museum cannot be understood or appreciated as they could be if they were to be seen in context. For example, would it not be better to walk into Tutankhamun's tomb and see the artefacts there, or to see the Parthenon Marbles in the Parthenon? Such a context would improve the experience for tourists and academics alike.

[6] The majority of the British Museum's collection is in storage and not on display. The Tun-huang statues are not on display in the British Museum – in Malaysia they would be given pride of place. Artefacts that do not matter to the British can be significant in their country of origin and should be displayed there for the world to appreciate them.

[7] Cultural treasures are an important part of a culture. They are tangible evidence of heritage and traditions and can act as unifying symbols and objects of national pride. They often also carry a religious significance. Glasgow returned the Sioux 'ghost shirt' because the city recognised its holy importance.

Possible motions

This House would return cultural treasures to their country of origin.

This House believes that the British should return the Parthenon Marbles to Greece.

This House believes in 'Finders keepers, losers weepers'.

Related topics

Arts funding by the state, abolition of
Indigenous languages, protection of

[4] We can guarantee that these treasures will be preserved in London – we cannot guarantee that in countries such as Nigeria or Afghanistan. If they fail to preserve them, due to either economic pressures or political strife, then the artefacts would be lost for the whole world.

[5] There is a legal principle of ownership. Many artefacts were acquired in good faith. If we insist they go back, what does that mean for ownership? If you were an art collector or a museum, would you risk buying a Monet if you thought in the future it might be taken from you and sent back to France?

[6] The British Museum has been preserving these artefacts for centuries. Without this, they would have been ruined. When Elgin took the marbles, the Parthenon was in disarray. The British saved the artefacts and have spent a fortune on them over the years – why should they now be punished?

[7] These artefacts represent an important part of British cultural heritage – the empire and the exploration and excavation periods. For example, school children in the UK study Howard Carter and the discovery of Tutankhamun. Objects can become important to their host country while their country of origin values them less.

Examinations, abolition of

Many education systems in the world use some form of examinations as part of their assessment of school children. In the UK in 2013, teenagers are examined at 16 years for their GCSEs, at 17 for their AS levels and 18 for their A2 levels, and many people think this represents too much testing. Some school systems use examinations once at the end of high school. Other countries such as the USA use a system of grade point averages (GPA) or coursework which rewards a child's performance over time. Is an examination a good way of capturing a pupil's knowledge and understanding, or does ongoing assessment and intelligence tests of aptitude provide a fairer view of attainment and intelligence?

Pros

[1] Examinations test the ability to memorise large amounts of information for short periods of time. It is well known that some students are much better at 'cramming' and revising than others and so do better at exams, despite performing consistently less well during the course of a year's study. Exams do not necessarily test creativity, imagination or even a flexible understanding of the principles involved in a subject; on the whole, they test the rote-learning of facts. It is therefore possible for students to idle for a year and then learn the course in a few days, just as they might successfully 'question spot' and only revise a few topics that might come up in the exam. It is unfair that university entrance and employment prospects are based to such a large degree on examination results.

[2] The pressure attached to exams, because of their significance both for the future and the stress involved in intense revision, is extremely detrimental to the student. Not only can this pressure cause a pupil to perform less well in the exam than he or she would in a stress-free environment, it can also lead to breakdowns or

Cons

[1] Examinations evaluate students' ability to apply the knowledge they have learned to an unfamiliar question, and to communicate their knowledge to the examiner. Exams should be retained – and perhaps improved – as part of a course involving other means of evaluation such as coursework and *viva voces* (oral examinations).

[2] Pressure is a fact of working life, as are deadlines, and both need to be prepared for and tested. The number of people who cannot handle pressure is very small, and there is no indication that they would manage the increased workload that curricula without exams would involve. They might feel under continual pressure. Parents and teachers should encourage students to relax for exams.

[3] Exams are intended to make pupils use what they have learned to answer a question they have not encountered before. They should not be spoon-fed the answer by teachers and should expect the examinations to surprise them.

[4] The disparity in mental maturity is significant only at primary-school level, where separate tests can be set for late

EXAMINATIONS, ABOLITION OF   175

worse. School drop-outs, discipline problems and even suicides are increasingly common, often due to worry about poor grades and the effect that failure in one set of exams will have on the future. Schools and parents are frequently culpable in reminding the student of the consequences of failure and hence increasing the pressure.

[3] Public exams (e.g. International Baccalaureate, A-levels) are set outside the school by examination boards, not by the teachers who are familiar with the students. This means one of two things. Either the pupils will find that the exams bear little relation to the course they have been studying, which can cause disillusionment and surprisingly poor results; or the teachers must anticipate the exams so carefully that they are enslaved to the curriculum, without the ability to adjust their syllabus to the needs of their classes. Creativity and initiative from the teachers are lost.

[4] For the most part, examinations are set and taken as if students had reached the same level of understanding at the same age. This is not true; boys and girls mature mentally at different rates, as do many individuals within the same sex. Exams make no allowance for this.

[5] Examination success frequently depends on the individual examiner who marks a certain paper. Since academics often disagree over interpretation of the same facts, a student's essay or opinion may be thought correct by one examiner and incorrect by another. Two examiners could indeed mark the same set of papers and grade them completely differently. This is why marks given for exams are

developers. It is also the school's responsibility, rather than the examining boards', to deal with pupils of different abilities, putting them into sets or forward for different examinations.

[5] At some point, opinions must be given about students, and their own teachers are much more likely to be partial than independent examiners who know them only as candidate numbers. Examiners mark primarily for knowledge and clarity of argument rather than for conclusion. Extensive moderation and examiner meetings guarantee that all papers are marked to the same standard. Whatever form of assessment you use, grade inflation could be an issue. It is not an exam-specific problem.

[6] Intelligence tests are highly controversial and can only differentiate between right and wrong answers. They cannot judge whether the pupil used the right thought process in reaching the answer, and cannot measure creativity, initiative, hard work, structure and the ability to communicate. All of these qualities are evaluated by examinations. Coursework is too open to cheating by candidates (see the increasing market for buying essays on the Internet) and to teacher corruption due to the huge pressure they are under to push up grades.

frequently moderated and raised or lowered by a second examiner – clearly the process does not provide an accurate evaluation of the candidate. Such a system also gives the impression that candidates from different years can be compared, when in fact, with 'grade inflation', a B grade achieved by a student a year ago may be worth an A[*] today.

[6] Intelligence tests should be used instead as a more reliable indicator of a student's potential, both for education and for employers. They do not favour the student with a good short-term memory. They may also be used to pinpoint exact strengths and weaknesses, profiling a pupil as, for example, being 'strong at logical inference while poor at lateral thinking'. These evaluations are much more useful to employers in selecting the right candidate for the right job. Meanwhile, coursework and regular evaluation should be used in school and university to make sure that students are working consistently and understanding their entire course.

Possible motions

This House would abolish the A-level.

This House would replace exams with coursework.

This House believes that exams undermine a good education.

Related topics

Co-education

Gambling, banning of

Gambling can cover many activities from betting on sports results, to buying a ticket for the national lottery, to playing cards or slot machines in a casino. Some forms of gambling are illegal or heavily regulated in many countries. In the twenty-first century, the debate has changed somewhat because of the emergence of the huge online gambling market. A debate could focus on Internet gambling or it could look at all forms of the activity.

Pros

[1] Gambling is immoral because it gives false hope to those least able to afford the financial outlay involved. This is particularly true of state lotteries and football pools. The psychological lure of a huge

Cons

[1] Gambling brings a bit of real excitement and hope to the lives of many, especially those whose daily realities bring them very little of either. *Someone* will win the jackpot in a lottery, and *some* people

prize is immorally used to lure the poor into parting with money they cannot afford for the sake of a near-zero chance of becoming a millionaire.

[2] The more widely acceptable and available gambling becomes, the more people will become addicted to it. Gambling is as addictive as any drug and as ruinous. Those who become addicted invariably turn to crime to fund their habit. All gamblers lose in the end – that is why bookmakers, lottery companies, fruit machine companies and casinos continue to make huge profits year after year. We should regard gambling with the same moral disapproval with which we regard other activities (e.g. taking hard drugs) that lead via addiction to anti-social behaviour, financial ruin and crime. Online gambling sites have made it possible for people to play, for example, poker for hours on end without ever having to leave their homes. This has greatly exacerbated the problems with gambling addiction.

[3] Freedom of choice should be limited in the case of gambling for two reasons: first, because once you are addicted you cannot freely choose to stop, especially if you believe your only way to pay off a big gambling debt is with a huge win; second, because gambling may also harm the families of the gamblers, who may lose their homes and face destitution through no fault of their own.

[4] The social toleration and state sanctioning of gambling inculcate materialistic values in society. People are led to believe that their greatest aspiration should be to increase their wealth by whatever means possible – the advertising of state lotteries suggests that huge amounts of money

win each time there is a horse race, dog race, etc. Those who say gambling is immoral are puritanical killjoys who do not appreciate the value that simple fun and escapism can add to life.

[2] Virtually anything can be the object of an addiction – sex, coffee, jogging, television, computer games – but that does not mean that we should ban them. Gambling is, for the huge majority, an affordable luxury, an inexpensive distraction, not a problem on a par with heroin addiction. A weekly lottery ticket, a night at the casino or a day at the races should not be denied to the masses because of a minority psychological disorder, though support such as gambling helplines should be offered to the vulnerable.

[3] People should be free to spend their money however they wish even if they make 'bad' choices which lead to financial strife. It may not be a good idea to get into debt buying a hundred pairs of expensive shoes, but we do not ban expensive shoes and we should not ban casinos which are a legitimate avenue for spending your money without harming others.

[4] People do not gamble expecting huge wealth – they gamble for fun, for the buzz, and they spend money on gambling as on any other form of entertainment. In any case, it is silly to assert that material wealth does not improve one's standard of living. It is all very well for someone who is financially secure to eschew the importance of material goods, but for the many who live in poverty, the acquisition of wealth could buy them security, education, healthcare and many other opportunities that are central to human fulfilment.

would transform a person's life immeasurably for the good. This is not the case. Many who have become millionaires through luck in a lottery have found that their marriages, families or friendships have been destroyed through greed, envy and bitterness. The materialistic life idealised by the gambling ethos is shallow and unfulfilling.

[5] There comes a time when – as with the firearms or drugs industries – we must take a stand against certain ways of making money. It may be hoped that those employed in the gambling industries could be employed in alternative, more constructive industries. In some cases, casinos provide criminals with a legal front for their other activities. Casinos have been associated with drugs, prostitution, money laundering and intimidation in debt recovery.

[6] We cannot shut down every private card game, but we can do a lot to limit people's exposure and opportunities. If there were no bookmakers on your high street and no online poker site on your browser, you would be less likely to fall into gambling in the first place, and thus less likely to become addicted, even if you do have a first experience of gambling. By removing advertising for state lotteries and casinos and taking away the flashing lights of slot machines, you also reduce the allure of gambling.

[5] The gambling industries provide services that bring people excitement, hope and sometimes wealth. The demand for gambling industries is there and its supply does not harm anybody other than those voluntarily taking risks for themselves. Banning gambling will harm the economy, lead to huge job losses and, in the case of state lotteries, reduce revenue to the government and charities.

[6] Given that anybody can host a card game in their home, it is virtually impossible to enforce a ban on gambling. If you take away legal avenues for gambling like betting shops and casinos, organised criminals will step in and provide the alternatives, getting rich as a result.

Possible motions

This House would ban all gambling for people under 21.

This House condemns gambling.

This House would ban online gambling.

This House would end all state lotteries.

Related topics

Protective legislation v. individual freedom

Alcohol, prohibition of

Music lyrics, censorship of

Indigenous languages, protection of

Many countries have minority, indigenous languages spoken within their borders (for example, the Basque language in France and Spain, or Welsh in the UK). There is a debate that can be had about the principle of protecting these languages, or you could look at specific policies such as broadcasting quotas or compulsory teaching in schools. There is also a related issue of protecting the purity of a country's dominant language (for example, protecting the French language from the influence of English).

Pros

[1] Languages are a rich and valuable part of culture in their own right and should be protected as part of a country's heritage like old buildings or works of art. Language provides the key to literature, history, traditions and psychology which cannot be properly understood or appreciated if a language becomes extinct.

[2] Allowing a more powerful language to subsume an indigenous language is an aggressive type of cultural imperialism. Speakers of dominant languages such as English and Spanish have a duty to protect what came before them, not trample other cultures out of existence just because they can.

[3] Indigenous languages do need state support to survive and thrive. Bilingual street signs, television programming, music, parliamentary business and classes in schools all keep the language alive and give it an equal status, thereby providing the incentive to speak it. The Welsh language is protected by legislation and this has helped to stop its demise.

Cons

[1] A language only has the value that people place on it. If people of a certain culture feel that the language is key to them, they will keep it alive. They may, however, feel that their culture has moved on and they should not be forced to remain static. A language can always be studied by academics so you do not lose the insight into the past. Latin and Ancient Greek are widely learned in order to study ancient civilisation; it does not matter that the languages are not living.

[2] Cultural practices, including languages, evolve. A dominant language may emerge, but it will have taken on features of the indigenous languages it has encountered and been enriched by them. The resulting 'soup' can be claimed and celebrated by all.

[3] It is the responsibility of communities to protect their own languages. Often it is the older generation who will need to persuade the youth of the value in carrying the language forward. A community that is proud of its culture and language will speak it as a badge of that pride. It is patronising and inappropriate for the state to intervene.

Possible motions

This House believes that the state should protect
indigenous languages.

This House believes that there is a duty to keep
endangered languages alive.

This House would protect its language from
outside influences.

Related topics

Arts funding by the state, abolition of
Cultural treasures, returning of

Music lyrics, censorship of

The censorship of music could cover lyrics containing expletive words, racism and
misogyny, espousing or glorifying violence, using explicit sexual imagery, condoning
drug use or any other such messages which support illegal behaviour. Rap and hip-hop
in particular have been accused of spreading social problems through their lyrics, but all
kinds of music could be targeted by this policy. Should freedom of artistic expression
be absolute, or should the government intervene in the name of protecting all its citizens
from violence and discrimination?

Pros

[1] Uncensored music is dangerous. The
right of expression is undermined by the
collective right to freedom from the
violence and poor societal values which
certain music promotes.

[2] Music artists are role models, having
influence over their fans. Those listening
to violent or discriminatory lyrics can be
influenced in their own actions by the
behaviour that their hero glorifies. Music
is not like films, TV or video games when
the audience knows that it is fantasy.
Musicians are themselves and are understood to be singing about their own lives.
Therefore, the lifestyle that they espouse
seems achievable and aspirational. In
particular, music which glamorises gang
culture can push people into joining
gangs.

[3] Music lyrics can affect the subconsci-
ous because they are listened to repeatedly,
but often without deliberate concentra-

Cons

[1] Freedom of speech must be protected.
The government should not be censoring
words, which can offend but not hurt its
citizens. The government should pass laws
against violence and intimidation and
enforce these, but go no further in restricting liberty.

[2] Music does not create reality, it reflects
reality. Gang culture, violence and prejudice are what many people grow up with
and they have as much right to sing about,
or listen to, their experiences as anyone
else. Romantic love and social tolerance
are not themes that resonate for everyone,
which is why earthier music is often very
popular. Artists often are singing or rap-
ping in character – for example, Eminem
as Slim Shady – and the listeners understand this even if wider society does not.

[3] Violence plays a part in most art forms
and always has, as it is part of the human
condition that art seeks to examine. Films,

tion. They are not therefore considered and challenged, but rather seep into people's thought processes in an insidious way. A continual diet of misogyny, homophobia and casual violence affects the societal norms for those listening in a highly damaging way.

[4] It is very difficult to keep children from listening to music, available as it is on the radio, TV and Internet. Children are particularly susceptible to being affected by the negative messages that are being sent. The Columbine High School massacre (2004) has been linked to the violent rock music that the perpetrators listened to.

[5] All of society would benefit from not having to hear the vile outpourings of the worst lyrics. You cannot shield yourself from music, and so many people are offended by having to listen to the boasting about violence to women and homosexuals, and the sexual conquests and drug taking of the singer or rapper. The more extreme the lyrics, the more notoriety the artist gets, so the culture purveys increasingly outrageous content.

TV and the visual arts all contain examples of gratuitous violence. Music along with literature may actually have less of an effect on the consumer as they do not contain the graphic images that make the violence so real and immediate. It is important to protect artistic expression from government control as art often seeks to challenge authority.

[4] Parents should be monitoring the music their children listen to along with monitoring their Internet use and viewing habits. Adults cannot have their liberty restricted because an activity is unsuitable for children.

[5] The fact that the privileged, educated, white chattering classes find street culture offensive does not give them the right to ban it. Shakespeare's plays can be gruesome, classic literature can be anti-Semitic and opera can be sexist, yet there are no calls for these to be banned. Society should be able to accommodate all art.

Possible motions
This House would censor music lyrics.
This House would censor rap and hip-hop.

Related topics
Censorship by the state
Pornography

Nursery education, free provision of by the state

Some countries, including Britain, provide free nursery or kindergarten education for one or two years before the start of school. But is this a good use of state funding? Should children be left to play at this age, or can these years be the foundation of success in education?

Pros

[1] Developmental psychology has demonstrated how crucial the early education of children is for their later progress. In other words, science has shown that nursery education should be a priority for any government. Many more doors are closed in the long term by a lack of education and stimulation at an early age than by the lack of free degree-level education. Specially trained nursery school teachers are needed to help to fully realise the development potential of all pre-school children, since most parents are not well equipped or trained to do this entirely by themselves. If a child has slipped behind in language development by the time they reach school, studies have shown that they are likely to continue to struggle with literacy throughout their education. This also means they will need costly interventions later on.

[2] If free nursery education is not provided by the state, then only the rich will continue to provide it for their children. This is particularly pernicious, as it means that social and economic inequalities are being engrained in the next generation from the first few years of their lives. Those whose parents could not afford nursery education will be at an intellectual and educational disadvantage from the outset. Free nursery education is a crucial way for a government to fight against the perpetuation of elitism and inequality. We should not be totally fatalistic about inequality – free nursery education will do *something* to redress the balance, even though it will not, of course, wipe out economic differences.

[3] Nursery schools provide crucial social training for young children as well as

Cons

[1] Up to the age of four or five, it is right and proper that children be educated in the home. Parents are biologically adapted to be the best carers for and educators of their children. Development during this period is important, but it can best be fostered by parental attention and stimulation. Children need to play and discover, but do not need any formal education at this age. Given that parents can fulfil this role, nursery education need not be seen as an essential part of a financially stretched public sector education system. Public education spending can properly be concentrated on the school years when specialist teachers are required, rather than being stretched and depleted to cover, in addition, nursery education, university education and museums.

[2] It is, sadly, already the case that the children of the rich will receive a better pre-school education, with or without nursery schools. It is the rich who can afford books, educational toys and advanced technology for their children, and who are often better educated themselves. With or without free nursery school education, socio-economic inequalities will be active in children's lives from the start.

[3] Young children can get the social development they need by going to playgroups, parent and toddler groups, classes (such as music or gymnastics) and by playing with siblings and friends. If they are closely supervised by a parent during their early social interactions then they are more likely to have lessons in proper behaviour, such as sharing and turn-taking. With a ratio of one adult to eight or 10 children in a nursery school, bad habits can be formed unnoticed.

preparation for academic work and school. Without free nursery education, more and more children will grow up socially underdeveloped – a real worry in our modern society where the idea of community has almost completely broken down. Socially undeveloped children can grow into anti-social and even criminal adolescents.

[4] Nursery schools also fulfil a pastoral, social-work role. Teachers can be on the lookout for disturbed or abused children. It will be harder for parents to hide the neglect or abuse of their child if nursery school is compulsory and the child is in regular contact with teachers from an early age. Hence, as well as enhancing equality of educational opportunity, socio-economic equality and social adaptation, free nursery education is a weapon against child abuse.

[5] A culture of nursery education means that parents (usually women) will take shorter career breaks when they have children. This is good for the economy, and in particular is good for women and gender equality, as studies show that the longer women are off work, the more their careers suffer.

[4] It is not clear that providing free nursery education for all is the most efficient way to deal with child abuse. The money would be better spent if it were targeted directly at child abuse, in particular via charities and social workers. This would be cheaper and more effective than having free nursery education for all. In addition, there have been cases where children have been abused in nurseries by the workers there.

[5] Most nursery hours are very short, perhaps 9 am to 2 pm, so this will not enable women to return to work. Either they will need wraparound childcare which means that their children will never see them, or they will be at home on their own during the day when they could have been looking after their children and saving the government money.

Possible motions

This House believes that nursery education is a right, not a privilege.

This House believes that the child is father of the man.

Related topics

Welfare state

University education, free for all

Performance-enhancing drugs in sport

There is a variety of substances and procedures which enhance physical performance that are banned in sports; for example, steroids, hormones and blood doping. Some sports such as cycling and athletics have seen many high-profile sports stars caught breaking the rules. Despite increased screening, some people believe that drug taking is still rife. The Proposition team must decide whether to allow everything in their definition, which will open them up to an attack of serious health risks; or whether to regulate the substances, which may undermine the point about a level playing field.

Pros

[1] Performance-enhancing drugs are a reality in sport that we cannot combat. Given that, it is fairer to allow everyone access to the drugs, thereby creating a level playing field. At present, the cheats have an advantage, and the honest are penalised.

[2] The current situation, with the exposure of drugs cheats, undermines sports. When Ben Johnson had to be stripped of his 100m sprint Olympic gold medal in 1988, or Lance Armstrong was stripped of seven Tour de France titles in 2012, it made a mockery of the sport and the fans who had been duped. People see their role models fall and children are sent the message that successful people cheat to win.

[3] The use of performance-enhancing drugs will make sport more exciting; it will literally become faster, higher, stronger. Imagine how fast Usain Bolt could run on steroids! It would be amazing to use drugs technology to push the limits of human performance in this way. It would still ultimately remain a competition between individuals and their training programmes. This would become one more enhancement like the right shoes, wetsuit, cycle, diet or altitude training. The athlete and his/her talent, drive and hard work would remain the most important factor (in fact, this would be truer because of the level playing field created by the policy).

[4] Athletes should be given the freedom of choice to take drugs, having been informed about the risks. Many athletes decide that the risk is worth it. There are risks associated with many sports already (paralysis in rugby, mental damage in box-

Cons

[1] Until all amounts of every drug are legalised, some people will always break the rules in order to gain an edge over their competitors. This measure would also disadvantage those who do not wish to compromise their health by taking steroids and other harmful drugs or who wish to achieve success naturally. You are not therefore creating a level playing field. The best way to create that is to continue improving detection technology, pursue thorough investigations and provide strong deterrents through lifetime bans for those who are caught.

[2] The exposure of drugs cheats shows that the status quo is working. People do not get away with cheating, and when they are caught they face public disgrace. The messages that are sent through this are that drug use is not acceptable and also that there are consequences to breaking the rules. Both of these are positive values to be communicating through sport.

[3] Sport would be damaged by this change. People want to watch human achievement, not a battle between pharmaceutical companies. It would also give an advantage to developed countries that have the funds for research and development of the substances. At the moment, there is no financial barrier to access sports such as running, in the way there is for sailing or horse riding. This will damage that. Because it will also discriminate against athletes who do not wish to take the health risks associated with drug taking, they may find they lose their places on teams, and sport could be denied some of its future talent.

[4] Taking performance-enhancing drugs can be extremely detrimental to an ath-

ing, possible death in motor sports), and we allow individuals to assess these risks. If the drugs were being taken in an open and regulated manner, then there would actually be fewer health risks (albeit to more people).

Possible motions
This House would legalise performance-enhancing drugs in sport.
This House believes that it is time to lift the doping ban in sports.

Related topics
Protective legislation v. individual freedom
Sport, regretting the commercialisation of
Boxing, banning of
Drugs, legalisation of

lete's health. The stakes are so high for athletes to win that there would be enormous pressure on them to take the drugs, risking their health and even their lives. In the 1980s, deaths of young cyclists were linked to taking the steroid EPO (Erythropoietin). Freedom of choice is compromised because of that pressure. Drug use would also trickle down from professional sport to amateur and junior leagues and young people would be harmed.

Press, state regulation of the

Renewed interest in state regulation of the press was spurred by the 2012 Leveson Inquiry in the UK, which examined the various models by which the media can be regulated. In essence, the two basic models used in most countries are 'self-regulation', in which the media establishes its own body to monitor and punish non-compliance with a Code of Ethics; whereas in a 'statutory regulation' model, an independent press regulator is created by the government, but run at arm's length. One important difference between the two systems is that with self-regulation, newspapers can opt out, so some may simply be unregulated. Statutory regulators often have greater powers, such as levelling fines, whereas self-regulators may be limited to powers of condemnation.

Pros

[1] The threat to freedom from state involvement in the media is not an automatic one; rather, it arises from the loss of independence from the government that might ensue, leading to the state being able to control what is said about it. However, this is not at all a necessary consequence of state regulation; rather, it can be prevented by a sufficient separation

Cons

[1] While it is attractive to believe that a government agency might be totally insulated from politics, this is simply not possible. Inevitably, things like funding arrangements and appointments will get some input from the government of the day, and this will allow it to influence the regulator, however indirectly. Moreover, there is no guarantee that, even if the

between the regulators and the government, such as making sure that the membership of the regulator is balanced, and none of the members can be fired by the government.

[2] The right to opt out of regulation is ultimately destructive of any system of regulation. First, it allows some people simply to get away with unacceptable stories; Britain's *Daily Express* opted out of the Press Complaints Commission, in large part because it was often cautioned against its invasions of privacy of public figures. Second, once one paper can opt out, others will follow, as being outside the regulatory system is profitable; it allows newspapers to capture readers by running stories that the self-regulated press could not.

[3] Laws against libel and harassment are not sufficient to prevent the serious threats posed by the media to a free society. First, full legal proceedings can be very expensive; a regulator can offer a fast, efficient system of arbitration to allow individuals to vindicate their legal rights against the press without recourse to the courts. Second, often there are gaps in the law where individuals still deserve protection; for instance, privacy may often be unacceptably breached without violating criminal laws on harassment.

[4] A major problem with self-regulation is that the Code of Ethics that a self-regulator applies is also set by the press; this means that it is often weak, and reflects a view of the role of the media in society that places press freedom ahead of privacy and accuracy. It should be up to democratic institutions to decide how the media should be constrained, which is only done when the state lays down the rules for its operation.

regulator is fairly appointed, it will not be politicised in a way that reflects certain powerful interests.

[2] The right to opt out of regulation is ultimately one that newspapers must possess. While it might seem like they can never have good reasons to do so, in fact, they may wish to pursue a course of the higher-risk, more investigative journalism that a regulator may try to prevent, even though it is ultimately in the public interest. For instance, Britain's *Private Eye* chose to opt out of the Press Complaints Commission because it wanted to pursue the more revelatory stories that the PCC was often dubious about.

[3] Laws against libel and criminal invasions of privacy are sufficient to provide individuals with the protection that they require from the press. If anything false and harmful is said about them, then they can sue for damages, and the same is true if their privacy is breached. In other words, if the media do anything illegal, they will be punished; but otherwise, they must be given a substantial area of freedom in which to operate.

[4] A state-imposed Code of Ethics will not be sufficiently attuned to the subtle difficulties that editors face when working under pressure, and so will not in fact be properly designed; it is better to let editors set their own code, as they are experts and understand the tasks that a newspaper is engaged in. Moreover, whereas a state-imposed code has to be written into statute and so cannot easily be changed, a self-regulated code can be more flexible, and so can be added to or adapted as circumstances change.

Possible motions
This House supports state regulation of the media.
This House would have a 'Press Law'.

Related topics
BBC, privatisation of
Privacy of public figures
Censorship by the state

Privacy of public figures

The 'tabloid' press has a particular reputation for relishing the details of the private lives of public figures. The death in Paris in a car crash of Diana, Princess of Wales in 1997 refuelled calls for restrictions on the paparazzi (press photographers) from whom she and Dodi Al Fayed had been fleeing. In 2012, *The News of the World* was shut down after it emerged that its journalists had been hacking the phones of some politicians and celebrities. The private lives (and particularly the sex lives) of politicians, actors, singers and sports personalities are constantly subjected to media scrutiny. In France, the media respect privacy much more. Is it fair that every aspect of the lives of public figures and celebrities should become public property, or should something be done to protect these figures' privacy? The arguments vary slightly if the debate is narrowed to just politicians or just celebrities. The debate may be argued in principle, or the definition may specify a privacy law, self-regulation or an independent regulatory body.

Pros

[1] Public figures and their families deserve privacy and protection from media intrusion. What they do in their private lives, unless it has implications for national security, for example, should not be investigated and reported by the media. The distress caused to politicians and their families by revelations about sexual indis-cretions is unjustifiable.

[2] What a politician does in private has no bearing on his or her ability to do the job. Throughout history there are examples of effective leaders who have had affairs. They may well have been forced to resign with today's media intrusion.

[3] Politicians are public servants, entrusted with running the economy and the public services in an efficient and responsible way. They should not be seen as moral

Cons

[1] Public exposure is one of the prices of fame and power. Politicians and celebrities realise this from the start, and if they do not like it, they should not enter the public sphere. These figures rely on the media for their fame and wealth – they cannot then complain if their lives become, to a large extent, public property. If a person goes into politics, has sexual affairs, and is caught, it is s/he who is to be blamed for the distress caused to his/her family, not the media.

[2] It is in the public interest to know whether a politician is unfaithful to his or her spouse. If someone cannot be trusted to keep a promise in their personal life, then it is to be doubted if they can be trusted more generally with important matters of state. The public have a right to

paragons. Religions are there to provide moral leadership. We should follow the example of France where there are strict privacy laws and the people accept that their politicians are not saints. The hounding of politicians by the press could be putting off many talented individuals from running for office. If you have to be 'whiter than white' and willing to put up with constant intrusion into your life, you have narrowed the pool of possible representatives.

[4] Giving public figures a right to privacy is not a form of censorship. Investigative journalism into immoral and criminal activities with a demonstrable element of public interest (rather than seedy gossip) will still be allowed.

[5] We should condemn the media for printing intrusive photographs of celebrities and 'kiss and tell' stories from their alleged lovers. Everybody should be allowed to be off duty sometimes. Stories are often unchecked, untrue or exaggerated. They may harm third parties (such as children) more than the celebrities themselves, and they have not chosen the spotlight. The bodies that regulate the media should take the lead in banning the printing of such material, and if that does not work, privacy laws will have to be introduced.

[6] Libel and slander laws are not good enough. People will assume that there is no smoke without fire, and so a politician or celebrity's name can be permanently smeared even if they subsequently win a libel suit or an apology is printed. Distress has already been caused to politicians and their families by revelations and the damage to their reputation has already been done.

take into account character when they elect their leaders.

[3] In an increasingly secular world, we need politicians to be the moral leaders that they claim to be. Hence it is right that the media scrutinise their personal life to reveal the all-too-frequent cases of hypocrisy (such as secretly gay politicians speaking out against the gay community, or a politician cheating on his wife and preaching 'family values'). The media perform an invaluable task as moral and political watchdogs and investigators. Public figures may well feel invulnerable to charges such as sexual harassment, and in these cases, it is the victims who need the protection of the press, not the powerful.

[4] Giving public figures a 'right to privacy' is in effect condoning media censorship and gagging the press. There is no clear line between what is in the public interest and what is not, so valuable investigative journalism will suffer. For example, when investigating the bogus expenses claims of British politicians, various personal details emerged, including secret relationships and the use of pornography.

[5] Interest in the private lives of public figures is an inevitable part of the modern media world. And as long as we keep on buying, in our millions, the newspapers and magazines that dish out the salacious stories and pictures, it is hypocritical to feign outrage at each new media intrusion. These stories sell because of our fascination with fame and celebrity.

[6] Libel and slander laws already exist to protect public figures from unfair press coverage. There is no need to introduce any more legislation.

[7] We are catching up with regulating new technologies. Twitter has taken down tweets which have gone against privacy injunctions and bloggers have been prosecuted. It is not perfect, but we cannot give up because of this. Any individual tweeter still has a small readership compared to *The Sun* in the UK or the *National Enquirer* in the USA, so it is still worth regulating the media even if an occasional blogger slips through the net.

[8] The hunger for salacious details about celebrities' lives has led to unacceptable behaviour from journalists. Many celebrities, including those who do not themselves court the media, have journalists camped outside their homes 24 hours a day and are intimidated by paparazzi who pursue them ruthlessly when they step outside. The incentives have also become high enough to encourage law-breaking, and the phone hacking scandal in the UK in 2012 revealed the appalling depths to which tabloids had sunk.

[7] The Internet and the profusion of individual bloggers and tweeters have meant that giving public figures protection in the media is meaningless. In 2012, the UK press may not have published topless pictures of the Duchess of Cambridge, but the pictures were online for everyone to see. When Manchester United footballer Ryan Giggs took out an injunction to stop details of his affair being reported, it did not stop the Internet from reporting it and so created a ludicrous two-tier system.

[8] It is possible to regulate the behaviour of journalists without censoring the content of articles. Believing in the freedom of the press does not mean supporting any means of gathering information. Phone hacking, in particular, is always wrong and members of the paper involved are facing criminal charges.

Possible motions

This House believes that public figures have a right to private lives.

This House condemns the paparazzi.

This House believes in the right to privacy.

Related topics

Censorship by the state

Politicians' outside interests, banning of

BBC, privatisation of

Homosexuals, outing of

Press, state regulation of the

Private schools

Private schools are those that receive no funding from the state and are instead usually financed through parental fees. They are sometimes called 'independent schools' and, confusingly, in the UK they are often referred to as 'public schools', whereas most of the world would use that term to describe state schools. Opponents of private schools usually point to the inequality that they believe the schools perpetuate in society, whereas supporters argue that parents should be able to spend their money how they wish.

Pros

[1] Freedom of choice is a fundamental principle of our democratic, capitalist society. If parents can afford to send their child to a private school, and wish to do so, why should any restrictions be put on that choice? We are, after all, allowed to buy the best car or the best stereo equipment if we have the money.

[2] A good education costs money. It is the government's responsibility to provide proper funding for state sector schools, but there is no doubt that private schools, with better funding raised from tuition fees, consistently achieve better academic results for their pupils – far better than any school could do if private schools were abolished. At present, parents who opt for private education pay twice – once through their taxes and once through their fees. If you abolished private schools, you would flood the state system with extra pupils without giving it any extra money, so the standards would fall.

[3] Many private schools offer facilities that are considered extremely worthwhile and are not found in most state schools. Many are still predominantly boarding schools, providing a secure community feeling which builds confidence in their students. Extra-curricular activities are strongly encouraged to complete a well-rounded and enjoyable education, instructing pupils in many skills useful for adult life. Some private schools exist in old manor houses in the countryside, where pupils have wider opportunities for sports. A large proportion of the schools are single-sex with all of the benefits that such a system brings.

[4] Following a national or a local school board curriculum results in two damaging

Cons

[1] In a moral society, freedom of choice is right because it is available to everyone. If a choice is available only to the few who can afford it, then it upholds the class-ridden, elitist society we are struggling to overthrow. Education is necessary for everyone and should be freely available – it is far more important than a car or a stereo and any comparison between them is fatuous.

[2] The wealth of private schools, no matter how good an education they provide, causes more problems than it solves. As long as these institutions exist, they will attract the best teachers, eager for high salaries, and the best resources. This means that schools in the state sector, which cater to the vast majority of students, receive disproportionately poor resources. Only when private schools are abolished will it be possible for staff and facilities to be distributed equitably. Standards will not fall because if the children of the elite are in these schools, then those parents will demand the highest standards.

[3] Most of these facilities are not as welcome in a modern world. Boarding schools offer sheltered existences where outdated traditions and prejudice flourish, leaving their alumni entirely inadequately prepared for adulthood. Co-educational schools provide a better education for all sorts of reasons. Extra-curricular activities should be encouraged in the state sector; where they do not exist, it is through lack of resources which are taken by the private schools.

[4] The whole point of standardised public examinations is that we can ensure that all students are given equal opportunity of

side-effects for the student. First, teachers become enslaved to the curriculum and lose their freedom for imaginative, unorthodox teaching techniques suited to their particular pupils. Second, the standards required to pass public examinations continue to fall and become meaningless for the most academic students. Teachers at private schools have far more leeway in how and what to teach. For example, they can choose to offer the International Baccalaureate instead of the A-level if they believe it would challenge their brightest students more effectively.

[5] Private schools have more freedom to specialise within an open market. The government may only be obsessed with inspecting state schools on their academic performance, but parents may choose to support a private school because of its strong artistic tradition, its child-led pastoral approach, its language of instruction or its extra support for children with dyslexia.

education; private schools opting out of this simply worsens the 'old school network' of academic elitism that already exists. Pupils should be judged by how successfully they passed the exams, not by which exams they were privileged to take. In terms of curriculum, movements within the state sector such as charter schools in the USA or free schools in the UK have given individual schools more freedom to set their own curriculum, and there is no reason why this should not be more widespread within the state sector.

[5] If children have special needs or special talents, then the state sector can accommodate these either in programmes within mainstream schools or in special schools. In general, however, the principle of choice is dangerous within the education market as the more privileged will always find a way to play the system to choose the 'best' schools for their offspring. Allocation by the state of all children to a local school, preferably through a lottery, is the only way to address inequality in education.

Possible motions
This House would pay for its education.
This House believes that private schools are not in the public interest.

Related topics
Capitalism v. socialism
Marxism
Privatisation
Welfare state

Religious teaching in schools

This entry looks at the teaching of religious studies (RS) as a subject rather than the existence of religious schools. Some countries, such as France, believe that religion has no place within state education. Other countries, such as the UK, offer RS, but allow parents to remove their children from the classes. A definition would need to clarify whether the debate was about instruction in one particular religion, or whether it was the study of all religions as a subject, or both.

Pros

[1] Religion has been so important to history – and is so important to a vast number of people alive today – that it clearly merits its place as an academic subject alongside History and Literature. In fact, the increasing secularisation and scientific progress of the world make it doubly important that the spiritual side of humanity is not ignored.

[2] Religious teaching can cover many faiths and denominations, outside specifically denominational schools (e.g. Roman Catholic), so it need not be discriminatory against minorities. In the UK, much of the teaching is analysis of the history and beliefs of different religions rather than instruction in any one set of doctrines.

[3] Religious teaching is the only framework for students to discuss morals and morality. That they should form a code of morals is clearly a useful benefit to responsible adulthood. In many Western democracies, the entire legal system is founded on the basis of Christian morality, so whether or not the theology is accepted, the morality of that religion is still considered 'right' in those countries. Generally, all faiths aim to improve society and to alleviate injustice.

[4] In increasingly multicultural, multifaith societies it is important to understand each other's religions in order to foster tolerance and respect. Traditions and practices can be mischaracterised by bigots, and RS can help to protect against this.

Cons

[1] A large number of people also happen to regard religious belief as unimportant or wrong. Religious history, where relevant, can be taught as part of a History syllabus, but religious and spiritual discussion should be entirely optional, the choice of the student or the student's family, and conducted outside school. Too many people regard religion as irrelevant to have it imposed on everyone.

[2] Even if religious teaching covers all faiths, it discriminates against the non-religious. Usually, however, it is focused largely on a small number of faiths or even the one relevant to the majority of its students; this is clearly unfair on the minority who may have another faith.

[3] Just because the law is based on religious morals does not mean that it needs to be studied in that context. Atheists can have a moral code. Morals should be discussed in school, as should the law, but in a modern setting dealing with citizenship.

[4] Tolerance is not promoted through knowing the names of religious festivals and clothing. Taking religion out of schools and asking all pupils to be treated equally regardless of their faith is a better way to encourage respect in a multicultural society. It concentrates on the similarities between all students rather than highlighting their differences.

[5] The danger is not that a child will not find their destined religion (religions are

[5] Religious Studies can expose young students to ideas that they have not, and would not otherwise, have come across. A teenager may be encouraged, for example, to find out more about Buddhism and may ultimately decide to follow this religion. Education should be about opening up the world of human existence to enquiring minds, not deeming some ideas as inappropriate to the classroom. If a child comes from a strongly atheist home, school may be their only chance to understand people of faith.

good recruiters of the eager and impressionable), but rather that they will be brainwashed into religious belief by a dynamic, religious teacher. Children should be free of indoctrination at school and RS provides too easy an avenue for bias to come through.

Possible motions
This House believes that religion has no place in our schools.
This House would keep schools secular.

Related topics
Churches in politics
Disestablishment of the Church of England
God, existence of

School sport, compulsory

Should sport form a part of compulsory education, should it be an optional extra on offer to pupils, or is it a complete waste of time and resources to have it on offer in schools? The debate is set against a backdrop of both rising obesity in the West and an increasingly stretched school timetable.

Pros

[1] A school education should involve much more than the simple acquisition of facts. All sorts of skills needed in adult life should be developed. Sport provides many of these: the value of keeping fit, teamwork and discipline in particular.

[2] Many children are unwilling to play sports simply because they have not been encouraged towards physical pursuits in the past: toddlers who are left to play or read in their bedrooms by their parents instead of being sent to play outside with friends. These children, when older, may choose to avoid sports if given the chance.

Cons

[1] There are far too many 'life skills' for all of them to be satisfactorily taught in school. An alternative to sport in many schools is involvement in charity work, where students visit local residents with special needs – surely these aspects of good citizenship should also be taught? When something is enforced, it tends to engender resentment which undoes the benefits it may bring when voluntarily chosen. Sport should therefore be optional, although encouraged.

[2] Students who start school sports as inexperienced, reluctant participants and

In fact, if forced to take part, they may well discover a surprising enthusiasm and talent for certain sports. Many notable sportsmen and sportswomen started their careers this way.

[3] Exercise is necessary to keep the body and mind healthy. While children are naturally more fit and energetic than adults, they need exercise to let off steam and to sleep properly; it is also advisable that they are prepared for a habit of regular exercise when reaching adulthood. It has been shown that academic work is generally better when coupled with exercise.

[4] Most aspects of school life are compulsory and the enforced teaching of anything is not usually regarded as controversial. Students accept sport as part of the curriculum just as they accept other mandatory subjects. Many students have no enthusiasm or talent for other subjects such as mathematics, but that does not stop us mandating them in the interest of the student.

[5] Most sports also entail social programmes and those who have chosen not to play sports miss out on these; they frequently feel excluded from events and social circles they would actually like to take part in.

[6] School sport need not be expensive. It could involve taking a football to the local park or running races through local fields. Many schools invest more in sport because they see the benefits for motivating their pupils and producing better rounded students with higher levels of concentration and discipline.

[7] Obesity levels are on the increase in the Western world and child obesity is a

then go on to shine are very few in number. Most of the resources – especially the attention of games teachers – are devoted to children who are already very sporty. Beginners are therefore ignored and lose enthusiasm. Or worse, they are bullied for their sporting ineptitude and put off sport for life.

[3] The fitness vogue of recent years has meant that adults are certainly aware of the value of exercise whether they choose to do it or not. They are more likely to continue sports they enjoy and have chosen to play. Many adults choose to get the benefits of exercise through using a gym rather than playing sport. If children are over-energetic, they will run around anyway.

[4] Most aspects of school are compulsory only for younger ages; teenagers develop discriminatory abilities that give them clear likes and dislikes. Curricula recognise this and allow students to choose between optional subjects. Those that are enforced are frequently resented.

[5] The competition of sport engenders an inevitable elitism among the best participants; poor sports players who take part are ridiculed far more than those who do not play them in the first place.

[6] Sport is one of the most expensive parts of a school curriculum. Many schools have facilities such as sports halls, playing fields or swimming pools. Almost all sports require special equipment and a high ratio of well-qualified staff to ensure safety. This money could be better spent, within an overstretched budget, on textbooks, computers, more staff and other investments that will advance pupils' academic achievement.

particular problem. Obesity can cause heart disease, strokes, diabetes and other serious health conditions. It is imperative that we do all we can to encourage healthy lifestyles and schools are the best way of forming positive habits in the young.

[7] Neither child nor adult obesity can be tackled through a couple of hours of school PE lessons. The time would be better spent on health awareness classes coupled with cookery lessons so that people have the knowledge about what they should eat and the skills to prepare it.

Possible motions
This House would make school sport voluntary.
This House believes that all students should take part in compulsory PE.

Related topics
Child curfews
Obese children, compulsory attendance at weight-loss camps
School uniform

School uniform

The norms for school dress code vary around the world from a strict uniform through dress codes to no, or very few, restrictions on clothing. This is usually a debate that school pupils themselves have very strong opinions on. A definition may want to address the age range it is targeting, and the anti-uniform side could clarify how free it wants dress to be.

Pros

[1] A school should encourage tidiness and discipline in its pupils. A uniform aids this, whereas freedom of dress tends to make pupils too eager to express their individuality, becoming obsessed with clothes and appearance. Teenagers may often choose clothes that are unsuitable such as skirts which are too short or trousers which are too tight. There is also a widely accepted connection between smart dress and good behaviour as the clothes help to create a work ethos.

Cons

[1] Many schools do not have uniforms, while still demanding certain standards of dress, such as banning jeans, or requiring long skirts while allowing a choice of colour. There is no reason why pupils not wearing uniform cannot still be smart. When pupils reach a certain age, they are old enough to behave responsibly while still making their own decisions, and this is what schools should be encouraging rather than a blind following of the rules. Why should they not be able to choose how to dress?

[2] School uniforms remove the opportunity for fashion-related bullying and the pressure to spend money on labels to impress friends and fit in with the crowd. A uniform is a leveller and emphasises the similarities between students rather than pointing out the differences.

[3] School teachers must manage a large number of pupils in a variety of situations. Uniforms inevitably make that task much easier when the pupils are out in public, on school trips. It is an administrative nightmare trying to monitor a group of pupils who are dressed casually. Uniforms also allow the public to recognise pupils and report bad (or good) behaviour back to the school.

[4] Uniforms prepare students for the smartness demanded in office life. Many people have no choice in what they wear to work, either wearing a uniform or the semi-uniform of jacket and tie. Children should not expect total freedom in their working lives.

[5] Uniforms reduce the cost for parents on their children's clothing, as they do not have to replace wardrobes every few months to follow the latest fashion trends.

[2] Expressing their individuality is important to many young people. Clothing can be a powerful way of establishing your identity. A uniform seeks to turn pupils into drones rather than allowing them to grow and experiment.

[3] Uniforms also help the pupils to stand out to other people as well; fights are frequently picked between pupils from different schools who recognise each other's uniforms. Sometimes anonymity is preferable!

[4] A relatively small percentage of jobs require uniforms to be worn. Why should pupils planning to be doctors not wear white coats, or future computer programmers not wear t-shirts and jeans?

[5] Uniforms are very expensive and have no value or chance of use outside school. Parents end up buying double as children still need clothes for the evenings and weekends.

Possible motions

This House believes school uniforms are a good idea.

This House would rather wear 'mufti'.

Related Topics

School sport, compulsory

Child curfews

Sex education

It is generally agreed that we are living in an increasingly sexualised society and that children are exposed to the world of sex earlier than ever before. Many countries are seeing increased teenage pregnancy, abortion and STD rates. How should schools respond to this? By teaching more sex education and doing it earlier or by preaching abstinence?

Pros

[1] The increase in sexually transmitted diseases (STDs) is due to ignorance about safe sex. In this age, when chlamydia, herpes, gonorrhoea and HIV are being passed on through sex, and only individual responsibility with condoms can prevent it, a full discussion is essential. Sex education must form a significant part of the curriculum.

[2] Sex education can help to prevent teenage pregnancies. Girls can be given information about how to access, and properly use, a range of contraception and about the 'morning after pill'. Both sexes can be educated about condoms. Myths such as 'you can't get pregnant if it's your first time' or 'you can't get pregnant if you have a bath afterwards' can be exploded. Teenage pregnancy is a major problem in many countries and schools must play their part in tackling it.

[3] There is also a need to understand sex and its role in society, whether in a stable relationship or outside it, to ensure it is treated responsibly and with respect. Too much distress is caused by sexual encounters where the two partners have different expectations. The media glamorise meaningless sex and yet are appalled by the rise in casual sex and date rape which they play a part in causing. Again, classroom discussion can engender a more responsible attitude among students.

[4] If you leave it to families to discuss sex, you will get widely different results. Some parents may leave it too late and others may not themselves be aware of the changes in contraception and STDs since they were young. Children will end up with a collection of half-facts and mis-

Cons

[1] Yes, awareness of the need for safe sex is important, but teachers are not the right people to raise it. Many countries whose STD and teenage pregnancy rates are soaring do have sex education programmes, so clearly this is not working if so many pupils are still careless. Safe sex (i.e. the use of condoms) is seen as unfashionable, and its espousal by teachers will only confirm that view. It is better to promote it through style magazines, television programmes and other sources that will emphasise how acceptable it is.

[2] The age of consent varies from country to country (in the UK, it is 16) and teaching sex education before that age is essentially asking schools to collude with young people in breaking the law. Sex education actually adds to the sexualisation of childhood. If you show 12 year olds how to put a condom on a test tube, you are sending the message that you are expecting them to be sexually active. This will only lead to more unwanted pregnancies and STDs. It is better to teach abstinence or nothing at all.

[3] School is not an arena in which teenagers take such things seriously. Any discussion of sex in a classroom is likely to lead to ridicule, especially in co-educational classes. Respect for sex can only be encouraged on a one-to-one basis, probably in the family by older siblings or parents. To try to teach it in school can only be detrimental.

[4] Schools are there to help children pass exams and develop their talents. Asking school staff to step into the personal lives of their students is not fair on the teachers who may not want to discuss sex with their pupils, and is particularly not fair on parents

understanding gathered from friends and magazines, and will not be equipped to deal responsibly with the choices they will face. Schools can provide a uniform knowledge and it is part of their role to develop young people socially and emotionally as well as academically.

who will want to decide how and when their children find out about sex. The 'facts of life' chat is for families, not the state.

Possible motions

This House would keep the bedroom out of the classroom.

This House would start sex education in primary schools.

This House believes that parents should not be allowed to remove their children from sex education.

Related topics

Censorship by the state

Population control

Co-education

Contraception for under-age girls

Size zero models, banning of

The modern fashion industry typically uses thin models; this debate focuses on the extreme of that trend, with (almost exclusively female) models becoming dangerously underweight. Reasons vary; many models simply profess a desire to improve their employment prospects, or the need to do so for a particular show, but the phenomenon is also linked very closely with eating disorders such as anorexia and bulimia. Public outcry reached its height when two Brazilian model sisters, Luisel and Eliana Ramos, died within six months of each other, both for reasons believed to be related to malnutrition. In 2007, the Madrid and Milan Fashion Weeks both banned size zero models, and Spain and Israel both have legislation preventing the use of underweight models. However, they are still legal, and widely deployed, in the USA, the UK and France.

Pros

[1] Most obviously, being size zero is highly dangerous for these models' health. While a ban would not guarantee that they would pursue a healthier lifestyle, it gives them a strong economic incentive to do so, because they have to gain weight to be employable. At the extreme end, this will prevent deaths, but it will also ensure

Cons

[1] There is no reliable measure for deciding what really constitutes a 'size zero'. Many people are simply naturally very thin, and this policy discriminates against them by preventing them earning a living in their chosen career. Moreover, for those people, this policy is simply unnecessary. 'Size zero' is not always absurdly thin; for

that far more young women avoid doing long-term damage to their bodies by being dangerously underweight for much of their teens and twenties.

[2] Size zero models can serve as very dangerous role models for young girls. Their fame and wealth often make their lifestyles seem highly desirable, and so girls seek to emulate them in every way; this often includes crash dieting, taking pills to speed up their metabolisms and competitive undereating. Banning such models is merely protecting some of the most vulnerable people in our society from highly dangerous influences.

[3] The decision to be size zero is not a free or rational one, but is typically driven by severe psychological illnesses. Anorexia, bulimia and other eating disorders are recognised medical conditions which impair these models' ability to think freely about their weight, quite literally distorting their self-perception so that they think themselves hideously fat even when they are in fact very thin. The state often steps in where people's decisions are ultimately harmful and they cannot rationally choose, and this is a paradigm case.

[4] Banning size zero models sends a powerful message that women should not be objectified. Much of the size zero trend rests on the idea that it is acceptable for anything to be demanded of women's bodies, even when extreme or unhealthy, as long as it makes them more attractive. This places a clear limit on that trend, and in doing so refocuses the fashion industry on normal, healthy body shapes, which do not require women to transform themselves because of a dominant perception of how they 'should' look.

many, it actually represents a perfectly healthy body shape.

[2] This policy is an unreasonable restriction on liberty. The state does not, in general, prevent people from doing harm to their own bodies, even where it might be fatal; cigarettes, alcohol and bungee-jumping are all examples of this. These women are perfectly capable of making rational decisions; many of them are not anorexic, and it is offensive to suppose that they are incapable of choosing to look a certain way of their own free will.

[3] Runway models simply do not have that much of an impact on the real problems of unhealthy body images within society. So it would be inconsistent to outlaw them, while keeping actors and musicians with unhealthy body images legal. Few people watch runway shows or read high-fashion magazines; indeed, adverts for the clothes that most ordinary women wear and buy are modelled by those with a much healthier body image. It is absurd to suggest that a size zero model does more damage to society than magazines running stories on which celebrities are 'looking fat this month'.

[4] This policy is ultimately counterproductive. Anorexic and bulimic women need help and support, not exclusion. The message of disapproval sent by the criminalisation of their activities does not encourage them to approach family, friends and medical professionals for support, but rather demonises them and blames them for their conduct. Particularly with an illness so strongly bound up with low self-esteem, this is obviously ineffective as a solution.

Possible motions

This House would ban size zero models.

This House would require all models to have a minimum BMI.

This House believes that models should also be role models.

Related topics

Beauty contests, banning of

Cosmetic surgery, banning of

Sport, equalise status of men and women in

The arguments below consider the general arguments for equalising the status of men and women in sport. You may debate this issue in principle or a motion may specifically ask you to look at equalising airtime, prizes or salaries. In all areas, the debate asks whether the market should be allowed to dictate terms or whether intervention is needed to produce equality.

Pros

[1] Men and women are equal and by giving different prizes or different coverage, you suggest otherwise and send out the message to society that women are inferior.

[2] Men's sport has had a head start in attracting a following. The current bias in reporting exacerbates this by giving less exposure and profile to women's sport. Many people assume that women's sports such as cricket or football are dull or slow without having seen them. If the media gave more attention to women's sports, then the fan base would follow. This can be seen with women's tennis which attracts large audiences.

[3] Women, and young girls in particular, need to see prominent role models in sport. At the moment, they see cheerleaders on television who are there to support the men, not to achieve success in their own right.

Cons

[1] Sport is commercial and is driven by the market. Prizes reflect what sponsors are willing to pay. Sky shows the fixtures that people will watch. Commercial TV companies are not, and should not be, asked to be, an engine for social change.

[2] If people want to watch more women's sport, they should start buying tickets and the money and profile will follow. Already women's sport has a higher profile than it used to, and it will continue to grow without intervention. There is no inherent sexism in coverage. In sports where there is an audience for watching women (athletics, gymnastics and tennis, for example), the events are shown on television. There is not the same audience for women's rugby or cricket. Similarly, since 2007, the prizes for Wimbledon champions are equal.

[3] Men's sport is faster, higher and stronger. People want the most entertaining spectacle and they find it watching

men. The fastest 100m will (probably) always be run by a man. Men's sport will probably always maintain an edge because of this and there is nothing wrong with that. Countries will always highlight the international success of their female sports stars (Russia and China celebrate their gymnasts, the USA their tennis stars and the UK their cyclists and sailors), so there will always be role models, even if domestic leagues are not given as much airtime.

Sport, regretting the commercialisation of

The influence of money in sport has long been present, but in recent years, the sums involved have risen exponentially. Gone are the days of local footballers earning small sums of money playing for a local team; in 2009, Real Madrid paid a whopping €98 million to sign Cristiano Ronaldo from Manchester United, while Lionel Messi's contract at FC Barcelona sees him earning €34 million. Outside football, the money is in fact even bigger; boxers Floyd Mayweather and Manny Pacquiao earned US$85 million and US$62 million respectively in 2011. All of this also means that prices rise as well; a season ticket is now beyond the reach of traditional supporters.

Pros

[1] The commercialisation of sport directly harms the sports themselves. The team loyalties that were once a major factor in many sports have been replaced by modern transfers, by which sportsmen and sportswomen move from one team to another in pursuit of a higher salary. Some events are staged for purely commercial purposes, especially in boxing, where ageing fighters are brought out of retirement and mismatched against younger opponents. Other sports are under pressure to alter their rules to make them more 'watchable'. For instance, professional cricket is now dominated by the T20 version of the game, a shorter version

Cons

[1] Far from harming sports, commercialisation aids them. With new money come better facilities and better training for sportsmen and sportswomen, allowing them to perform at their very best and fulfil their potential. Better competitors make for better events; therefore, increasing investment in sport can only be a good thing for the sports themselves. Although there are occasional abuses, the spirit of sport – and the desire to win on the field as well as with the bank balance – is as vibrant as ever.

[2] The extra money in sport is in fact good for the sports fan. Obviously, the

for those with poor attention spans or limited time to spare.

[2] Commercialised sport is also bad for the viewer. As covering major events has become more expensive, rights to do so have been bought by subscription and pay-per-view channels; public broadcasting can compete only with the aid of state intervention, which is heavily opposed by sporting bodies greedy for more cash, leaving fans out of pocket. Coverage is in danger of becoming ever more revenue-led – football in particular is under pressure to become a game of four quarters to allow more advertising.

[3] Sportsmen and sportswomen simply do not deserve the inflated salaries they earn. For boxers such as Mayweather to have earned US$85 million in a year for just two fights is obscene when teachers and nurses are paid barely enough to make a living. The market is no longer paying what these people are worth; rather, structural problems in the market mean that sportsmen and sportswomen are systematically overpaid.

[4] The amount of money in sport damages competition, because only teams with enormous sums of money have any meaningful chance of being competitive; for instance, big-money takeovers of Chelsea and Manchester City have unbalanced Premiership football heavily in favour of a small number of wealthy clubs. That group is very hard to break into, and as that will only happen rarely, the sport will become more predictable.

more highly trained athletes result in a more exciting spectacle. Also, major sporting fixtures have become national events. For those dedicated enough to attend in person, expensive new stadia provide room for more fans in more comfort and safety than ever before; for others, well thought-out comprehensive coverage is provided on television and radio. Even though rights are increasingly bought up by satellite and cable channels, deregulation of the broadcasting market means that ever more people have access to these. Moreover, national governments can, and do, stop the sale of certain events to pay-per-view channels, to ensure universal access.

[3] Modern sportsmen and sportswomen deserve the money they are paid. Their activities entertain millions worldwide, yet their professional lives are often short. Recognition should be given to those who have given their all in pursuit of a sporting ideal, and who are often heroes to many members of the public. They also train obsessively all year round; it is not as though they are lazy or just lucky.

[4] In fact, large cash injections improve competition because they give previously unsuccessful clubs a means of challenging the dominance of the previous top tier. Chelsea's takeover allowed the club to buy players who would never previously have joined the club, and so challenge Manchester United's dominance over the sport.

Related topics

Capitalism v. socialism

Salary capping, mandatory

Performance-enhancing drugs in sport

Sports teams punished for the behaviour of fans

Many football matches have been marred in recent years by the violent or abusive behaviour of the fans. This has included mass rioting as in the Juventus v. Liverpool European Cup Final in 1985. More often the behaviour manifests itself in the throwing of objects at players, or insulting players because of their racial/ethnic background. Nowadays, CCTV may bring the perpetrators to justice, but there is a feeling that since the club is a community, the team should also face the consequences.

Pros

[1] There is a problem in some sports (especially soccer) in that racism and violence are rife. The crowd situation makes it hard to target individuals. This means there are few consequences for offending and if some perpetrators are caught, plenty are left to continue making trouble. It is essential to find a solution that tackles the group nature of the issue and this proposal does just that.

[2] This action would be effective. Fans love their teams and do not want them to suffer, therefore this will act as a powerful deterrent. This deterrent will act on an individual level, but also especially at a group level where peer pressure will act to stamp out anti-social behaviour to protect a team's success. It also incentivises teams to promote the good behaviour of their fans. They know they need their fans to behave for their own self-interest and so will get involved more in policing and setting a good example.

Cons

[1] If there is a problem with the behaviour of fans, then it is better to tackle the fans themselves. It is possible to identify and strongly punish offenders. If necessary, hold games with no spectators so that it is the fans who suffer and not the team.

[2] This policy will not be effective as a combination of alcohol and the high emotion of matches mean that bad behaviour is not a rational decision, but an out-of-control response to stimulus. Deterrents only work when people are thinking logically about consequences.

[3] Sport already works hard to send strong messages on values and behaviour; for example, through the UEFA Respect campaign. We should work with not against teams to stamp out problems.

[4] This is exceptionally unfair. A team cannot control their fans' behaviour and yet their hard work is overturned by the actions of others. Sporting results should

[3] This policy carries a strong message that racism and violence are not acceptable and will not be tolerated. This is good for the sport and for the whole of society. Many young people are obsessive about sport and they can learn lessons through this arena about values and about the consequences of their actions.

[4] This punishment is consistent with other policies. For example, in Premiership football, a club can be penalised for its financial mismanagement, which is not the fault of the players. Games can also be held in private which affects all fans even if only a minority have engaged in hooliganism. This is accepted as fair, as a club is seen as more than just the players.

be based on sporting skill and nothing else. It is also open to abuse. How do you know if someone is really a fan or trying to sabotage a team?

Possible motions

This House would punish sports teams for the behaviour of their fans.

This House would penalise football clubs for the hooliganism of their fans.

Related topics

Zero tolerance

Sport, regretting the commercialisation of

Parents, responsibility for the criminal acts of their children

University education, free for all

University education is very expensive and there are a number of models for funding it. Some countries such as Germany, France and Sweden fund it fully through taxation and it is free to the students. Other countries such as the USA, Australia and England expect students to pay some or all of the fees. There may be loans available so that the students do not have to pay the fees until they are earning, and there may be exemptions for the poorest students. Another option is a graduate tax to raise money for higher education funding. It is not essential for the Opposition team to put forward a model of how they would make students pay, but they may choose to, to clarify the terms of the debate.

Pros

[1] As developed countries become more technologically advanced and richer, there is a need for a fuller education for young people, and there are the resources to pay for it. Where there is the political will, university education can still be free – even if that might involve raising taxes by 1 per cent or 2 per cent. We should campaign for free university education for all as part of the education the state provides to each citizen as a right.

Cons

[1] There is always only a finite amount of money available that can be spent on education by the government. It is right that the focus should be on the years of compulsory schooling (e.g. 5–18 or 7–16) as this is the core period of education to which everybody is entitled. Higher education is not part of the core education that the state must provide free of charge for all. University education, like nursery education, is a bonus, a privilege that

[2] Individuals do not exist in a vacuum – we are all part of one organic society. Just as students are dependent on the work of others (e.g. parents, teachers, cleaners) for their educational opportunities, so society is dependent on well-educated graduates (e.g. academics, scientists, economists, bankers, doctors) to prosper and flourish. Society at large benefits from the skills and wealth generation of graduates, and so society at large (i.e. the state) should pay. It is in the nature of taxation that people pay for services that they do not use, and if graduates earn more, then they will contribute more through their taxes.

[3] Charging tuition fees discriminates against the poor and perpetuates elitism in the university system. Those from poorer backgrounds are particularly unwilling to take on debt in order to gain a university education, so those young people who happen to have rich parents will, on average, get a better education. University education should be a key engine in social mobility and equality by allowing everyone to make the most of their academic abilities.

[4] A free system removes barriers to entry and the disincentive of debt and therefore leads to a greater percentage of society attending university, which benefits society. Industry, commerce, science and the culture of a country all need the benefit of graduates, and society should be prepared to invest in having a well-educated population.

[5] It is patronising and elitist to say that some people who go to university are not really up to it. It is up to the students and the universities to decide whether these people have the ability to do a degree. Employers continue to prefer graduates

people opt for rather than a right. It is therefore acceptable to raise money for higher education by charging fees.

[2] It is right to follow the principle that the consumer pays. It is the students themselves who benefit most directly from their university education – earning as much as 50 per cent more, on average, than a non-graduate in later life. It is therefore they themselves who should pay for their university fees. Why should cleaners or bus drivers who never went to university themselves pay for those who do? A majority of university students come from more affluent backgrounds, while most taxpayers are poorer; clearly it is inequitable to make them pay.

[3] The important consideration is equality of access and opportunity – a system that discriminated against the poor would be elitist and unacceptable. Such equality can be guaranteed by a loan system where those who cannot afford fees will not have to pay them until they are earning enough to pay them back, or by having bursaries for the poorest in society. There is no need to have university as a universal benefit in order just to promote access.

[4] There is no conclusive evidence that charging tuition fees leads to a drop in student numbers. With awareness of the different ways of paying and the benefits of a university education, most people choose it as worth paying for.

[5] It would not necessarily be a bad thing if fewer people applied to university. Not everyone is suited to an academic degree, and it is questionable whether so many people should be encouraged to go to university. Politicians often boast of the

over non-graduates, and so in the interest of equality, a free university education should be available for all. University education is a right, not a privilege.

[6] Some people will always be lazy and prefer socialising to studying. Tuition fees will not change this as the student will not feel the effect of them until after their degree. Students may, however, feel under extra pressure to get paid work through-out their time at university to reduce their debts, and this acts as a distraction to the diligent.

Possible motions

This House believes in free university education.
This House would charge university tuition fees.
This House believes in a 'graduate tax'.

Related topics

Capitalism v. socialism
Privatisation
Welfare state
Private schools
Nursery education, free provision of by the state

increasing numbers of people going to university, but this, in fact, means that standards drop, resources are stretched to breaking point, and many young people find themselves spending three more years studying for little long-term gain when they could have been working. Introducing tuition fees teaches people to value a university education as a privilege rather than a right – if this means a drop in numbers and a raising of standards, then that is no bad thing.

[6] Tuition fees ensure that students make the most of the opportunity. When it is free, some students skip lectures, do the minimum work and see the experience as the chance to party. If they are paying, they are more likely to value the experience. Additionally, if they are customers, then they have more chance of guaranteeing that the university is providing them with the best education.

Violent video games, banning of

This debate considers whether state censorship can be justified by the harms caused by violent video games. Games such as Grand Theft Auto have attracted increasing criticism over recent years as the amount of violence has escalated.

Pros

[1] Violent video games encourage a more violent society. The constant exposure to horrific acts desensitises the user to assault and killing. The extent of the brutality in today's games is shocking and people play them for hours a day, meaning they are on

Cons

[1] Violent video games are just enter-tainment and the government should not intervene to limit people's freedom of choice to play them, as they do not harm the player or anyone else. People know that it is make-believe and it does not

a constant diet of shooting, beating and bludgeoning. This normalises violence in society. There is also a specific issue of copycat crimes where a player enacts in real life the atrocities that they have played. Recently in Britain, a 14-year-old boy committed murder with a hammer after repeatedly playing Manhunt which rewards the same type of attack.

[2] Video games are a particularly harmful medium because of their immersive quality. Violence in film and TV should also be limited, but video games are the worst culprit because the player is in control, committing the violence themselves, rather than watching somebody else do it. It is this feature which leads to a programming effect and can embed violence in the brain of those using the games.

[3] Violent video games are especially harmful to impressionable children and it is very hard to prevent access to them. There has always been a problem with older friends and siblings buying games for youngsters, but now that you can download games straight to your computer, children can access the games themselves with ease.

[4] Violence as entertainment is immoral. If society wants to take a stand against violence, then it should not allow entertainment media to glorify it. This only muddies the message and undermines our values.

therefore influence their views of reality. People who are psychologically disturbed and commit awful crimes would do so without video games. The games cannot be blamed when the overwhelming majority of people play and are unaffected. In fact it may be that video games can channel aggression which might otherwise come out in real violence.

[2] It is wrong to target video games. Film and television have just as much gratuitous violence as video games, and some music genres also feature violence in their lyrics. If anything, these media are worse as they show real people rather than graphics, and they create action heroes for the audience to admire.

[3] Video games have age certification to make sure that they are used appropriately. It is up to parents to monitor use, just as it is with films. Adults should not be denied access to video games in order to protect children any more than they should be denied access to alcohol or gambling.

[4] There always has and always will be violence in entertainment because people find it entertaining. Before the technology for video games was here, children played with toy guns and when there are no toys, children will still engage in imaginative play using their fingers as shooters. Computer games are just a different way of doing the same thing.

Possible motions

This House would ban violent video games.

This House believes that violent video games damage society.

Related topics

Boxing, banning of

Music lyrics, censorship of

Zoos, abolition of

See the introduction to the debate on 'animal experimentation and vivisection, banning of' (Section E) and the entry on 'animal rights' (Section A). The conditions of animals in captivity vary hugely around the world. If the debate is set in your own country, you will need to consider the specific treatment of the animals. The definition could also include or exclude safari parks, where the animals roam around an open area that visitors drive through, rather than living in cages.

Pros

[1] Animals have rights just as humans do. They have evolved from nature and each belongs undisturbed in its own natural habitat, left alone to live, breed and seek food. To remove them against their will from this habitat is immoral.

[2] Even if animals do not have rights, we as humans still have a duty to treat them humanely in our role as 'stewards of the Earth'. Although we may breed them for our purposes, to use for entertainment, for company, or to wear or eat, we must still avoid causing them to suffer. Zoos do this in two ways. First, the animals frequently suffer abuse, neglect and even death, through boredom, unfamiliarity with their new habitats and cruel treatment by zookeepers. A San Francisco zookeeper, explaining an incident in which an African elephant was beaten with axe handles for two days, described the treatment as 'the only way to motivate them'. Birds' wings may be clipped, aquatic animals may have too little water, herd animals are kept alone or in pairs, and many animals contract 'zoochosis' – abnormal and self-destructive behaviour caused by their confinement. Second, the exhibition of animals in captivity tells an impressionable public that cruelty to animals can be condoned.

Cons

[1] Animals do not have rights. It is entirely at our discretion how we treat them, since we are a stronger predatory species. The use of a weaker species for the needs of a stronger one is entirely natural.

[2] It is easy to pick shocking, isolated examples of animal cruelty. In fact, the general treatment afforded to most animals in zoos is very good. They are given regular food and water, comfortable environments suited to their particular needs, and most importantly, medical treatment – something they would not benefit from in the wild. In many cases, their chance of survival is better than in their 'natural' habitat. It is certainly not worse than a life as a pet or on a farm. Zoos do not condone cruelty to animals; the public is taught that all animals are interesting and precious.

[3] By all means close down roadside zoos, or at least subject them to the same stringent safeguards as municipal zoos.

[4] Zoos are useful for educational purposes. In particular, they allow children an opportunity to observe closely animals from other countries that they might never have a chance to see, as well as learn about all the species of the animal kingdom and how they are related.

[3] Few zoos approach satisfactory standards of care for their animals. Many make no attempt to do so, such as 'roadside' zoos or menageries, where the primary purpose of the animals is to attract customers to another facility such as a restaurant, store or hotel. There is no educational benefit to these zoos.

[4] Larger zoos that claim to be for educational benefit are kidding themselves; visitors usually spend no more than a few minutes at each exhibit, using the animals rather for entertainment. The public can watch nature documentaries and find out about how animals act in their own habitat, which is more educational than seeing them in cages. Their primary use for research is to devise ways to breed and maintain more animals in captivity. If zoos ceased to exist, so would the need for their research.

[5] Animals chosen for zoos are usually the popular breeds, which will attract crowds. Endangered species in need of protection may not necessarily attract audiences.

[5] Endangered species may be protected from extinction in zoos, or in wildlife sanctuaries. Scientists are also afforded valuable opportunities to study animals in strange environments, and draw conclusions about how we can affect their natural habitats.

Possible motions

This House would free the animals.
This House would shut down zoos.

Related topics

Animal experimentation and vivisection, banning of
Blood sports, abolition of
Animal rights
Vegetarianism

SECTION G

Crime and punishment

Capital punishment

In 2013, 58 countries still use the death penalty as a form of punishment. The vast majority of executions take place in China, which is thought to execute more than 4,000 people a year; Iran comes second with about 400; no other state executes more than 100 prisoners a year. As such, it is a punishment mostly used sparingly and for the most serious crimes; murder is the primary one, though some countries retain it for drug-related offences as well. The methods of capital punishment also vary; some US states retain the use of gas chambers to execute prisoners, but most use lethal injection.

Pros

[1] In any country – democracy or dictatorship – one of the roles of the state is to punish criminals. In the case of serial murderers, terrorists, 'cop killers' etc., they should be punished by death. Our human rights are given to us as part of a contract – which says that we can do anything we want as long as it does not hurt anyone else – and so, if we take away the life of another person, then surely we forfeit the right to our own life.

[2] Use of the death penalty deters criminals from murdering. Numerous studies in the USA show a noticeable drop in murder rates in the months directly following any execution. One study concludes that each execution prevents, on average, 18 further murders. Since capital punishment was abolished in the UK in 1965 (for all crimes except treason), the murder rate has doubled.

[3] Executing murderers prevents them from killing again. Given that the rate of re-offending is so high, these people must be removed from society altogether. Serial killers – those who are so 'evil' or hardened as to be incapable of reform – can be removed permanently from society.

[4] The death penalty is only given when the facts are certain and the jury has no

Cons

[1] If killing is a crime and immoral in the eyes of society, then for the state to kill its citizens is equally barbaric. Two wrongs do not make a right, and it is never right to put someone to death, no matter what the crime. The death penalty is a 'cruel and unusual punishment', especially in view of the psychological torture inflicted on those on Death Row, who know that they are going to be executed, but do not know when.

[2] If the death penalty is such a deterrent, then why is the murder rate so high in the USA? There has been virtually no change in the overall rate since 1976 when the death penalty was reinstated, despite an enormous increase in the number of executions. Also, death penalty states often have a higher murder rate than their neighbouring states that do not use the death penalty. A distinction also needs to be made between local short-term deterrents (immediately after executions in particular places) and long-term deterrents that have an effect on national crime rates, for which there is less evidence.

[3] Execution may remove some killers from society, but in return, it brutalises society and invests killing with state-sanctioned acceptability. Not only is capital

doubt whatsoever, and only carried out when every right to appeal has been exhausted. There have admittedly been some cases of wrongful conviction leading to execution in the UK (notably Timothy Evans in 1950 and, probably, James Hanratty in 1962), but although it may seem harsh, this is negligible when compared with the number of murders prevented by the death penalty. The discrimination between various degrees of homicide or manslaughter allows the jury plenty of opportunity for clemency, and insane murderers are never executed.

[5] If there is no death penalty, then there is no incentive for prisoners sentenced to life without parole not to commit crimes while in prison – to kill warders, other prisoners, or to try to escape and kill again. Nothing they can do can result in further punishment.

Possible motions

This House would reintroduce the death penalty.
This House would hang murderers.

Related topics

Smacking, remove parents' right to
Mandatory prison sentences
Prison v. rehabilitation
Zero tolerance
Dictators, assassination of

punishment not a deterrent, but it can even increase the murder rate; California's rate showed its biggest increases between 1952 and 1967, when executions occurred every two months on average.

[4] A single mistaken execution of an innocent person, among no matter how many thousands of cases, is utterly unjustifiable and is enough to destroy our trust in the death penalty and in any judicial system that uses it. Rehabilitation is part of the purpose of punishment, and who is to say that any guilty criminal cannot be reformed? Any prisoner must be given every chance to come to terms with their wrongdoing and perhaps be rehabilitated into society – a chance that execution denies.

[5] There are several ways of dealing with misbehaving prisoners: the revoking of privileges if their disorder is on a minor scale, and solitary confinement in a maximum-security cell if they are violent. There will always be psychopaths who need to be confined in this way. Those who are not psychopaths should not be sentenced to life without parole – if they have the chance of parole, they have an incentive towards good behaviour.

Child curfews

Punishing children and preventing them from committing crimes poses a peculiar problem for law enforcement. Often it is harder to prosecute children, and the available punishments are less severe; in addition, governments are keen to emphasise the need for softer measures to deal with youth crime, which focus on enhancing parental involvement in crime prevention. Curfews can be part of a broader strategy to prevent youth crime before it takes place, rather than only punishing it after the event.

Pros

[1] There is a worrying increase in anti-social and criminal behaviour among young children. There have been horrific cases of crimes perpetrated by children under the age of 13; many of the participants in the 2011 London riots were very young. We need to take action to stem this tide of young offending. Children pick up anti-social and criminal behaviour and habits from older children with whom they associate. Much of this crime (car theft, drugs, vandalism, gang fights) takes place at night, and child curfews will give the police an additional weapon with which to fight offending by young people.

[2] Parents would also have a responsibility to enforce the curfew. Any policy to combat youth crime must include an important role for parents who must be made to take responsibility for their children. They, along with their child, would be liable to punishment if the curfew is broken. This would serve as an incentive to better and more responsible parenting.

[3] Curfews also protect young people from crime; it is much harder to protect them at night, when there are fewer passers-by or people looking out of their windows, than during the day, when the eyes and ears of a community are all around to watch out for them. Parents cannot know where their children are at all times; thus, the state should assist them in making sure that they are at home when they are most in danger.

Cons

[1] The sort of children who would murder, or even those who would get involved in gangs, drugs and car theft, will not take the slightest bit of notice of a curfew. Children who behave in these criminal and anti-social ways are well past taking notice of bedtimes. Youth crime is a radical and alarming problem that calls for a more radical solution. The age of criminal responsibility should be lowered to eight, and sentences for young offenders should be more severe, and imposed after a single 'final warning', rather than children receiving several 'cautions' before any punishment is dished out.

[2] Most young offenders learn violent behaviour, lack of respect for property, indiscipline and dishonesty from their parents. Others learn it from their peers, and the need to impress these peers and be included by them outweighs any worthy parental entreaties. In the first case, the parent would not care whether a curfew was enforced; and in the second case, they would be powerless to see that it was. So introducing a curfew would be an empty and futile gesture.

[3] If anything, curfews put children in more danger, because they discourage them from seeking help from the police or other adults if they are out late at night and get into trouble; this is because they will fear admitting that they have broken the curfew rules. Moreover, parents may wrongly assume that their children are not breaching curfew, and so fail to protect them sufficiently.

Possible motions
This House would put a curfew on children.
This House would not allow kids out after dark.

Related topics
Smacking, remove parents' right to
School uniform
Zero tolerance
Parents, responsibility for the criminal acts of
their children

Community sentencing

Most legal systems that allow local communities to play a prominent role in sentencing limit this right to relatively cohesive and isolated indigenous or religious communities, but there is no reason in principle that this must be so. A crucial distinction is made between setting the law, conducting the trial to see if a suspect is guilty, and then sentencing; these debates only allow the local community in at the final stage, while retaining the state's power to set the law and administer it. However, there are profound implications in those areas as well. The most prominent example is 'sentencing circles' in Australia and Canada, where judges sit with indigenous elders to determine sentences and explain them to both offender and victim. Such circles often take into account different considerations from normal courts focusing on healing and restoring the community rather than a strict emphasis on retribution.

Pros

[1] The main damage done by a crime is done, after that to the victim, to the community in which it is committed; any secondary impact on 'the state' is minimal. As such, it should be up to the community to determine appropriate sentences, rather than judges who may have little or no involvement with the real lives of those affected by crime. This can cut both ways. Communities may want to punish some crimes more harshly; for instance, gun crime in a neighbourhood where those offences are especially prevalent might be seen as a particularly serious crime. But equally, they may want to display more mercy; poor areas might display greater understanding about burglary driven by desperation, for example.

Cons

[1] The state depends for its legitimacy on the ability to enforce its laws, and this policy undermines that. While the law may remain the same, it is only meaningful if punishment follows a breach. Here, the state loses its power to punish breaches of particular laws, and so risks individual communities weakening the state's ability to prevent certain social harms. Moreover, because different areas will choose to punish things differently, this creates 'patchwork justice', where a crime may be punished more harshly in one area than in its neighbour, which is dangerous and illogical.

[2] The state also loses the power to protect internal minority groups. Sentencing circles may reflect biases against a 'minority within a minority', such as the 'Native

COMMUNITY SENTENCING   217

[2] The world contains many different moral value sets, and the state should be less stubborn about privileging one at the expense of all others. Many indigenous communities do not have firmly fixed conceptions of 'rights', but instead think of moral relationships in a more community-focused way, which places special emphasis on mercy and restoration of past relationships. The state should be more open to bringing these moral concepts into its operations, especially where all the parties understand them better.

[3] These punishments will be more effective. Often, minority communities feel disconnected from the justice system, because its primary role in their lives is the arrest and prosecution of their young men. As such, they have little respect for the justice system, and so do not acknowledge the moral force of its punishments. Community sentencing makes it more likely that both the offender and his/her community will acknowledge the punishment as valid, making re-offending less likely.

[4] Mainstream justice in these societies is far from perfect; indeed, often its emphasis on retribution over rehabilitation is substantially flawed. The justice system potentially has much to learn from other value systems. It is not enough merely to listen to them; they must be seen to be put into practice and experimented with, in order that the lessons from them can be seen in action and then deployed by judges and juries in all courts.

Freeman' in the USA, who are the descendants of African-American slaves that belong to Native American groups, so crimes against them will be punished less harshly. Moreover, it may simply be that certain crimes are ignored within a community; for instance, if a community decides to sentence rape less harshly, then women are left vulnerable within that group. This also means that the state loses its power to propel social change; if a minority group lags behind mainstream society in reducing homophobia, they may also punish homophobic violence less harshly.

[3] Rather than improving relations with these groups, this policy undermines these groups' relationships with the state, by emphasising their cultural and social differences. This sends the message that those differences are so deep that they cannot be contained by the criminal justice system. If we need separate sentencing, why not also have separate police forces and courts? This proposal will ultimately increase crime, as minority groups become less willing to avail themselves of the justice system altogether.

[4] Such sentencing powers actually risk doing significant damage to cohesion within these communities, as it is far from clear who is to control these sentencing powers, or how they will do so. If it is elected leaders in these communities, then those elections will become vastly more intense, and may spill over into violence. But more dangerous still is the possibility that decisions will be made on familial or patrimonial lines, based on traditional connections, rather than as a fair reflection of the group's beliefs.

Possible motions

This House believes that criminals should be sentenced in their communities rather than in the courts.

This House would allow indigenous groups to sentence their own.

This House supports sentencing circles.

Related topics

Judges, election of

Jury trials, abolition of

Mandatory prison sentences

Zero tolerance

Right to bear arms

International Criminal Court, abolition of the

The International Criminal Court (ICC) came into being on 1 July 2002. Located in The Hague, the ICC is intended to prosecute the most important war criminals, replacing special regional tribunals for Rwanda, the former Yugoslavia and Sierra Leone that had represented the world's first attempt at taking a strong stand against the most heinous atrocities. There are three routes by which a case can come to the court. First, if the crime took place in one of the states that are parties to the case. Second, if the accused is a national of a state that is a party to the case. Third, if it is referred by the UN Security Council. At the time of writing, of 30 people indicted by the ICC, 13 remain at large, 7 are being held before trial, 4 have been acquitted, 2 are appealing convictions, 2 are on trial, and 2 have died.

Pros

[1] The ICC is a violation of national sovereignty. Criminal law is the responsibility of individual states, which should be able to decide when to punish their citizens. The ICC violates that, especially because states do not even have to sign up, but can be 'referred' by the UN Security Council.

[2] The ICC is often unable to secure a conviction. Of six prosecutions to date, four have resulted in acquittals, and two are on appeal. In 2012, Thomas Lubanga was only sentenced to 14 years in prison for war crimes committed in the Democratic Republic of the Congo because the prosecutors could not make all their charges against him stick. This makes the ICC pointless, insulting to victims and unable to do justice.

Cons

[1] National sovereignty is not absolute, and does not extend to cases where states are 'unable or unwilling' to prosecute the worst crimes on earth, which are the only occasions on which the ICC intervenes. Moreover, in most cases, the ICC mainly intervenes in cases where national governments have requested assistance (like Uganda) or the perpetrators are abroad (e.g. the prosecution of Jean-Pierre Bemba who fled to the Central African Republic after committing crimes in Eastern Congo).

[2] The ICC is far from incompetent. First, some acquittals are to be expected; that is how criminal justice works. Second, although slow to get off the ground, it only has jurisdiction over post-2002 crimes, so in its early years it was

[3] The ICC is too rigid in its pursuit of justice over peace. Often, prosecutions, rather than ending a conflict, simply perpetuate it and revive old wounds. Moreover, they inhibit the possibility of using amnesties to end conflicts. Joseph Kony (the Ugandan leader of the Lord's Resistance Army) fled peace talks because he was indicted by the ICC; Laurent Gbagbo (President of Ivory Coast from 2000 to 2011) would have stepped down peacefully had he been guaranteed that he would not face prosecution, but ICC rules did not allow it.

[4] The ICC comes across to victims as Western justice; the majority of their voices are never heard, because it is located in The Hague, not their homelands. Moreover, by focusing not on the actual crimes, but the need to score political points by getting any kind of prosecution, it misses the extent of the harm. Lubanga's conviction was only for using child soldiers, a minor component of the devastation he wreaked in the DRC.

effectively waiting for crimes to occur. Now it prosecutes frequently, and will only get better at it.

[3] Apolitical justice is a necessity in post-conflict societies, especially where national judiciaries may be perceived as biased and unfair. For example, in Kenya after the 2008 election violence, referring people on both political sides to the ICC was a key component of the peace deal.

[4] International Criminal Court justice is not Western at all; crimes against humanity are so severe as to be seen as such regardless of cultural background. Moreover, most atrocity victims want a strong seal of international condemnation on their oppressors, which the ICC provides.

Possible motions
This House believes that war crimes are a global responsibility.
This House would abolish the ICC.

Related topics
Pacifism
Dictators, assassination of

Judges, election of

In the USA, most judges at a state level are elected, but federal judges are appointed by the president, subject to confirmation by the senate. In the UK and most other 'common law' countries, judges are appointed, usually by independent and expert commissions. It is important to realise that there are many indirect consequences of elections of judges, most prominently the increase in politicisation of the judiciary. Judicial appointments outside the USA receive very little public scrutiny, whereas in America they are front-page news. It is important to recognise that judges perform a wide range of functions, which may differ in their relevance to politics; interpreting the Insolvency Acts is unlikely to be a highly political activity, but reducing murderers' sentences obviously is.

Pros

[1] Being a judge is an inherently political activity; judges make decisions all the time about how rights in constitutions or human rights laws are to be interpreted, which define the limits of what governments can do to their citizens. For instance, there is nothing exclusively 'legal' about the decision as to whether abortion or gay marriage are legal, or the limits of the right to strike; these decisions should thus be governed in the same way as other political ones.

[2] If judges are appointed, then the government of the day will be able to appoint judges who are sympathetic with their legislative programme and policies. If judges are elected, on the other hand, they will often be figures who are critical of the government of the day, as happens in mid-term local government elections, which almost always favour the opposition parties over the governing party.

[3] It is right that the law should be open to indirect influence over time by public opinion, rather than being entrusted entirely to an often out-of-touch, elitist, establishment-appointed judiciary. Electing judges with known views on crime and punishment (e.g. for or against the death penalty, in favour of retribution or rehabilitation, tough or lenient on drugs and prostitution, etc.) means that the judicial process is democratised, and figures can be elected in order to shape democratically the way that law is interpreted, implemented and evolves.

[4] Elections do not need to put their candidates at the mercy of large corporations. There are plenty of other funding bodies that could get involved, such

Cons

[1] Most judicial decisions are not really political; they involve arid, technical debates about the correct approach to interpreting contracts, or causation in medical negligence claims, or the rules for transferring property; such decisions are best made by experts in those fields, and should not be swayed by democratic pressure. Moreover, big constitutional decisions on abortion or gay marriage *are* legal; they involve interpreting statutes which have been laid down.

[2] If judges are elected at the same time as the government, then far from dissenting from the government, they will be far more likely to share its views. If they are elected at a different time, then there will simply be insufficient interest in these elections, and so they will be hijacked by extremists.

[3] In a civilised society we should seek to minimise the influence of 'mob rule'. Democratic and judicial processes are set up specifically to remove important judicial decisions from emotive public pressure and prejudice. Elected judges will pander to public opinion (e.g. turning down appeals against death penalty sentences), seeking votes rather than justice. Second, public opinion already has enough influence on the judicial process. Punishments and laws are set by elected politicians, and the judiciary typically shows considerable deference to those politicians on matters of public policy.

[4] Elections in the modern world can involve huge amounts of money; which may mean prospective judges would need to raise money. In certain jurisdictions, like the USA, this may mean that candidates might have to seek funds from corpora-

as trades unions or legal campaigning groups. Moreover, it would be perfectly viable simply to cap funding, or provide state funding, to prevent these problems.

Possible motions
This House would elect its judges.
This House believes that supreme court officials should be elected.

Related topics
Democracy
Social movements: courts v. legislatures
Jury trials, abolition of
Community sentencing
Mandatory prison sentences

tions. This would make judges who win elections more vulnerable to corporate pressure, which undermines their role in enforcing the law – particularly in disputes involving the companies which funded their election campaigns.

Jury trials, abolition of

Juries are an integral part of the criminal justice system in most 'common law" countries, such as the UK, the USA and Australia, but are totally alien in 'civil law' systems like France and Germany. They were abolished in South Africa in 1969 as the apartheid government did not want black jurors sitting in judgement on their peers. In some cases, jurors may also sit in non-criminal claims cases; in the USA, juries sit in personal injury or medical negligence cases, which has led to very high pay-outs in those trials. Similar worries have emerged in the UK where juries occasionally sit in libel claims cases, and often tend to give huge pay-outs for damage to reputation which are even larger than those for physical harm.

Pros

[1] In the modern world, there is no longer any need for protection against unscrupulous or politically biased judges. Therefore, we do not need a jury, which used to provide this safeguard.

[2] Judges can be relied on to enforce the law more faithfully, as it has been made by democratic institutions, and because they have had a lifetime of believing that this is the correct way for a system to operate.

Cons

[1] Judges, even if they do have fewer pro-government biases, may still have a range of other prejudices. They are often drawn from a white, male, middle-class elite. It could be argued that because of the narrow demographic pool from which judges are currently drawn, they may be more likely to sympathise with the police, and so are more willing to accept evidence given by the police.

Indeed it is; democratic institutions should make the laws, and the legal system should then enforce them. Anything else represents a troubling breakdown in the separation of powers.

[3] Jurors are unreliable lay people, uninformed about the law and with no training, and no proven skills of attentiveness, analysis or fairness. They, unlike legal experts, will be swayed by prejudice and preconception (e.g. judging defendants by their appearance). It is not in the interest of justice to have such people decide the fate of those accused of serious crimes, whose futures, or even lives, hang in the balance. Particularly in the case of fraud trials which last months or years and are full of complex legal technicalities, juries cannot be expected to follow the case or know how to reach a verdict. Juries should be replaced by panels of lawyers (as already happens with appeal court judges who sit in panels) or magistrates, the latter being a compromise between the untutored lay person and the professional lawyer.

[4] Most jurors, especially if they have not understood or followed the case closely, will be swayed by the summing up of the judge. A panel of lawyers or magistrates would have their own understanding of the case to balance that of the judge. So replacing jurors with an expert panel will in fact provide a more efficient check on the influence which a single judge can bring to bear on the outcome of a case.

[2] Juries inject an element of common-sense morality into the justice process; whether someone can prove that, for instance, they were coerced into committing a crime is not a legal judgement, but one based on what the reasonable person thinks. Moreover, juries may help to prevent the enforcement of highly regressive laws; for instance, although abortion is illegal, for most circumstances, in the Australian state of Queensland, juries have simply acquitted the accused in recent trials, because the law is now widely accepted as unjust.

[3] The jury system forces lawyers and judges to make the law lucid and comprehensible. Without a jury, barristers and judges would have no obligation to make a comprehensible case, and the courtroom would become an alienating and incomprehensible preserve of legalistic jargon in which defendants were left not understanding the accusations made against them, nor the process by which they were acquitted or convicted. While they are, indeed, untrained in legal matters, jurors bring an open mind and commonsense judgement to bear that expert panels would lack. Expert panels would tend to become 'case-hardened' and cynical, disbelieving often-heard defences simply because they were frequently encountered, not judging them on their merits.

[4] There is already the appeals process to deal with cases where judges have misdirected the jury. And expert panels would be inclined towards the opposite danger – trusting too much to their own ability at legal interpretation and tending, arrogantly, to ignore the judge's direction as inferior to their own analysis.

Possible motions
This House would abolish jury trials.
This House would not use juries in civil cases.
This House would leave tough cases to judges.

Mandatory prison sentences

In many countries, certain crimes carry mandatory prison sentences; that is, there is a level beyond which a judge cannot go, whatever the circumstances of the case. In some cases, such sentences are for a specific crime; for instance, many jurisdictions demand that murder carries a life sentence, and the USA has 'mandatory minimums' for particular drugs offences. In other cases, sentences are mandatory only if the offender has committed previous crimes; for instance, a 'three strikes and you're out' policy which demands prison time for a third-time offender, whatever the crime.

Pros

[1] Governments need to be tough on crime to counteract the alarming increases in crime that characterise some modern societies. Mandatory prison sentences of, for instance, five years for a third burglary conviction, and 10-year (or life) prison sentences for a third conviction for serious violent or sexual crimes are powerful and effective deterrents in the fight against crime.

[2] Political gestures are important for public confidence. The government must be *seen* to be tough on crime. Mandatory sentencing will increase public confidence in the judicial process and make people feel safer in the face of the threat of serious crime.

[3] It is particularly important for more serious crimes that there is consistency of sentencing. For prison sentences to be effective deterrents and for them to be seen to be justly and uniformly imposed, they must be imposed at the same level for

Cons

[1] The fact that mandatory sentences *may* have a deterrent effect does not begin to compensate for the injustices that such a system produces. A third offence in exceptional extenuating circumstances can technically qualify for a mandatory 10-year or life sentence despite clearly not deserving it. In an infamous case in California, the third felony that carried the mandatory life sentence for one unfortunate young man was the theft of a slice of pizza from a child on a beach. In another case, a man was sentenced to 51 years for owning a forged driving licence, because it was his third felony. Judicial discretion must be allowed to decide each case on its merits. Also, prison sentences are an expensive way to make bad people worse and we should not be seeking to increase them. Probation and rehabilitation through community work and social reintegration (through measures such as help to return to employment) are the really effective ways to tackle crime.

the same crime by all judges. If repeat offences against property (theft and burglary) are given substantial custodial sentences by some judges and not by others, then the sentence will not serve as a deterrent, but instead the criminal will be tempted to take the risk. Allowing judicial discretion will result in too many freak verdicts of over-lenient sentences, and hence an erosion of the deterrent effect. The sentence received should be determined by the crime, not by the biases of the judge.

[4] It is already the case that a criminal's previous convictions are taken into account when a judge passes sentence. A first-time offender is always sentenced more leniently, and a repeat offender will be treated more harshly. Mandatory sentencing for third-time burglars, sexual and violent offenders is simply a formalisation and standardisation of this existing judicial procedure.

[5] It is a concern that crackdowns on crime often seem to have harsher consequences on black, Hispanic and Asian individuals than on white members of the community. But mandatory sentencing is not the cause of this discrepancy – it is an endemic problem for the judicial system and for society as a whole, and has complex socio-economic causes. Black communities are often poorer than white – a hangover of centuries of discrimination and inequalities – and poverty causes crime.

[2] Mandatory sentencing is an unnecessary political gesture, and an inappropriate meddling by politicians with a judiciary that should be kept apolitical and independent. There are already sentencing guidelines which are laid down by appellate courts and statute, and prosecutors have the power to appeal (often successfully) against sentences they consider to be too lenient. There are already mechanisms in place to ensure that appropriately severe punishments are meted out.

[3] The whole problem with mandatory sentencing is that it makes sentencing *artificially* 'consistent', whereas every crime and every criminal is in fact unique. The punishment should fit the crime. That is why we should rely on judges to use their experience, expertise and discretion to apply sentencing guidelines in a fair and appropriate way. Governments legislating for mandatory sentences send out the message that the judiciary cannot be trusted to pass the correct sentence. Far from bolstering public confidence, this will undermine confidence in the fairness and reliability of the judiciary.

[4] There are already mechanisms and guidelines that ensure that a criminal's previous convictions are taken into account in the appropriate way. Mandatory sentencing is an unnecessary and unwelcome political gesture.

[5] Mandatory sentencing has been seen to hit ethnic minorities disproportionately hard. It is a worrying fact that law-and-order crackdowns are often used by law enforcement officers and the judicial system as an occasion for racist oppression of non-white communities. The best example of this is in the USA, where the

Possible motions

This House would give mandatory sentences to repeat offenders.

This House believes in 'Three strikes and you're out'.

Related topics

Zero tolerance

Prison v. rehabilitation

Capital punishment

'mandatory minimums' for crack cocaine are substantially higher than those for powdered cocaine; crack is cheaper, and therefore mainly a drug used by black youth, while powder is often used by white people.

Parents, responsibility for the criminal acts of their children

This is a policy that sits ill with the long-held legal doctrine that for most crimes, a person must have the relevant *mens rea* (state of mind) for that crime; it is hard to see how parents can have the state of mind for a crime committed by someone else. But it is easy to borrow from other areas of law, such as the doctrine of 'vicarious liability' which holds employers civilly liable for the actions of their employees, to make this work. While there are no examples of this policy being enacted in a complete way, there are some smaller-scale examples of it, such as punishing parents for their children playing truant from school or bullying other children (the former in Florida, the latter in Michigan).

Pros

[1] Parents are responsible for giving their children a sense of morality and bringing them up from an early age to have good moral habits. Committing a crime is a violation of those moral norms and attitudes that parents should have instilled in their children from a young age, so it is perfectly reasonable to hold them responsible.

[2] Influence is not just about moral values, but about practical control. Parents have substantial control over their children's lives; they control their money, when they can go out, etc. Parents should know where their children are, and if they

Cons

[1] It is wrong to punish somebody for something they could not have prevented. Even if parents instil sound values in their children, there are numerous other sources of influence that mean that could go wrong: peers, schools, a social culture of violence, etc. It is ridiculous to say that bad parenting is the only cause of criminal behaviour; as such, it is wrong to punish parents for it.

[2] This is a romanticised view of parenting. Some parents may have that control, but many do not; a single mother who is substantially weaker than her violent son might have little control over him,

are with the kind of people who might influence them to commit crimes. If they are, then they should stop them; this is the duty of a parent, which they ought to be given serious incentives to fulfil.

[3] This will act as a powerful deterrent against children committing crimes. If children love their parents, they will think twice before committing crimes, knowing that they could not only land themselves in prison, but potentially leave themselves and their siblings parentless. It is thus highly useful to manipulate potential criminals into behaving themselves.

Possible motions

This House would punish parents for their children's crimes.

This House would visit the sins of the son upon the father.

Related topics

Smacking, remove parents' right to

Child curfews

physically or mentally. Moreover, it is not practical for parents to have total control over their children's lives; children have a degree of autonomy which they can use to sneak out, work for or steal money, etc. It would be undesirable for this autonomy to be shut down.

[3] This will not deter children from crimes; the reason that children commit crimes is not because of a rational cost-benefit analysis, but because they believe they will not get caught. Moreover, some children may not love their parents, but will see this as an opportunity for revenge, especially if they themselves are too young to be sent to prison for the crime as well; that is a win-win scenario for a child criminal.

Prisoners' right to vote, denial of

This debate was made prominent by a series of rulings by the European Court of Human Rights and the United States Supreme Court, which aimed to oblige governments to grant prisoners the right to vote. There are several forms that denial of voting rights can take, ranging in severity from a lifelong ban for felony commission (Kentucky and Louisiana in the USA), a ban for all prisoners (the UK, Italy) or disenfranchisement for particular crimes, as in most of the rest of Europe. An interesting side issue is about the severity of crime at which the threshold should be set, and in particular, for property crimes, how inflation has slowly made certain offences felonies 'by creep'; for example, in Massachusetts, it has been law for decades that a property crime of more than US$250 is a felony, for which you lose voting rights, but inflation has made that a much larger range of crimes.

Pros

[1] Voting is a right, but with rights come responsibilities, and one of those responsibilities is to obey the law. Once you refuse to obey the law, you lose certain rights, and voting is an obvious candidate. If you have shown a flagrant disregard for the law, you should have no say in making it; you should not be allowed to benefit from the democratic system that you have rejected.

[2] Taking away voting rights from criminals represents a strong deterrent for committing crime. The right to vote is not just practically important in terms of influencing government policy, but also symbolically important as a clear statement of social membership. No one wants to be made an outcast from society, which is what the deprivation of votes does.

[3] Rehabilitation is not the primary purpose of criminal justice. But even if it were, this policy would not primarily be about that. Rather, governments will be encouraged to pander to prisoners, making short-term promises for their benefit, such as more lenient punishments, which hurt the rest of society.

Possible motions

This House would give prisoners the vote.
This House believes that if you lose your right to freedom, you should lose your vote.

Related topics

Democracy
Social contract, existence of the
Prison v. rehabilitation

Cons

[1] Voting is an absolute right which should never be denied. The point of voting is to allow people to hold governments accountable and represent their interests, but prisoners undeniably have interests that deserve to be represented: being treated properly in prison, fair sentencing, etc. Breaking the law is not always a matter of failure of moral responsibility; many people do so because of psychological difficulties, drugs or poverty, that are not necessarily blameworthy.

[2] It is ridiculous to suggest that people considering committing crimes would care about the right to vote. They are, after all, willing to give up their rights to freedom of movement, and of association, so it hardly seems as though they are thinking through permutations for the future. Rather, they commit crimes rashly or out of necessity, and something as minor as voting rights for the one election they will likely be in prison for will not influence them.

[3] Giving prisoners the vote is an integral part of allowing them to rehabilitate and integrate fully into society. Telling prisoners that they have no say encourages them to perpetuate precisely the kind of beliefs about politics that led to them committing crimes in the first place, namely that no one listens to them. By giving them the vote, they will be encouraged to develop political opinions, which can give them a real focus in prison.

Prison v. rehabilitation

This debate is clearly a broad one, about a spectrum of different cases; no one would advocate abolishing prison altogether, but equally, very few people think it should be possible to imprison someone for literally *any* crime. The central theme is about a comparison between different systems. In Norway, prison sentences are very rare, and the country has just a single prison, which is broadly quite 'soft'; prisoners are allowed to leave their cells at most times, and are referred to primarily as 'students', as they spend most of their time in education. By contrast, in the USA, more than 2 million people are imprisoned at any one time, with a further 5 million on parole or probation (allowing them to be called back if they misbehave); this means that fully 2.2 per cent of the US population is under 'correctional supervision'.

Pros

[1] Prison is the right punishment for all crimes against property and all violent crimes. The primary purposes of punishment are deterrent, retribution and prevention. Prison serves all of these purposes well. The threat of the complete loss of liberty in a prison sentence deters potential criminals; criminals who are in prison are prevented, for that period, from committing further crimes; and prison is also society's way to gain retribution from an offender for what he or she has done. Rehabilitation is not part of the purpose of punishment and is very much a secondary concern of the justice system.

[2] Prison works. Rehabilitation (counselling, psychiatric treatment, and work in the community) is a soft option for criminals who will simply feel that they can continue to offend with virtual impunity so long as they volunteer for counselling and community work. The justice system must be seen to be strong in its imposition of punishments if the fight against crime is to be won. Prison is the best form of punishment to send out this strong message.

Cons

[1] Prison is the wrong form of punishment for all but the most serious crimes (e.g. rape, murder). If we really want to reduce crime and live in a safer society, we need to understand criminals as well as having our retribution against them for the wrongs they have done. Punishment without rehabilitation is merely dealing temporarily with the symptoms rather than addressing the root causes. A criminal who is put in prison cannot offend for that period of time, but when s/he comes out, s/he will be the same person – or worse – and will simply go straight back to a life of crime. Rehabilitation must go together with deterrence, retribution and prevention as an integral primary concern of the justice system.

[2] Prison does not work. Centuries of reliance on the retributive imprisonment system have failed to stem the increasing crime rate. The way to reduce crime is to change people's beliefs and habits of behaviour – this is most effectively done by counselling and especially by integration into the community. If young people can be set to work on community

[3] For society to function we must maintain a strong sense of individual moral responsibility. We cannot allow people to absolve themselves of moral responsibility on the grounds of 'medical', 'psychological' or 'social' dysfunction. People have even claimed in their defence that they are genetically predisposed to crime and so should be treated leniently. These excuses are simply ways of hiding from the fact of moral transgression. A culture of rehabilitation denies individual responsibility and thus erodes the moral fabric of society. Prison sentences, enforced strictly, reinforce the crucial notion of individual responsibility for actions.

Possible motions

This House would condemn more and understand less.
This House would be tough on crime.
This House would only use prison for violent offenders.

Related topics

Mandatory prison sentences
Capital punishment
Prisoners' right to vote, denial of
Zero tolerance
Community sentencing

regeneration projects rather than sent to young offenders' centres – which in effect are often little more than 'academies of crime' – they will have a greatly increased chance of living a life free of crime in the future. In one American study, drugs offenders who spent 12 months in prison followed by 6 months' drugs rehabilitation and training in skills for future employment had a 50 per cent lower re-offence rate than those imprisoned for similar offences for the whole 18 months.

[3] The autonomous morally responsible self is a myth. The victims of sexual abusers do not go on to become sexual abusers themselves just because, by coincidence, they are morally wicked people too. Children brought up with poverty, drugs and violence do not grow up to be criminals or drug users because they are just morally bad individuals. The advocate of radical individual responsibility is peddling an ineffective, simplistic and vindictive myth. In truth, criminal behaviours have complex psychological and social causes that stretch well beyond the boundary of the individual. Parents, teachers and society at large must be responsible for teaching by example and understanding and healing disturbed individuals. Social regeneration through employment, reintegration of offenders into communities, the renewal of the family, counselling and psychiatry, rather than blank retribution through imprisonment, are the ways to reduce crime.

Racial profiling

Racial profiling refers to the policing policy of focusing efforts in crime prevention on particular minority groups who are thought to be involved more often in certain types of crime. The policy is *not* about acting on specific pieces of intelligence ('There is a suspect, who is 6 foot 3 and Afro-Caribbean'), but about a more general approach to the use of stop-and-search powers, extra checks at airports and so on. Clearly, which minorities are targeted is a contextual factor; if seeking to prevent Islamic terrorism, it will probably involve searching South Asian men more often at airports, but if concerned about gun crime in inner-city Baltimore, it will focus on young male African Americans.

Pros

[1] Racial profiling is the best way of deploying scarce police resources. We cannot search everyone, so we should search those whom we can, based on factors which make them more likely to be involved in criminal activity. Nothing about this says that such relationships are innate, or that 'all of X minority are criminals', but simply works off statistical facts that we know exist.

[2] This policy will catch criminals. Too often, gangs are based on race; in New York, for instance, many gangs divide along the lines of the African countries from which they first migrated. This makes it easy to identify specific types of crime, and catch the potential perpetrators and prevent them.

[3] This policy will not radicalise minorities. In fact, they will welcome it, as criminal acts often disproportionately affect the minorities from which they emanate. Ultimately, if we are able to reduce violent and drug-related crime among African Americans, for instance, that is something for which they will be grateful. That is particularly so as, often, predominantly minority areas are abandoned by the police altogether – an approach this policy reverses.

Cons

[1] It is unacceptable to tar whole groups with the brush of a particularly trouble-some subgroup. No one should be treated unfairly just on the basis of their race, but this policy does exactly that; people are more likely to have their liberties invaded by being searched, merely because they are black or Muslim.

[2] Terrorists will readily be able to cir-cumvent this policy, because terrorist groups represent ideological, not purely ethnic, causes, and so they will use non-stereotypical ethnicities to conduct their terrorist acts. For instance, the hijacking of an El Al plane from Israel to Entebbe, Uganda, in 1976 was conducted on behalf of Palestinian terrorists, but by white members of Germany's Baader-Meinhof gang; such sharing agreements between terror groups will simply be revived.

[3] This policy will massively radicalise minorities. If we treat every member of a minority as though they are a criminal or a terrorist, they will rightly and under-standably be hugely offended. That in turn makes them turn against the state, and so be less likely to co-operate with the police. But this becomes particularly prob-lematic when people are falsely accused or convicted, cementing the impression of the state and police as evil, and driving people into the arms of terrorists.

Right to bear arms

The continued and rising death toll from gun crime in the USA often makes it seem baffling that that country has stuck so closely to the right to bear arms contained in the Second Amendment to its Constitution, but there is still strong public support for it. The most high-profile incidents tend to occur in schools and universities (Columbine High, Virginia Tech, Sandy Hook), but gun crime clearly in fact kills far more people as a result of gang violence and other more run-of-the-mill crime. This debate requires the Proposition team to take a strong, principled stance on self-defence, but even so, they cannot ignore practical consequences.

Pros

[1] Ownership of guns must be allowed because it is necessary to vindicate the basic human right to self-defence. We acknowledge that the state cannot be everywhere at all times for us, and in those instances, we need the ability to defend ourselves. Given that criminals will always have guns, individual citizens must be able to protect themselves against them in a similarly effective manner.

[2] Tragedies involving the use of handguns by criminals and by psychopaths and other unbalanced individuals will always occur. Such people will not be deterred by legislation any more than they are by reason, humanity or conscience. The incidence of such tragedies will not be affected by banning handguns.

[3] Ownership of guns actually reduces aggregate crime, because it makes criminals less willing to start criminal activities

Cons

[1] Self-defence is, of course, important, but handguns are not the answer. When an assailant or intruder is armed with a gun, pulling a gun oneself is merely dangerous and inflammatory, greatly increasing the chance that one or both parties will be injured or killed. Allowing the ownership of handguns (rather than teaching unarmed forms of self-defence) will engender a mentality of vigilantism, encouraged further by rhetoric about 'criminals getting the upper hand'. It is the job of the police, not of private citizens, to be armed and capable of tackling armed criminals.

[2] Tragedies such as the massacre at Sandy Hook in November 2012 are the indirect result of the ownership of handguns. The Columbine High School shooter (2004) had been able to own guns in advance of his shooting and practise his actions; if that had not been allowed, he would not have

because of the fear of armed retaliation. Finland, Israel and Switzerland all have very low rates of crime and allow people to own guns and carry them in public; if they see an attack beginning, they are able to intervene and end it instantaneously.

Possible motions

This House believes that the right to bear arms is dependent on the existence of a 'well-regulated militia'.

This House would legalise handguns.

Related topics

Police, arming of the

been able to use a gun and the tragedy would most likely not have occurred. Banning handguns would not eliminate such tragedies altogether, but would significantly reduce their incidence. There would simply be fewer guns in circulation and fewer people capable of using them.

[3] The correlation between gun ownership and higher death rates is not a perfect one; there are some outliers, like the countries mentioned by the Proposition team, but all of them have compulsory national service, and so anyone using a gun is trained. By contrast, in the USA, where the users of guns are untrained, they are highly dangerous; they may misfire, or not be able to defend themselves in time to prevent their attacker also opening fire. Overall, citizen gun ownership creates an 'arms race' with criminals, making them more likely to use offensive weapons in their crimes.

Sex offenders, chemical castration of

Castration is the removal of any sexual gland (the testes or ovaries) in males or females. This debate is about the process of administering drugs to sex offenders to remove all function in those glands; the main drug used to destroy testicular function is called Depo-Provera. Policies are of two types: voluntary and mandatory. Voluntary castrations are less contentious; sex offenders may opt to take the drugs. Mandatory ones are the meat of this debate. In some US states, castration is mandatory after two sexual offences; in others, it is at the judge's discretion. In some countries including Poland, Moldova and Estonia, castration can be compulsory immediately upon conviction.

Pros

[1] One of the principal purposes of the punishment for any crime is prevention of re-offence. Chemical castration would take away the sex drive of sex offenders and thus guarantee that they would not re-offend. It would also be a strong deter-

Cons

[1] Chemical castration is not an acceptable form of punishment. In a civilised society, we do not permanently physically alter people as a form of punishment, but always allow for rehabilitation of some kind after a prison sentence has been

rent. It is therefore an effective and appropriate punishment.

[2] Sex offenders currently pose a problem for the criminal justice system. They are often victimised in prison and subjected to a witch-hunt and, on their release, are hounded out of each new community by concerned members of the public. Chemical castration would make these people safe – they could live in the community without posing a threat. This would avoid their abuse in prisons, would help reduce the ever-increasing prison population and would allay the fears of concerned members of a community.

[3] For the sake of the offender, chemical castration is the best solution. Offenders often feel that they are ill, or possessed by a physical force outside their control from which they long to be freed. Chemical castration would liberate them from the mental torture and resulting crimes of their condition by removing their sexual drive.

served. Also, as with the death penalty, miscarriages of justice would have disastrous permanent consequences if chemical castration were the sentence for all sex offences. Would first-time sex offenders be chemically castrated? The punishment is extreme and crude. Prison sentences and psychiatric treatment are to be preferred.

[2] We cannot be confident that chemical castration would be such a magical cure. If sex offending really is just the result of chemical drives, then whatever the punishment, it will not work as a deterrent. Prison would still be needed as a form of deterrent and also to protect society even from those who have been chemically castrated. As for the public's response, the fear of parents and other members of the community will not be allayed by a chemical procedure – sex offenders will still be feared and hated and the objects of witch-hunts.

[3] Our first thought should be to punish the sex offender. Second, when it comes to treating the sex offender, a more subtle form of counselling and rehabilitation is required, rather than just putting our faith in a one-off physical treatment.

Possible motions

This House would chemically castrate sex offenders.

This House believes that sex offending can be chemically cured.

Related topics

Prison v. rehabilitation

Televised trials

In some countries, especially the USA, criminal trials are commonly televised, and can be both broadcast live in full, or shown in highlight form. In other countries, especially the UK, there has generally been a strong ban on such coverage, although in 2004 it was briefly experimented with. This debate is about *criminal* trials; civil cases are rarely dramatic enough, or of enough public interest, for anyone to care about broadcasting them (although the UK Supreme Court does live-stream its hearings on the Internet, without many viewers!). Perhaps the most famous example is the 1995 trial of former American footballer O. J. Simpson for the murder of his ex-wife and a male friend, but other high-profile cases, such as singer Michael Jackson's sexual abuse trial, have also been broadcast.

Pros

[1] The judicial process is currently mysterious and threatening to most ordinary people. If they find themselves in court, they will be baffled and intimidated by the strange language and procedures. The televising of trials and other judicial proceedings will demystify the legal process and serve to educate the public about the judicial process. Only real court proceedings can truly perform this educative function – TV and film portrayals are over-dramatised, glamorised and unrealistic. Nobody will watch a public information film, but people will watch a real trial.

[2] Currently, judicial proceedings are only accessible to the public at large via news reports in the media, which are partial and potentially biased. The television camera does not lie. Allowing TV cameras in courts will provide full, accurate and honest coverage of exactly what happens in any given case. Whatever media spin or reportage is laid over the TV coverage, the proceedings will be in full view of the public, which at the moment they are not.

[3] It is democratic to allow cameras in courts. The scrutiny made widely possible by television coverage of court proceedings will create healthy criticism of the process and personnel of the judicial system, and will make them answerable. Unfair laws, prejudicial practices and

Cons

[1] Mock trials in films and soap operas are often realistic and give everybody a very good idea of what happens in a courtroom. Increasingly great attention is paid to detail in historical and popular films, and the picture of the judicial system portrayed is reliable and accurate. If this is not considered enough, public information films of mock trials or reconstructions of famous past trials can be shown – television coverage of actual trials is not necessary.

[2] There are already full and accurate records of court proceedings available to anyone who is interested in them. Legal reports in reputable newspapers are reliable and objective. Anyone truly interested in the judicial system can also sit in the public gallery of most courts. The TV media will in fact invariably create a much more distorted picture of a trial – as in the famous case of the O. J. Simpson trial which became a 'media zoo'. Most people will not have the time or inclination to sit and watch every minute of the process of a trial, but will rely on 30-second 'sound bites' in the evening news with the biased spin of the TV journalists presenting the case. Cameras in courts will increase media distortion of trials.

[3] Injustices in the judicial system and incompetence of judges and lawyers are already fully reported in the press and broadcast media. There is no need to see

incompetent lawyers and judges will be exposed to a wide public.

[4] If trials are televised, a huge audience is made aware of the case and the evidence, and crucial witnesses may come forward who would otherwise have been ignorant of the case and their potential role in it. Televising trials will thus increase the chance of a fair trial.

Possible motions

This House would put cameras in the courtroom.

This House believes that justice should be blind.

Related topics

Community sentencing
Judges, election of
Privacy of public figures

actual pictures of scenes in a courtroom to believe these news stories or to act upon them. Judges have been forced to resign for widely publicised incompetence in Britain, despite the lack of television cameras in courts. There are also many groups campaigning for fairer legal status; for instance, for homosexual rights, despite the lack of televised judicial proceedings. Unfairness and incompetence will be reported on and campaigned against with or without cameras in courts.

[4] Far from creating fairer trials, TV coverage will create more miscarriages of justice. Jurors will inevitably be swayed by high-profile TV reporting of cases and people will come forward as witnesses not because they have crucial evidence, but because they want to become TV stars. American TV talk shows demonstrate what people are prepared to do and say to get on television – the same cannot be said about getting into the legal pages of a national newspaper. Also, in countries such as the USA where judges are elected, the televising of trials will lead to judges performing to the electorate by, for example, imposing harsher sentences than they otherwise might.

Terrorist suspects, torture of

It is hard to know precisely how widespread torture by security services is, because it is typically kept secret, since it is a clear violation of international, European and (in most states) domestic law, which governments do not want to admit to. It is often referred to by euphemisms, of which 'enhanced interrogation' has recently become the best known. Torture techniques vary; some countries are thought to use beatings or electric shocks to torture, but Western techniques tend to be more clinical; IRA suspects were often forced to stand in uncomfortable positions for hours on end, or subjected to light and noise torture, while the US military at Guantanamo Bay used 'water-boarding', where suspects are wrapped in cling film and have water poured on them to simulate drowning. It is hard to know exactly how much information is obtained from torture, given that it is so secret. It is also hard to deal with the problem of complicity with torture, because many security services who practise it routinely are those with whom Western intelligence must co-operate (in the Middle East and South Asia); in consequence, even when they do not know about it directly, the CIA and MI6 will often be working from information obtained via torture.

Pros

[1] Sometimes torture is necessary to save lives. Where a terrorist possesses information that might lead to the prevention of imminent terrorist attacks, it is legitimate to violate their rights to ensure the protection of many others' lives. This argument has two components. First, while torture is undeniably a serious invasion of someone's bodily autonomy, that is less bad than death; thus, if just one life can be saved as a result, we should use torture. Second, because terrorist acts often have high death tolls, many lives may be saved by torturing just one person. As such, balancing the competing interests involved favours torture.

[2] While torture is typically used on those who have not yet been convicted, that should not be a bar to using it. First, it will rarely be the case that someone who is totally innocent is tortured; they are only being detained in the first instance because security services have some reasonable suspicion of their guilt. Moreover, if the occasional innocent person is tortured, that is an acceptable cost of the need to protect the public.

[3] The 'ticking bomb' scenario is perhaps the best illustration of why torture will sometimes be morally acceptable. Suppose we knew that a bomb was located somewhere, but were not sure where that was, and further knew that a particular terrorist

Cons

[1] The right not to be tortured is not the kind of right that can be overridden for mere utilitarian considerations. The invasion of rights is so serious that it is not the kind of thing that civilised societies should ever be complicit in. In particular, the deliberate infliction of pain on fellow human beings is something we should treat with great caution, especially when it involves such cruel and dehumanising practices.

[2] Torture involves punishing those who have not been found guilty of the offence on which information is being sought. This is an unacceptable curtailment of due process, especially as it creates a very real risk that innocent people will be subjected to the cruellest punishments available to us, when they have done nothing wrong.

[3] In fact, there is no known example of a real 'ticking bomb' scenario ever occurring; rather, this commonly made argument for torture rests on an imaginary and distant set of facts coming about, which in practice rarely would, if ever. Rather, torture becomes a crutch for security services, who do not look to alternative ways of obtaining the information, and so it becomes far more widespread than it needs to be.

[4] Rather than producing large amounts of information, torture is necessarily highly

in our custody did possess that information, but was unwilling to give it to us. In that scenario, not torturing is to choose the deaths of a large number of innocent civilians, when they are clearly preventable. This highlights the fact that, while some might oppose torture on the grounds that there are alternative ways of gathering information, sometimes, in the short run, torture will be necessary.

[4] Terrorists tend to be highly ideological, with a belief in the correctness of their cause drilled into them. Often this is because they are religious, and so they believe that Heaven awaits them if they successfully fulfil their terrorist objectives. Such people are highly unlikely to ever give information unless they are coerced, so torture is necessary to acquire any real information from terrorist cells. Moreover, it is rarely possible to acquire such information via other routes; terrorists tend not to leave paper trails, or even make many phone calls that could be intercepted, and are located in complex networks all around the world. So when a terrorist is in our custody, it is vital that we act accordingly to get this information.

[5] Torture can help reduce radicalisation. If torture can be used in a targeted way, this reduces the need for blanket, more invasive measures like racial profiling, stop-and-search, phone tapping, etc., which are far more likely to alienate minority communities, as they actually touch the everyday lives of far more people.

limited for two reasons. First, terrorists can give false information, which may in fact lead us down the wrong path in the short term; such false 'leads' can in fact damage anti-terrorist measures overall. Second, they may well not possess the information being sought, and so will say anything to get out of the situation. Again, this leads to incorrect information.

[5] Torture runs the risk of radicalising large groups of people to further acts of terrorism. Evidence from Israel, for instance, shows that the families of victims of torture by the Israeli Defense Forces are much more likely to become terrorists themselves; having witnessed people close to them being harmed, they are understandably angry, and more likely to turn to violence. Moreover, torture serves as a recruitment tool for terrorist groups by advertising that the claims of Western liberal democracies to be more 'civilised' and respectful of human rights are, in fact, far from true.

Possible motions

This House believes that torture is a necessary evil.

This House would use torture in the war on terror.

This House would never allow evidence obtained by torture to be used in court.

Related topics

Terrorists, negotiation with
Terrorism, justifiability of
Dictators, assassination of

Zero tolerance

'Zero tolerance' is a phrase that first came to light as a description of the crackdown on petty crime in New York City by William Bratton, police commissioner for that city, appointed by Mayor Rudolph Giuliani in January 1994. The aim of zero tolerance is to prevent petty criminals graduating to serious crime by imposing immediate and harsh sentences for petty offences such as underage drinking, small-scale drug use and dealing, shoplifting or vandalism (rather than using cautions or fines). It is this particular law-and-order policy that the arguments below are about. 'Zero tolerance' is, however, a phrase that has come to be used in a panoply of other contexts to mean, for example, a tough and uncompromising approach to racism, fascism or violence against women.

Pros

[1] We need to find innovative and effective new weapons in the ongoing fight against crime. Zero tolerance is just such a weapon. It sends a clear, tough message that the state will condemn and punish rather than be soft and 'understanding'. This stance functions as an effective deterrent to potential offenders, especially potential young offenders, and also raises public confidence in the police and judiciary.

[2] Zero tolerance works. Murders in New York City fell by 40 per cent between 1993 and 1997, while robberies and shootings fell by 30 per cent and 35 per cent respectively. These are phenomenally impressive results. Cities in Britain (e.g. Coventry) and Australia (e.g. Melbourne) have achieved similar impressive results through implementing zero tolerance of the use of drugs and alcohol in public places. Racism in police forces and in society at large is a problem, but it is long-term and endemic, not the result of this particular policing initiative.

[3] Zero tolerance not only prevents young offenders from graduating to serious crime,

Cons

[1] Zero tolerance is precisely the wrong way to approach crime. Understanding and rehabilitation rather than the macho rhetoric of punishment and condemnation are the key to reducing crime. And far from raising public confidence in the police and judiciary, it makes them alienating and inflexible figures set against society, rather than agencies that can work with and for members of their community.

[2] New York's gain is its neighbours' loss. A high-profile crackdown on petty crime in one place simply makes the petty criminal move elsewhere to ply his/her trade. These results are bought at a heavy cost. Complaints of brutality against the New York Police Department have soared since the introduction of zero tolerance. Some police seem to have used the initiative as an occasion to oppress black communities. Zero tolerance may not cause racism, but it serves to increase and exacerbate it. Also, like mandatory sentencing, zero tolerance necessarily reduces judicial discretion in individual cases. A harsh fine or prison sentence may be inappropriate and counterproductive in

it also breaks the back of organised crime by depleting the ranks of the 'foot soldiers', especially small-time drug dealers who together provide the power base and financial resources for drugs barons and Mafia bosses. Without these petty criminals on the streets, organised crime ceases to flourish.

Possible motions

This House would have zero tolerance.

This House would crack down on petty crime.

This House would be tough on crime.

Related topics

Mandatory prison sentences

Child curfews

Capital punishment

Sports teams punished for the behaviour of fans

Prison v. rehabilitation

many cases, but zero tolerance insists that no leniency, subtlety or professional judgement be shown by judges.

[3] Small-time drug dealers and petty thieves are not the real criminals. They are unfortunates trying to escape from poverty and deprivation through the income they can make through petty crime. Not only are they not the real criminals, they are also indefinitely replaceable from among the ranks of the poor and deprived. Once one set of petty criminals is locked up, a new set will emerge to replace them. The multi-million dollar fraudsters, money launderers and drug barons are the ones who must really be removed to bring down the criminal system.

SECTION H

Health, science and technology

Cars in city centres, banning of

City centres around the world have taken different approaches to dealing with the gridlock and pollution that an abundance of cars can cause. London has a congestion charge, Los Angeles and Sydney have 'carpool' lanes and Athens restricts the days on which cars can enter the city. This debate suggests going further with an outright ban on cars in city centres. A definition should make sure to detail any exemptions the Proposition team wishes to make, such as emergency vehicles, taxis, deliveries or cars for people with disabilities, but be aware that too many exemptions could weaken the case.

Pros

[1] We must lower CO_2 emission levels to address global warming and cars are major contributors. If we were to ban cars from city centres, we would significantly reduce the overall number of journeys taken by car and we might well see lower car ownership overall. This would be good for the planet.

[2] Car emissions are worse in city centres because of their concentration. Pollution from car fumes causes serious health problems including asthma, especially for children who grow up living near busy roads. The same fumes also damage historic buildings. In some cities, the smog is so bad it is visible.

[3] In many more economically developed countries, road accidents are the single biggest cause of deaths in children and teenagers. Banning cars from city centres would slash accident rates and save lives as many schools and houses are on busy roads. Bus drivers do not drink and drive, speed, or talk on their phones while driving; it is private car drivers who cause accidents. With the trend for more cycling, we have also seen increased rates of cyclist fatalities that could be prevented.

[4] Traffic in many city centres is horrendous. Banning cars would get the city

Cons

[1] Emissions of CO_2 must be cut, but this is not the way to do it. Banning cars from city centres simply displaces the traffic to the suburbs and out of town. It possibly causes longer journeys leading to more emissions overall. CO_2 levels should be tackled at the level of industry and energy reduction.

[2] Car emissions can be cut in city centres without banning cars outright. This could be done by incentivising car pools or charging people to drive in the city. These measures encourage people to make only essential journeys and to think about fuel efficiency without removing the liberty to drive. Technology continues to clean up cars. Catalytic converters and unleaded petrol make a big difference to air quality and the future may lie with hybrid or electric cars.

[3] Road safety should be a priority and speed limits and other driving regulations should be pursued with zero tolerance to keep accidents to a minimum. Road safety education is also essential in schools. With these measures, it is not necessary to ban cars from city centres where traffic and low speed limits keep accident rates down.

moving again as buses and taxis would no longer be stuck in gridlock. This would also benefit emergency vehicles.

[5] Banning cars would see an improvement in public transport as more money would be in the system. This in turn would remove the reason that many people wish to drive (that public transport is not good enough) and so would create a virtuous cycle.

[6] Shops and businesses would get a boost as pedestrian areas are pleasant and attract visitors. *Al fresco* dining and street entertainment would replace congested roads, and this would improve everyone's quality of life. Many businesses are already seeing an increase in online shopping and this may increase as people find it more convenient, but there would be no net drop in sales as demand would not decrease.

[7] Banning cars would also encourage more people to walk and cycle which would lead to a public health benefit in the reduction of conditions such as obesity, heart disease and strokes.

Possible motions

This House would ban cars from city centres.
This House believes that the modern city should be car-free.

Related topics

Vegetarianism
Global warming: binding emission targets for

[4] People can choose whether they wish to drive in traffic or find an alternative way of travelling. Bus lanes can protect buses from the worst traffic and cars make way for emergency vehicles, so this is not a problem. London operates a congestion charge to discourage car journeys, which is preferable to a ban.

[5] Public transport is not reliable. It is often an unpleasant experience where one may be squashed in a crowded carriage. People should have an alternative choice for travel. Public transport is also not appropriate for many journeys; for example, a shopping trip where you have to carry heavy bags. It is also hard for those travelling with children or those with illness or disabilities.

[6] Banning cars from city centres would have negative economic effects. Shops and businesses would be forced to close as poor access to them would drive away customers who would instead visit supermarkets and malls outside the centre. There would also be job losses in the car industry and related businesses which exist in cities, such as garages, car parks and car washes.

[7] It is not the job of the government to force people to exercise. People should be informed of the benefits and then be allowed to choose for themselves. The government can seek to influence people's behaviour through measures such as increasing fuel duty, but freedom of choice should not be restricted.

Contraception for under-age girls

Most countries have an 'age of consent' for sex of 16 or 18, under which it is illegal for young people to engage in sexual activity. In spite of this, many such jurisdictions will make contraceptives available, sometimes even free, to girls under the age of 16. This debate questions whether that juxtaposition makes sense. The objectives of policy in this area are, on the one hand, to prevent teenage pregnancy and the spread of sexually transmitted diseases (STDs); and, on the other hand, to preserve young people's opportunities to live their lives free from the pressures and potential harms of sexual activity.

Pros

[1] Young people will experiment with sex regardless of what the state, their doctor or anyone else says. In recent years, teen pregnancy has been rising dramatically in many countries. There has also been an increase in STDs. The relative difficulty of access to free contraception is one of the most obvious reasons for this. If we know that young people will have sex anyway, we should do whatever we can to make sure that it is as safe as possible.

[2] Young women should be given the information and resources to stand up for themselves and make informed choices. Not all parents are able or willing to give their daughters these resources. Contraception must be just one facet of a comprehensive sexual health and education programme, encompassing schools and society at large. Research suggests that such programmes delay sexual activity rather than promoting it.

[3] Children should not be kept ignorant and in the dark about sex, and then be expected suddenly to be 'grown up' when they hit 16. Delaying problems is no substitute for solving them. Parents often find it difficult to raise issues of sex with their children – and yet under 5 per cent

Cons

[1] If it is illegal for an under-age girl to have sex, it should surely be illegal for anybody to aid and abet her in that activity. Moreover, the apparent official sanctioning of such behaviour can only encourage it. This is not just about the enforcement of Victorian-era morality. There are very sound policy reasons for under-age sex to be prohibited. First of all, if it is with an older person, there is a serious risk of emotional manipulation, such that real consent is absent. But even with parties of the same age, young people may not be ready for the emotional consequences of sex.

[2] We should not be encouraging young people to have sex at an early age. Contraception is far from being 100 per cent effective, and failure can lead to unwanted pregnancy and/or STDs. Most contraception, even if effective, cannot prevent sexually transmitted diseases; in all cases, it is not certain that transmission will be prevented. Our resources would be better targeted at discouraging under-age sexual intercourse.

[3] Children already have to cope with a barrage of sexual images from a multitude of sources (pop videos, magazines, films,

of parents opt out of optional sex education lessons for their children. Far from fighting against sex education, parents are crying out for it.

the Internet); the state should not be joining in the assault. It is parents who should be empowered to provide a moral framework for their children, rather than doctors or the government.

Possible motions
This House would make contraception freely available.
This House believes that if you are old enough to be having sex, then you are old enough to use contraception.

Related topics
Sex education
Parents, responsibility for the criminal acts of their children

Cosmetic surgery, banning of

Cosmetic surgery is a sub-category of 'plastic' surgery, which is the use of surgical techniques to change physical appearance, and derives from the Greek word *plastikos* for 'able to be moulded'. The other category, which this debate is not about, is 'reconstructive' surgery, which helps people recovering from severely deforming accidents to look as they did before. Cosmetic surgery is about procedures to make subjects more attractive. In 2011, there were over 1.6 million cosmetic procedures in the USA alone; 91 per cent of those were performed on women.

Pros

[1] Cosmetic surgery reflects an unhealthy social obsession with physical appearance, which is not one which we should accept. Individuals are unlikely to be happy with the way they see themselves after the procedure, because they have falsely been promised an unreasonable idea of beauty which they cannot in fact attain. Many people become 'addicted' to cosmetic surgery, having endless procedures in pursuit of this unreasonable ideal.

Cons

[1] It is not clear that caring about physical appearance is 'unhealthy'; we allow people to work hard to improve their intelligence, and taking steps to make themselves more attractive is not different. Second, even if it were, surgery cannot be meaningfully distinguished from extreme dieting, the use of huge quantities of make-up or the huge numbers of non-surgical cosmetic 'procedures' like Botox injections; if those things are to be allowed, then surely cosmetic surgery is

[2] Cosmetic surgery is high-risk; many people end up with serious complications because, like any surgery, there are unexpected surprises, such as infections or surgical errors. Given this possibility, individuals should not be allowed to make the irrational decision to take such risks with their physical safety, especially for such trivial gains.

[3] Cosmetic surgery objectifies women. Although there are cosmetic procedures for men, they are the overwhelming minority; for the most part, such procedures are conceived for, marketed at and performed on women. This encourages women to believe that their physical appearance is of primary importance, which is particularly bad for young girls, who should not be taught that they must be permanently seeking to make themselves more attractive, even if it entails physical harm.

Possible motions

This House would ban cosmetic surgery.
This House believes that going under the knife for the sake of appearance is a step too far.

Related topics

Protective legislation v. individual freedom
Beauty contests, banning of
Size zero models, banning of

merely a route by which something more successfully transformative could be achieved.

[2] Cosmetic surgery may have some risks, but it is far less risky than other forms of surgery, including those such as eye surgery which aim not at saving life, but simply making it better. Those are risks that individuals have to be allowed to balance for themselves. Moreover, for individuals with body dysmorphic disorder (where they grow to hate a certain aspect of their physical appearance), the pain of living with that may be much greater than any risks from surgery.

[3] Cosmetic surgery is increasingly becoming a cross-gender choice, which plenty of men make too. Moreover, who is the government to tell individual women what they should and should not consider to be the 'feminist' choice? If women believe that having cosmetic surgery is something that will make them happy, then regardless of the social structures that might condition that choice, they should be allowed to do so.

DNA database, universal

Many countries have set up DNA databases of convicted criminals. Britain has controversially included the DNA of all those suspected of a crime even if there was no conviction, but now must delete those records after two years if there has been no conviction. But should governments set up DNA databases for all their citizens? Such DNA databases could have wide-ranging uses for research, health and crime, but many think the invasion of privacy is too great. A debate could be had just about criminal databases, but this article looks at the introduction of a universal database.

Pros

[1] A universal database would be an invaluable tool in fighting crime. Many crime scenes contain blood, saliva or semen and these could be matched against a database. Alongside more traditional investigative methods, this could lead to more criminals being caught faster and more criminals being caught overall.

[2] A DNA database would also be useful to the judicial process; it can help a jury reach a verdict more expeditiously. It may even act as a deterrent to crimes as people would know that their DNA would identify and convict them.

[3] There are public health benefits to a universal DNA database. Researchers would be able to use the database to track genes and advance our understanding of predictive and preventative medicine. As the Human Genome Project progresses, this is the next step in understanding our genetic make-up.

[4] There are a range of other miscellaneous benefits including identifying bodies, establishing paternity and tracing missing children.

[5] We should not be concerned about the loss of privacy here. The information would be protected and its use would be regulated; for example, legislation could be passed to prevent employers or insurance companies having access to an individual's genetic information. Innocent people have nothing to fear from the police being able to run a DNA search on them. Research would be done with anonymised data.

[6] The cost of producing and maintaining a database may well be balanced out by the saving of police time and the advances in preventative medicine.

Cons

[1] The police can already search for the DNA of convicted criminals. Additionally, they can take samples from suspects to check. DNA is most useful in violent and sexual crimes, not many of which are committed by first-time criminals who do not know the victims. The effect of this, therefore, would be minimal and would not justify keeping the DNA of the whole population, most of whom will never commit a crime. The state should not treat its citizens as potential criminals from birth.

[2] Once a suspect has been identified by traditional policing methods, DNA evidence can be used. A sample can then be taken that can help to clear somebody's name or to establish a guilty verdict. If the only available evidence is a DNA match from the database, then something may well be wrong, but juries can be unduly swayed by what they see as 'indisputable' evidence.

[3] The scientific community needs to convince people to donate their DNA in order to further research – it cannot expect it to be taken without consent. Blood and organs also have large medical benefits, but we accept that consent must be given before they can be used, even after death.

[4] People should be able voluntarily to give DNA samples if the situation arises; for example, to establish paternity or to check for hereditary diseases, but the choice should be theirs and the information should not be stored afterwards. That way, many of the benefits of DNA technology can be gained without the downsides.

Possible motions

This House would establish a universal DNA database.

This House asks the government to keep its hands off my DNA.

Related topics

Eugenics: IVF and genetic screening

Genetic engineering

National identity cards

[5] This is a huge invasion of privacy and a step towards a Big Brother state. The government should not be able to store the very essence of our identity and information about our genetic propensities which we do not even know ourselves. The potential for abuse of the database is huge. Insurance companies, employers and even the government itself may all want to see what is encoded in our genes, but that is our private information. In addition, we do not know what else we will discover that DNA carries, so we do not even understand the scale of the risk. Governments do not have a good record of keeping large amounts of information secure, and if this data were hacked, anybody could then have access to the secrets of our genes.

[6] The financial cost of a DNA database would be very high and cannot be justified by the limited benefits.

Environmental responsibility, developed world should take more

The debate about how to tackle global warming presents a paradox. On the one hand, most of the damage done to the environment historically was done by Western nations, which industrialised first, and reaped the economic benefits. On the other hand, many of the world's most significant producers of CO_2 today are developing countries, which are only just industrialising, and their role in CO_2 emissions is only growing. China is the largest single polluter (though it pollutes less per person than the USA), with 16.4 per cent of the global emissions total in 2011, with America a close second with 15.7 per cent. Brazil, Indonesia, Russia and India (all developing as middle-income nations) occupy places three to six in the league table of carbon producers (though if the EU is counted as one entity rather than 27 separate countries, it rises to third place). This paradox therefore presents a difficult question: should developed countries bear more of the burden for reducing emissions and preventing global warming?

Pros

[1] Most of the CO_2 in the atmosphere as a result of man-made action today was put there by the developed world; thus, they are the ones primarily responsible for the damage. Moreover, they are also the ones who have benefited from it historically, getting rich by industrialising before the developing world could catch up, and so are more able to absorb the substantial economic costs of reducing emissions.

[2] The developed world still produces a significant, if not the most significant, share of global emissions. As such, it would be perfectly viable and successful for these countries to prevent climate change by reducing their own emissions. For instance, the G8 Club of rich nations produces one-third of emissions on their own; they could make substantial inroads into the problem of carbon emissions simply by cutting that number.

[3] Who is *affected* by emissions is not the question; what is important is who *causes* them. If we accept that it is possible for countries to owe obligations to those outside their borders, then surely the obligation not to create brutal environmental destruction is one of them? Moreover, if we were to deny that obligation, then treating the 'developing world' as a whole would make no sense; it is not a coherent collective that shares any kind of identity, so could not be expected to act in collective interests.

Cons

[1] The developed world did emit a lot of CO_2 in the past, but it did not know that what it was doing was damaging; at the time that industrialisation began, we did not realise that global warming was occurring, and certainly not that it was a man-made phenomenon. By contrast, the developing world's current refusal means that it is wilfully and with foresight destroying the environment.

[2] It is simply not possible to create the kind of change we need without involving the developing world. Not only do less developed countries now represent the bulk of the world's emissions, but their emissions are rising; as such, even if developed countries were to cut their emissions, the emissions would simply be replaced. Moreover, a global political consensus is required to attain change, which cannot be done if the developing world shirks responsibility.

[3] The developing world should take the lead in preventing emissions, because it is these countries that will be most affected if they rise. For instance, flooding, one of the primary environmental consequences of global warming, threatens to largely wipe out Bangladesh and create a refugee crisis in that region. That is a burden that the developing world must deal with.

Eugenics: IVF and genetic screening

'Eugenics', meaning 'good breeding', was first used by the English scientist Francis Galton in 1883 to refer to the study of ways to improve the mental and physical characteristics of the human race through targeted mating. It did not then have the sinister overtones that it has since acquired through association with the attempts in Nazi Germany to exterminate entire racial and social groups. Modern techniques such as genetic engineering – and in particular, the genetic screening of embryos created by *in vitro* fertilisation (IVF) – have again raised the question of whether we should intervene to determine the biological make-up of our children.

Pros

[1] The process of IVF does not involve any pernicious manipulation of genes, and is already widely used. Using IVF, a large number of embryos can be made from the sperm and eggs of the parents. A cell biopsy can be done on each embryo and the DNA from the cell can be screened. This will tell the parents which of the embryos has the lowest risk of heart disease, cancer or diabetes and which will contract genetic diseases such as Alzheimer's, muscular dystrophy, haemophilia or cystic fibrosis later in life. This technology already exists, and it is inevitable and understandable that parents will want to use it to ensure that their baby is as healthy as possible.

[2] It is also right that the technology should be used. If we have the power to decide whether we bring a baby into the world with or without cystic fibrosis, with

Cons

[1] It is right that those couples using IVF because they cannot conceive by other methods should be told whether their embryos have certain serious genetic defects, but a line must be drawn between this and the widespread use of genetic screening to make 'designer babies'. Apart from its being an affront to people with disabilities to suggest that those born with physical or mental impairments should be 'bred out' of the human race, to use genetic screening is to open up existing technology to widespread abuse. It is not inevitable that genetic screening will become widespread, but it is inevitable that if there is not an international moratorium on this development (as there should be), people will use it to select embryos conforming to stereotypes of intelligence, physical beauty, athleticism and so on.

or without a genetic neurological disease such as Huntington's chorea (which brings on rapid and extreme mental dementia in middle age), then we surely have a duty to choose the latter. This is not genetic engineering – it is merely a case of choosing which of the embryos 'naturally' created from the parents' sperm and egg should be implanted in the womb. At present, there is an *in utero* anomaly scan and parents can choose to abort an embryo if it is found to have Down's syndrome or another genetic disorder. IVF screening is morally preferable to that and less distressing for the parents.

[3] Healthy embryos not chosen after screening can be frozen (as surplus IVF embryos often are) and offered up for 'adoption' by childless couples. Government agencies can be set up (as opposed to the private clinics that trade in these embryos in some states of America), analogous to adoption agencies, to administer and oversee this process. Couples will not be allowed to dictate the genetic make-up of the embryo, but could be offered a selection of healthy embryos from which to choose. This method has two principal advantages over traditional adoption: first, the parents have an assurance that the embryo is genetically screened and so their child will be healthy; and second, the mother will carry the child to term herself, thus forming an important additional physical and emotional bond with her child.

[2] This is objectionable for three reasons. First, it envisages the use of human embryos as commodities and as resources of medical technology – as mere 'things' rather than potential people. Those embryos that are rejected will be disposed of or indefinitely frozen. This is a dangerously cavalier attitude to take to human life. Second, it perpetuates the idea that those with physical 'defects' are inferior human beings. This is a narrow and discriminatory approach, which is offensive to people with disabilities.

[3] This proposal would make embryos into commodities to be chosen between like objects on a supermarket shelf. Moreover, it is a fallacy to assume that everyone has a fundamental right to be a parent of their own biological children. Those who cannot have children should foster or adopt children without homes of their own, given the enormous number of orphans desperately in need of a family.

Possible motions
This House supports universal genetic screening.
This House would choose its babies.

Related topics
Genetic engineering
Surrogate mothers, payment of
Abortion on demand
Euthanasia, legalisation of

Genetic engineering

One must be careful to distinguish between genetic engineering – actual tampering with the genetic code of a being or an embryo – and other forms of intervention in the natural process. This debate focuses on both the genetic modification of crops, which is generally done to produce better commercial and agricultural plant life by making them last longer or be more resistant to disease, and genetic modification of human and animal cells. Most debates will naturally focus on one of these or the other, but they do contain overlapping issues (some of the issues in the human type are also dealt with in the previous debate on 'eugenics: IVF and genetic screening').

Pros

[1] Genetic engineering may sound spooky, but in fact, it is a harmless and welcome initiative. There is nothing special about genetic code that distinguishes intervention in it from any of the other ways in which we intervene in natural biological processes. Moreover, we know more and more about genetics with every passing year; now is the time to seize on that knowledge.

[2] There are many benefits to the plant world with the use of genetic engineering, and these are of immense significance to the world's starving millions. Perhaps the most immediate is the creation of crop varieties that are resistant to disease, thereby requiring fewer pesticides and thus safeguarding the environment. Even more important, the development of varieties that require little in the way of expensive chemical treatments will be a boon to the developing world.

[3] Genetic engineering is nothing new. Man has been 'genetically engineering' crops and livestock by artificial selection for thousands of years. Wheat could never have evolved in the wild without it; the domestic cat is an artificial animal, the result of 4,000 years of 'unnatural'

Cons

[1] We should not readily intervene in genetic codes, because we do not know what the consequences will be. While we believe that we are starting to understand genetics better, we do not really understand properly how genes interact; that is different from visible, tested interventions in medicine and science, because it is so speculative.

[2] Genetic engineering involves human beings acting in a sphere that should be the preserve of God, or at least of natural evolution. In the quest for ever greater profits, we are meddling with processes that we barely understand.

[3] The promises made now about genetic engineering are reminiscent of those made about pesticides in the 1950s and 1960s (e.g. DDT which threatened wildlife), which proved disastrous for the food chain. Like all science from nuclear power to the 'green revolution', we can be sure that genetic engineering will promise far more than it will deliver, and create problems no one can predict.

[4] Genetic engineering poses serious risks which we barely understand. For example, a soybean variety that had been

breeding. But in the past we had to geneti-cally engineer indirectly, by painstaking cross-breeding with the hope of keeping certain genes. Genetic engineering allows us to transfer genes one at a time, and with a far greater degree of certainty. It is a revolution only in technique.

[4] Problems of dysfunctional varieties that may arise are nothing to be alarmed about. They would equally have arisen from cross-breeding and simply illustrate that genetic engineering should be employed with as much care as any other cross-breeding technique.

[5] Genetic engineering can be used in humans in two ways – either germ-line therapy or somatic therapy. The former involves engineering genes in the sex cells of potential parents to alter the genetic material inherited by their offspring (e.g. seeking to remove the gene for Alzheimer's or MS) and thus has long-term repercussions. Somatic therapy deals only with the individual during his or her lifetime and is not inherited – for example, giving a diabetic person a gene to produce insulin internally. We should be more cautious with germ-line therapy, but both can be used for the medical benefit of humanity.

engineered to resist a herbicide was withdrawn from sale after it was dis-covered that a Brazil nut gene inserted into the soybean DNA caused an allergic reaction in people allergic to nuts. Genetically altered cotton plants lose their own immune system, thus leaving them vulnerable to aphid attack.

[5] Genes are related to each other in complex ways that we do not always understand. We know that some genes with negative effects (e.g. the gene for sickle cell anaemia) survive because of the positive benefits they also bring (immu-nity from malaria). We do not know what benefits and essential human traits we are playing with when we permanently alter genetic make-up at the germ-line level. We should err on the side of caution and have a moratorium on genetic engineer-ing until our knowledge is better devel-oped. The prejudices of the current age (in favour, perhaps, of very narrow sporting, economic or intellectual abilities) will be inscribed into our genetic heritage for centuries to come. This sort of mentality was behind the Nazi ideology that resulted in the Jewish Holocaust.

Possible motions
This House supports the use of genetic engineering in the natural world.
This House calls for a stop to all research on human genetic engineering.

Related topics
Eugenics: IVF and genetic screening

Global warming, binding emission targets for

There have been numerous global attempts to agree on limits to greenhouse gas emissions, but thus far, nothing on the global scale has succeeded; the Kyoto Protocol was rejected by the USA, withdrawn from by Canada, and had not imposed binding targets on the developing world anyway. The closest thing to a serious inter-country accord was the European Union's cap-and-trade scheme, but that was largely disastrous, with limits set too high to be effective. This debate represents a radical departure from existing practice, to impose internationally binding obligations that require immediate action.

Pros

[1] The pollution we have pumped into our atmosphere since the industrial revolution threatens to cause long-term climate change. In particular, CO_2 from the burning of fossil fuels is thought to build up in the upper atmosphere and act like a greenhouse – letting sunlight in, but preventing heat from escaping. Projections show global temperatures rising by 3° Celsius in the next century, sufficient to melt the polar ice caps and cause widespread flooding. The four hottest years in recorded history have been in the last decade. Extreme weather phenomena have become more common, from droughts and floods in sub-Saharan Africa to water shortages in South-East England. Countries such as Bangladesh and some of the Pacific island states are in danger of being totally submerged in the near future if current levels of global warming continue. Binding targets are necessary to solve this problem.

[2] Tighter controls on emissions must be introduced, but this need not sacrifice economic growth. Western countries should be allowed to 'buy' the emission quotas of developing countries that succeed in bringing their levels down. This

Cons

[1] The environmental lobbyists have been prophesying doom for decades, but the world still seems to continue with relative stability. There have always been natural climactic cycles – ever since the last Ice Age, the world has been getting warmer. There is no conclusive evidence that man is responsible for the current change – in fact, the earth's temperature fell between 1940 and 1970 despite a rapid injection of CO_2 into the atmosphere, and there has been no warming in the Arctic despite 'computer predictions'. So binding targets are simply unnecessary.

[2] The West has built its prosperity upon industrial growth. Pollution controls will have the effect of preventing such growth in the developing world – such controls amount to environmental imperialism. It is inevitable that at this economic stage, emissions will be greater and it is hypocritical of the West to insist that developing countries do not do what they themselves have done for centuries. In the absence of hard evidence for the causes of global warming, emission limits should not be further reduced.

[3] Environmentalists wish to destroy jobs and reduce our nation's wealth on the basis

will reduce total global emissions while also providing investment in, and financial incentives for, 'green' forms of industrial development in developing countries.

[3] When the potential harm is so great, we cannot sit around waiting for 'certainty'. Putting economics ahead of the environment will mean that some countries cease to exist – presumably the worst economic scenario for any nation. The environment is fundamental to the flourishing of life from the most basic to the most prosperous and must be our number one priority. Also, pollution controls have many beneficial side-effects – improving the quality of life for people choking in polluted cities and encouraging energy conservation rather than consumption.

of an unproven theory. Their scaremongering and indoctrination (particularly of children) threatens our very way of life. Energy conservation and pollution controls should be encouraged up to a point (as they already are), but economic productivity and improved standards of living must remain our number one priority.

Possible motions

This House supports internationally binding emission targets for all countries.

This House believes that only binding emission targets can save the planet from global warming.

Related topics

Cars in city centres, banning of

Environmental responsibility, developed world should take more

Vegetarianism

Nuclear energy

The disaster at Fukushima Daiichi, Japan in 2011, in which an earthquake triggered meltdown at a major nuclear power plant, reignited the debate about nuclear energy. Prior to that, the world appeared to be marching slowly towards the greater use of nuclear power, but that progress is now somewhat in doubt. Fukushima caused five deaths; however, it is hard to estimate the precise number of deaths, as many are likely to occur in subsequent years from radiation increasing the risk of cancer. What seems certain is that it will not be comparable to the 1986 Chernobyl disaster, which killed 6,000 people directly, and anywhere between 27,000 and 985,000 indirectly.

Pros

[1] The world needs energy, and nuclear power is the only way to get it. Fossil fuels will run out soon, and the truth is that 'renewable energy' is simply not ready yet to provide the level of power that we require. Nuclear energy is cheap and efficient, and the technology is certain, which makes it a much better choice than speculative renewables development.

Cons

[1] Nuclear energy is not a viable alternative to renewables. First of all, it can take 20–30 years to build a nuclear power plant, and it is hugely expensive. Second, many existing nuclear power plants are in fact about to be decommissioned. This means that the existing network will also have to be replaced, which makes such a project unreasonably expensive.

[2] Nuclear power is safe. Far from revealing that it is not safe, Fukushima showed just how safe it is. In literally the worst possible combination of circumstances, a 40-year-old power plant, on a tectonic fault, was hit by an earthquake, and still there are currently fewer than 100 deaths. Technology has improved immeasurably since Chernobyl, and that makes it substantially safer.

[3] Sources of uranium are mainly stable countries with open trading relations, which are traditional allies of the Western world. Australia controls 30 per cent of the world's uranium reserves, and Canada a further 9 per cent. Moreover, they are diversely located, with 12 per cent of reserves in Kazakhstan, and 6 per cent in South Africa, while Brazil and Namibia each have 5 per cent. This means that most countries would have access to a secure supply, and in the event of political difficulties with a supplier, could switch readily to another. This is in contrast to oil and gas, where energy needs can influence foreign policy and providers are able to hold importers to ransom.

[4] Nuclear energy is green and clean. Many environmental charities such as Greenpeace are now supporting nuclear energy as they see it as the best way quickly to reduce the burning of emission-producing fossil fuels.

[5] The problems of the nuclear energy programme have been a result of bureaucracy and obsessive secrecy resulting from nuclear energy's roots in military research. These are problems of the past. In the future, we can improve on even this – the development of nuclear fusion in the next 30 years will provide a virtually limitless energy source with no pollution.

[2] Nuclear power is far from safe. As Fukushima showed, the potential consequences of a nuclear power disaster are catastrophic. We were very lucky that Fukushima's meltdown did not spread, but even so, it is highly likely that large numbers of deaths will result. Moreover, the consequences of such a meltdown are so catastrophic as to outweigh any potential benefits.

[3] Renewable energy is the only truly secure form of energy, because it is almost all domestic. Solar, wind, wave and hydro-electric power are all created in-country, and so do not suffer from the risks of international conflict or discord.

[4] Nuclear energy may be greener than fossil fuels in the short term, but that ignores the problem of nuclear waste. We could be storing up a catastrophe for generations who come after us.

[5] In the 1950s, we were promised that nuclear energy would be so cheap that it would be uneconomic to meter electricity. Today, nuclear energy is still subsidised by the taxpayer. Old power stations require decommissioning; that will take 100 years and cost billions.

Possible motions
This House says 'Yes, please' to nuclear power.
This House would extend the use of nuclear power.

Related topics
Cars in city centres, banning of
Environmental responsibility, developed world should take more
Global warming: binding emission targets for
Vegetarianism
Nuclear weapons, right to possess

Obese children, compulsory attendance at weight-loss camps

This debate draws on the presence and growing use of voluntary 'fat camps', or weight-loss camps, in the USA, the UK and Canada to deal with the problem of obesity, especially childhood obesity. They involve people voluntarily checking into residential camps where they eat carefully prescribed diets, away from temptation, and exercise heavily. They can also involve nutrition classes and cognitive behavioural therapy designed to achieve positive long-term outcomes. This policy obviously varies in making them compulsory.

Pros

[1] Children who are severely overweight are in urgent need of intervention. Their weight exposes them to the risk of long-term health damage, such as the development of diabetes and heart damage, as well as significant short-term problems, including chronic fatigue. The state must step in immediately to protect them.

[2] The reason for serious obesity is often bad habits and/or psychological disorders. Weight-loss camps help to fix these by offering participants counselling, and educating them about ways to eat and live more healthily. Often weight loss is about developing alternative diversionary activities when stressed, or learning how to cook with fresh ingredients. This policy makes weight loss durable.

[3] Rather than stigmatising them, a trip to a 'weight-loss camp' will be beneficial to children's self-esteem. As they lose weight, they will be able to be more active, and so go out more and play with their friends. They will no longer be labelled as 'the fat kid', and so will in fact thrive socially.

[4] Parents who allow their children to get severely obese are so irresponsible as to lose their absolute right to control their

Cons

[1] Although the harms of obesity are undeniably great, they are rarely so urgent as to warrant immediate intervention. Slow but steady weight loss is healthier, more durable and more appropriate to the problem at hand.

[2] This policy is simply a short-term fix, which will quickly spring back as children do not understand how to cope outside their controlled environment. We must teach children how to lose weight and exercise while facing their normal daily circumstances, which this will not assist with.

[3] The stigma of having been sent away to 'fat camp' will be significant. When children are released from such camps, they could become pariahs within their social networks, and be unable to lead normal lives. This would only increase the stresses that made them overweight in the first place.

[4] This is a violation of parents' rights to parent as they see fit. Moreover, this is an area in which parents need to be 'on side' with the government's efforts to reduce their children's obesity. This will make them angry and resentful, and is thus ultimately counterproductive.

children. When their children are so in danger, and at risk of such severe harm, the state has a solemn obligation to step in to protect them. Moreover, often their parents need a shock to make them realise that their attitude to their children's weight is unacceptable; once they receive it, they will become more supportive.

Possible motions

This House would force obese children to attend weight-loss camps.

Related topics

Protective legislation v. individual freedom

School sport, compulsory

Child curfews

Organ donation: priority for healthy lifestyle

Debates about organ donation fall into two categories: those about how to increase the overall size of the donor pool, to reduce scarcity of organs; and those about how to allocate scarce organs. While the former are more common, the latter are also vitally important. Given that organ scarcity is not going away any time soon, we also need to think about the questions of principle and policy about how we give them out. Most states adopt a broadly similar system of allocating organs based on need, without regard to other factors, which means that patients typically have to wait until they are very ill for transplant organs. The policy proposed here is already often enforced in a minimal form; for instance, by denying liver transplants to alcoholics who have failed to stop drinking. The policy is not mutually exclusive of other systems of allocation, such as the sale of organs or prioritising those who are registered donors themselves, but gives substantially greater weight to people's prior choices. There is also a related debate about prioritising a healthy lifestyle in other medical treatment such as changing the order on waiting lists for surgery in favour of those who follow a healthy lifestyle, or (in national health services) denying costly treatment to smokers or the obese.

Pros

[1] Given that organs are scarce, we should make them do as much good as possible. Those who have lived healthy lifestyles are more likely to recover from their illnesses, and more likely to live longer after their transplant; for instance, a smoker who requires a kidney transplant is more likely to die from other illnesses than a non-smoker. This system of allocation thus maximises the number of healthy years of life that it is possible to create by allocating organs, and is thus the best we can do in the bad situation of organ scarcity.

Cons

[1] It is true that organs should do as much good as possible, but this policy does not achieve that. The existing system of allocation by need, however, does exactly that; when patients most need organs, they are available. Denying those who most need the organs is obviously counterproductive, and will prevent doctors from saving many lives. In particular, it is just not correct to claim that people who have led unhealthy lifestyles are less likely to recover; in fact, they may have a very high chance of recovery, which this policy ignores.

[2] It is a fundamental principle of a liberal society that people are held responsible for their choices, and judged accordingly. In this situation, we are in effect faced with a straight choice as to whose life we should save; the person who has led the healthy lifestyle, or the person who has not. As the latter will often be to blame for their illnesses (for instance, by drinking to excess and so damaging their livers), it is more appropriate to save the former, because their illnesses are mere chance, and not self-induced.

[3] This policy does not have a differential impact on the poor. That is to mischaracterise how poor people actually live. It is simply not that difficult to live a healthy lifestyle; it requires moderation in alcohol consumption, avoiding illegal substances, and sensible calorie intake. None of these things require enormous incomes; indeed, it is important to send the message that poor people are equally expected to live healthily and sensibly, and should not be stigmatised as unable to do so.

[4] This policy acts as an incentive for people to live more healthily. While it is obviously not plausible that teenagers will radically change their behaviour, many people who persistently engage in unhealthy practices, like drinking to excess or smoking, are aware that they will probably make themselves ill by doing so, but persist in this anyway. It is important for the government to send a signal that this type of behaviour is unacceptable; individuals must be encouraged to clean up their lives and behave in a way that is conducive to public health generally.

[5] This policy also encourages the donation of organs. It is important to signify that governments take organ donation

[2] We do hold people responsible for their choices, but we also acknowledge that sometimes it is important to protect people from them. We do not, in general, deny medical care to anyone who has caused their own illness; rather, the state recognises the importance of providing a safety net against people's irrational or short-term choices. A death sentence does not give someone a chance to learn from their choices, which is also a very important part of living in a free society.

[3] The main consequences of this policy fall overwhelmingly on the poor. Obesity, alcoholism and drugs are all, for various tragic social reasons, problems which occur predominantly in poor areas. For instance, ready meals tend to be cheaper than fresh food, and so eating healthily is much harder on a lower income. This policy thus disproportionately punishes those who, through no fault of their own, have less money, which also sends the message that the state considers the poor less worthy of life.

[4] It is just unrealistic to suppose that anyone will in fact live more healthily because of this policy, because no one expects that they will need an organ transplant; after all, if they did, getting so ill would presumably be a sufficient deterrent, without much attention to the added worry of an organ transplant. Moreover, many of the lifestyle choices that are under discussion (drinking, smoking, drug taking, etc.) are addictive; those who engage in them do not rationally calculate costs and benefits, especially about the distant future.

[5] This policy will not increase the overall number of organs donated; if anything, it will reduce it. That is because it is harder to understand why people who have lived

seriously, and value it; in that way, being an organ donor becomes a 'badge of honour', which makes people more likely to want to do it. At the moment, the fact that many organs are 'wasted' on those who do not take adequate precautions with their lives and lifestyles sends a message that organs are not important. This policy creates a link between the individual virtues of those who are donating with those of the recipients, establishing both as social role models.

healthily for their entire lives would need organ transplants, so the PR effect of this policy is actually to reduce the perceived demand for organs, thus discouraging donation. Moreover, this policy seems like an acceptance that there will never be enough organs; that undermines the strongest arguments for new policies on donation (such as opt-out systems).

Possible motions

This House would prioritise those who have lived healthy lives when allocating organs for transplants.

This House would deny liver transplants to alcoholics.

This House believes that if the state is going to take care of you, you should have taken care of yourself.

Related topics

Organs, legal sale of

Organs, legal sale of

One thing that is indisputable in all debates about organs is that there is a shortage of them in almost every country in the world; people die daily waiting for donor organs. However, as soon as we proceed to the vexed question of how to solve that problem, huge ethical and economic debates open up. Aside from compulsory organ donation, creating a trade in organs is widely seen as the most common possible method by which we could increase organ availability. There are few examples of this policy in practice; only Iran currently allows the sale of human organs, although India did until 1994 and the Philippines until 2008. The Proposition team can, though they are not required to, bite the bullet and make the ability to obtain an organ depend on the ability to pay, but more commonly, will seek to buy organs through a national health system.

Pros

[1] The overarching goal of any organ policy must be to increase the supply of organs. This policy achieves that by incentivising people to donate financially. It is

Cons

[1] We should strive to obtain more organs, but this proposal will not achieve that goal. Many people at the moment donate out of a sense of altruism; as soon

possible either to pay people while they are still alive for certain organs (like a kidney or part of the liver) or to leave that money to their family after they are dead. Either way, that represents a real cash incentive to donate that is presently lacking.

[2] A belief in the principle of autonomy dictates that we allow payment for donations. We already allow people to donate their organs, but if that is a legitimate choice (so that there can be no objection from them about damaging their bodies, for instance), then adding money into the equation cannot possibly make that choice less legitimate. Indeed, all it does is make someone who decides to make that choice financially better off.

[3] Legalisation will wipe out the black market in organs. We know that there is a thriving black market, especially in India after it banned organ sales, because people will always be willing to go to extreme lengths to protect their lives. In a black market, exploitation and donation without informed consent are more likely, as are unsafe medical procedures that threaten to kill people as a result of donating.

as organs become a product with a monetary value, that sense of altruism is lost. This policy means we would lose some organs. Moreover, if the state is paying for these organs, that will represent an enormous burden on the taxpayer that may hurt other areas of healthcare. If it is being left to the private sector, then though there may be more organs, the poor will be unable to obtain them, which is unacceptable.

[2] The difference between the choice made without money involved and one with it is huge; namely, the possibility for economic coercion. Under this policy, the poor may find themselves selling their organs, in spite of serious reservations about this as a health decision, just to get some money quickly. It is wrong that people might be forced into a choice that is so fundamental.

[3] Far from wiping out the black market, this policy will only encourage it. First, if organs can now be sold legally, that increases incentives to obtain them for free (by kidnap, or illegal purchase from countries like China that allegedly sell the organs of executed prisoners). Second, people will try to undercut the regulated market by reducing costs, meaning that all the problems remain.

Possible motions
This House would legalise the sale of organs.
This House believes in a free market in body parts.

Related topics
Protective legislation v. individual freedom
Surrogate mothers, payment of
Prostitution, legalisation of
Organ donation: priority for healthy lifestyle

Social networking has improved our lives

It is a tribute to the speed of the rise of the online social network that, when this book's last edition was published in 1999, it is arguable that not a single social network existed. Early context-specific social networks like Friends Reunited and Classmates emerged in 2000, followed by more general ones such as Myspace, Bebo and Friendster in 2002 and 2003. But perhaps equally telling is that a teenager using Facebook today may well not even have heard of the above, let alone used them, because Facebook and Twitter, founded in 2004 and 2006 respectively, have swept through all competition, and become the all-consuming means of online communication. This debate understandably focuses on them.

Pros

[1] Social networking allows unprecedented ability to communicate at high speed in many different forms, across huge distances. The ability to contact friends on the other side of the world allows for the maintenance of cross-border friendships, while the flexibility of communication is a huge advantage; 'Events' allow us to organise parties, while 'Groups' allow us to create communities for a specific purpose, in a much easier way than anything we have seen before.

[2] Social networks allow rapid political campaigning over issues, connecting people who would otherwise never be able to meet to rally together. Hashtags on Twitter allow us to attach a message to a particular issue, so that like-minded people can get a range of views. This also makes youth a powerful political constituency, as politicians and campaigners check social networks to observe their opinions and capture votes.

[3] Social networks allow us to have greater control over our identities. We can let others know more precisely what our preferences are by 'liking' the relevant movies, bands or brands. We can post

Cons

[1] This speed of communication is present, but disastrous. Face-to-face interaction has died; we no longer make time to catch up with friends because we always know their news anyway. Moreover, we are under constant stress to convey the right social media 'presence'; it is oppressive to feel the need to 'check in' at every location we go to or answer messages in seconds.

[2] This kind of campaigning is pointless talk, and encourages a 'slacktivist' mentality, with a superficial understanding of issues and no actual intention of pressuring politicians for change; for example, hundreds of millions of people shared the Kony 2012 video which demanded action on the crimes of warlords by the end of 2012 – the deadline passed, and no one cared.

[3] This is an unhelpful way to think about identity. We should live naturally, and let our identities be expressed through our actions, rather than requiring a hugely contrived set of publicly available ways of portraying ourselves.

quotations which express our political or philosophical views. All of this allows us to cultivate a personality that goes beyond a few short personal meetings, and also to seek out like-minded people more easily; we do not need to have an initial conversation with them, because we know they share our interests from their online presence.

[4] Social networks are only 'coercive' in the sense that they provide us with huge benefits, which we typically accept, but there is nothing about them that restricts our liberty; we can choose to opt out if we so wish. Moreover, as long as we are careful in protecting our data, social networks do not own anything damaging.

[4] Social networks coerce us into joining; it is virtually impossible not to be a member of one, and so we do not exercise meaningful choice over whether we use it to run our lives. Once we do, they control all our data, in an invasive way.

Possible motions

This House believes that social networking has made us better off.

This House 'likes' Facebook.

Space exploration

In 1957, Sputnik 1 was put into space by the USSR, and in 1961, Yuri Gagarin became the first man in space. The Cold War was a focal point for the early years of space travel, with the USA landing on the moon in 1969. In the following years, focus has shifted towards the possibility of using space for technological and scientific advancement, with 1998 seeing the launch of the International Space Station, a joint NASA–Russian project to further develop space travel. In 1986, a stark reminder of the risks of space travel was delivered with the disaster aboard the Space Shuttle Challenger, in which seven astronauts perished, resulting in the USA grounding its shuttle fleet for two-and-a-half years.

Pros

[1] Scientific understanding of the origins, nature and destiny of the universe we live in is both one of the crowning achievements of human civilisation and a goal to be pursued for its own sake. The pictures of nebulae, distant galaxies, white dwarfs and other extraordinary phenomena, produced by the Hubble Space Telescope, may not be of immediate material use in terms of day-to-day economics, but they are wonderful and fascinating achieve-

Cons

[1] We cannot afford to spend billions on space telescopes, space shuttles, space probes, space stations and the like when poverty and starvation exist on earth. Quality of life for all must take priority over knowledge for its own sake. As for the existential dimension – scientific space research and cosmology have created a bleak and depressing worldview of an impersonal and purposeless universe, condemned either to thermodynamic

ments. It is also of great existential importance that we know where we came from and what our place is in the universe. The Big Bang theory and speculations about the future of the universe fulfil that existential need that used to be fulfilled by religion.

[2] Astronomy has always been used to understand and predict our own planet better. Ancient Egyptians used the stars to predict when the Nile would flood, and astronomy has always been used for navigation and meteorology as well. Studying the behaviour of light and chemical elements in conditions characterised by extremes of time, space, distance, heat and gravity tells us about the fundamental laws of nature and characteristics of matter – the same laws and matter that we seek to manipulate and predict here on earth. Space exploration may lead to the longed-for 'Theory of Everything' sought by scientists such as Stephen Hawking, who are trying to unify general relativity and quantum mechanics.

[3] Through space exploration and the need to construct probes and satellites, satellite technology has been developed that has provided us with massively increased and improved broadcasting, telecommunications and weather-predicting capabilities. This alone would justify the expenditure that has been put into space research.

[4] Space research, especially experimentation done in zero-gravity conditions in space stations, has resulted in many scientific and technological spin-offs, from super-conductors and miniaturised microchips to non-stick frying pans. We should continue to fund space research to allow more such breakthroughs to be made.

heat death or a 'big crunch' in which we are meaningless specks of cosmic dust.

[2] The earth itself provides ample testimony to the laws of nature and the nature of matter – testimony found in the discoveries of geologists, biologists, chemists and particle physicists. We will never encounter a black hole or a super-nova or an object travelling at the speed of light and so do not need to understand them. Only scientists who are not content with everyday reality and earthly interactions seek comfort and escape in the speculative fantasies of cosmology and space research.

[3] Satellites are not really examples of space exploration technology. They would have been discovered without exploring space *per se*. They are essentially examples of terrestrial technology developed for purely terrestrial purposes.

[4] It is misleading to suggest that space exploration was a necessary prerequisite for all these discoveries. In the case of computer technology, as with so many technologies, the driving force was large-scale military investment in research and development. We should also look at the negative spin-offs – the Reagan administration's Strategic Defense Initiative or 'Star Wars' project which developed technology for space-based nuclear missile interceptors, and the escalation of the Cold War arms race.

Possible motions

This House would increase funding for space exploration.

This House would boldly go where no House has gone before.

This House believes the truth is out there.

Surrogate mothers, payment of

A surrogate mother is a woman who carries and gives birth to a baby for another couple who are unable to have children in the normal way. A couple in which the woman is infertile might use the man's sperm and the surrogate mother's egg to produce the foetus – the surrogate would not need to have sex with the man, but could be inseminated in another way. Alternatively, if the woman and man are both fertile but the woman cannot, for some other reason, conceive and bear a child, one of the woman's eggs, fertilised by the man, can be implanted into the womb of the surrogate. When he or she is born, the child is handed over by the surrogate to be adopted by the couple. In some US states, and in India and Russia among others, it is legal to pay surrogate mothers for their services; whereas in other countries such as the UK, Australia and France, only altruistic surrogacy is allowed, which merely permits the payment of reasonable costs. Some countries such as Italy have outlawed all forms of surrogacy, paid or not.

Pros

[1] Surrogate motherhood is to be encouraged as it is a way for people who could not otherwise do so to start their own family. For some infertile couples, surrogacy is the only chance to have their own baby as procedures such as IVF require the woman to be able to implant an embryo and then carry the baby to term and many women cannot do this. It is also a way for gay men to father children with a donated egg. Surrogacy allows people to fulfil their deep desire to be biological parents.

[2] Commercial surrogacy makes the procedure accessible to all. Countries such as India have set up clinics to facilitate matches. This is better than a couple relying on finding a relative, friend or kindly stranger to help. It prevents pressure being felt to comply and a sense of debt afterwards.

[3] When formal and commercial, the process can be carried out within strict medical and legal guidelines. This offers more protection both to the surrogate and

Cons

[1] Being a parent is not a right that everybody is born with. If a couple are unable to have children themselves, then they should adopt or foster a child rather than bringing yet another child into the world, particularly through surrogacy, which is a method beset by emotional, legal and financial wrangling.

[2] It is wrong to make a trade in human lives. The result of commercial surrogacy will be that only the rich can afford to buy babies in this way. That is not the way that parenthood should be decided.

[3] It is naïve to believe that there will not be disputes in these instances of surrogacy. Surrogate mothers have been known to change their minds and keep the child due to the strong biological and emotional links made between mother and baby during pregnancy. There have also been disputes where the parents have sued the surrogate for her behaviour during pregnancy and refused to take the child.

those who have hired her. In countries that allow altruistic surrogacy, the law is often murky, with an adoption needed after birth.

[4] A surrogate mother should be paid for her services. She is meeting a demand, at some inconvenience, discomfort and risk to herself. It is only right to recognise this through a fee.

[5] In principle, there should be no objection to financial gain through surrogacy. A surrogate mother can weigh up the advantages and disadvantages of hiring out her womb and should be free to do so if the arrangement is between consenting adults and nobody is harmed. The surrogate mother may feel fulfilled knowing that her work is helping people who are infertile. Both parties benefit from the transaction and the only role of the state should be to make sure that contracts are enforced. Many other jobs are far riskier.

[4] Surrogacy, if it is practised at all, should be an altruistic gift. Carrying a baby is not a 'job' any more than any other bodily function. Paying for surrogacy is equivalent to paying for an organ rather than relying on donations.

[5] There are physical risks to pregnancy and childbirth and psychological harms in surrogacy, and women should not be financially incentivised to go through this. It may seem like an easy choice of a career – money for nothing – but when complications arise, it can be devastating. In principle, we should not treat the body as a commodity that can be bought and sold.

Possible motions

This House would allow paid surrogate motherhood.

This House would let a woman rent out her womb.

Related topics

Abortion on demand

Eugenics: IVF and genetic screening

Genetic engineering

Organs, legal sale of

Vegetarianism

Vegetarianism has always been an alternative lifestyle that has been practised by some proponents of animal rights, by a faction of the health-conscious and by some religions. In recent years, however, it has taken on an environmental dimension with some green campaigners saying that widespread vegetarianism could be crucial to the planet's future. It is unlikely that this debate would call for a law banning the eating of meat; rather, it should debate the practical and moral advantages and disadvantages of the lifestyle choice. See the introduction to the debate on 'animal experimentation and vivisection, banning of' (Section E) and the entry on 'animal rights' (Section A) for an overview on the issues of animal welfare.

Pros

[1] We are animals ourselves, with shared ancestors with all other creatures. We should take responsibility for our animal cousins rather than exploiting and eating them unnecessarily. Furthermore, we cannot know exactly what feelings and emotions other animals can have. There is good evidence that they feel fear and pain like us. Therefore, we must err on the side of caution and not farm and kill animals at all. As Jeremy Bentham said, the question about animals is not 'Can they think?', but 'Can they feel pain?'

[2] Most mass meat-farming techniques are barbaric, especially the battery farming of chickens and the force-feeding of veal calves. Supposedly quick slaughter techniques are often botched – leaving animals half-alive and in pain for hours when they were supposed to be dead. Cows are pumped full of antibiotics and steroids to force them to grow to an unnatural size, and are forced to produce an unnatural quantity of milk, so that they become exhausted and die at half the age they would in nature. By buying and eating meat, the non-vegetarian is indirectly torturing animals that have unnaturally short, miserable and confined lives.

[3] There is no need for meat in a balanced diet. All sorts of fruits, vegetables and pulses provide the variety of carbohydrates, proteins, fibre, minerals and vitamins that we need. Our closest animal relatives – the apes – have all-vegetarian diets. It has been suggested that this is our natural diet too. Meat consumption has been linked to high blood pressure, high cholesterol, heart disease and some cancers. In addition, almost all of the worst

Cons

[1] It is natural for people to farm and eat other creatures. Humans have come to flourish and dominate through their successful adaptation to and manipulation of other species. It is a strange and unnatural idea that we have 'duties' to other animals – rights and duties are exclusively applicable to humans. It is true that we cannot know what feelings or emotions animals have, but we can assume that they are minimal. Vegetarianism rests on sentimentalism and anthropomorphism. It is natural for us, like many other animals, to kill and eat other species to survive.

[2] Modern farming techniques may often be cramped, but we cannot assume that chickens or calves really have much of an awareness of their quality of life anyway. Their slaughter is generally swift and painless. If it is thought to be very important, free-range chickens, eggs and meat can be purchased to ensure that the animal one is eating had a natural and more varied life.

[3] Humans have evolved as an omnivorous species. Therefore, the omnivorous diet (meat and vegetables) is what we are adapted to flourish on. By cutting out half of this natural diet, we are bound to lose the natural balance and variety we need. Meat is a rich source of minerals such as iron and zinc, which are not easily found in a vegetarian diet. Excessive meat consumption might be bad for the health, but this is not a reason to cut it out completely.

[4] The effects on the environment arising from meat eating are disputed, as we would need vast amounts of land to farm

forms of food poisoning are transmitted from meat (E. coli, BSE, salmonella). Vegetarian diets are often lower in fat and healthier all round.

[4] There is an environmental cost attached to livestock farming. It is estimated that the farming of animals causes more greenhouse gas emissions than the world's entire transport system. The land needed to farm animals has led to mass deforestation, with over 70 per cent of deforestation in the Amazon rainforest occurring for the raising of cattle. Meat is also a wasteful use of water. The only environmentally responsible thing to do is to go vegetarian.

[5] Factory farming is increasingly dangerous for human health. Agricultural slurry is poisoning our rivers and nitrates entering our water supply have been linked to increased rates of cancer. Antibiotics fed to animals in vast quantities are causing the evolution of 'super-bugs' – bacteria that are resistant or immune to antibiotics. The inclusion of animal brains in their own feed has led to the disastrous spread of Bovine Spongiform Encephalopathy ('mad cow disease') and the human equivalent, Creutzfeldt–Jakob Disease (CJD). Epidemics of foot and mouth disease, bird flu and swine flu have all been linked to intensive livestock farming.

the extra vegetables and meat substitutes needed; it may also increase the importation of food, thereby adding more food miles to our menus. Unless we all go vegan, livestock farming would still have to continue to produce dairy products and eggs. It may well be true that we should eat less meat and not consider it the main component of every meal, but switching to a vegetarian diet is going too far.

[5] Intensive farming allows the masses to access cheap food. A vegetarian diet may be healthy (if unbalanced), but it is exceedingly expensive. Vegetarianism is a luxury for the middle classes – fresh vegetables are prohibitively expensive, compared with processed meats, burgers and so on, which are affordable and filling. Safer farming techniques and increased health awareness, not a wholesale switch to an unnatural vegetarian diet, are the solutions to the problems of unsafe meat farming.

Possible motions

This House believes that meat is murder.
This House believes that we should all be vegetarians.

Related topics

Protective legislation v. individual freedom
Animal experimentation and vivisection, banning of
Animal rights
Blood sports, abolition of
Zoos, abolition of

SECTION I

United Kingdom issues

BBC, privatisation of

The British Broadcasting Service (BBC) is a public service broadcasting corporation funded from a licence fee. Anybody who has a television set or uses a computer or phone to watch television in real time must pay the licence fee. The fee is set by government and in 2013, stood at £145.50. The BBC was set up in the 1920s and has grown to encompass eight television channels, 10 radio stations and a website. Many people believe that the BBC is a national treasure which must be protected, but there is a growing voice calling for it to be privatised.

Pros

[1] The licence fee is unfair in principle as you have to pay it even if you never watch the BBC. People should not be made to pay for a non-essential service that they do not want, need or use.

[2] The quality of BBC productions does not merit special treatment. The BBC reproduces the same mix of quiz shows, lifestyle programmes and soaps as the other channels. Its drama, documentaries and news are no better than programmes on offer elsewhere. Home Box Office (HBO) (a US TV channel) shows that a private channel can produce quality programming that is watched around the world.

[3] State involvement in the media should be avoided. A totally independent media free to criticise the government is what is needed. The board of governors of the BBC is appointed by the government and this is not sufficiently detached.

[4] The BBC is a bloated bureaucracy that has been badly governed and has been involved in innumerable scandals since the early 2000s. A privatised channel would be more efficient and offer better value for money. Advertisements, sponsorship and product placement can provide the funding for all the television we need.

Cons

[1] There are many services that are paid for out of taxpayers' money that not everyone uses, and the licence fee is the equivalent of a tax but is more independent. You can opt out altogether if you do not wish to own a television set.

[2] The lack of commercial pressure means that the BBC has the ability to innovate and take risks with its programming. It also allows the BBC to produce special interest and local shows that would not attract large enough audiences to be viable for a commercial provider. The BBC is famous worldwide for its drama and comedy and is seen as a badge of quality.

[3] Funding through the licence fee does not lead to lack of independence. The BBC is very effective at holding the government to account; you only have to watch a government minister being grilled by Jeremy Paxman or listen to John Humphrys on Radio 4 for evidence of the independence of the news. Commercial stations like Sky or Fox produce much more biased coverage than the BBC.

[4] With commercial stations come commercial interests. It is good to have the option of television which is not interrupted by advertisements or artistically

[5] The notion of a centrally funded television and radio service is outdated. It is a throwback to when BBC One was the only channel. In an age of multi-channel digital TV, on demand services and Internet downloads, there is no place for a nationalised media institution which is given funding above all others.

Possible motions

This House believes that the BBC should be privatised.

This House would scrap the licence fee.

Related topics

Arts funding by the state, abolition of

Press, state regulation of the

Privatisation

undermined by product placement. Parents like the option of advert-free TV for their children and sports fans prefer to watch a match uninterrupted. In the 2010 World Cup, ITV were on a commercial break and so missed the only England goal against the USA.

[5] There is something fair about guaranteeing that everybody has access to national events such as the Olympics, Wimbledon or a royal wedding even if they cannot afford a Sky box. The BBC regularly attracts viewing figures of over 10 million, so even in a multi-channel market it is still immensely popular. It has also stayed up to date with the BBC iPlayer and a well-respected website.

Disestablishment of the Church of England

Currently in Britain, the Church of England is 'established'. This means that Anglican Christianity is the official religion of Great Britain. The monarch is head of the Church of England. In addition, senior bishops of the Church of England can sit in the House of Lords. There have been increasing calls for the disestablishment of the Church of England – the ending of its privileged status as the official religion of Britain – from many quarters, both within and outside the Church itself.

Pros

[1] The case against the establishment of the Church of England is simple – it is an embarrassing anachronism. It fails to reflect our largely secular multicultural society. In Britain today, believers are a minority, Christians an even smaller minority, and Church of England worshippers a tiny fraction of the population. To provide such a minority with a legally and constitutionally privileged position is bizarre. The secularisation of the past two

Cons

[1] The Church of England has been central to British history for 400 years and still plays a vital role. Historically, Christianity has been fully engaged with secular laws, wars and social policies. The separation of church and state is a development of the past century or two. It is right that moral and spiritual leaders should be involved in political decision making. It cannot be denied that religion is still vitally important for a great many

centuries and the rise of an atheistic and scientific worldview make all forms of traditional religion irrelevant. Moral issues are discussed by philosophers, scientists and bio-ethicists – there is no need for the superstitious angle provided by religions.

[2] Establishment is not just philosophically objectionable, but embodies religious discrimination in practice. The monarch has to swear an oath of allegiance to uphold the Church of England. Bishops sit in the House of Lords – no other religious leaders do. More perniciously, the heir to the throne cannot marry a Catholic, and the prime minister cannot be a Catholic. These mediaeval hangovers contribute to a Catholic sense of victimisation, particularly in Northern Ireland. To end this religious discrimination, the Church of England should lose its secular privileges and be disestablished.

[3] Ironically, establishment has actually been dangerous for the Church of England. Parliament can block church reforms as church law needs to be voted through both Houses. The prime minister also has to approve church appointments and it is believed that Margaret Thatcher appointed some of her own choices as bishops. Parliament also finds it easier to meddle in church issues, as in the debate over the ordination of women.

people. The Christianity represented by the Church of England is not an exclusivist religion – there are few of other faiths who view it with hostility. Indeed, Muslim and Jewish leaders oppose disestablishment.

[2] These are academic niceties of symbolic importance only. Attacking establishment can accomplish little in practice, and ignores the real problems of prejudice and religious mistrust. Disestablishment would send out a strong signal that there is no place for religion in modern society. Instead of taking away the secular and political role of the Church of England, all major religions should be given some degree of representation in parliament and by the royal family. Leaders of other religions should be given a place in the House of Lords. Charles, Prince of Wales, has already stated that he sees himself as a 'Defender of Faith' in a multicultural Britain rather than 'Defender of the (Christian) Faith'. Religious discrimination can be ended by making the establishment multi-faith rather than no-faith.

[3] So-called secular societies have not proved a success. Stalinist Russia's suppression of religion resulted in the revival of superstition on an unprecedented scale. The constitutional separation of church and state in the USA sits uneasily with vulgar and extreme expressions of fundamentalism.

Possible motions

This House calls for the disestablishment of the Church of England.

This House believes that religion and politics do not mix.

Related topics

Churches in politics

Monarchy, abolition of

Religious teaching in schools

English Parliament

Since the establishment of the Scottish Parliament and the Assemblies in Northern Ireland and Wales, there has been a discussion of whether England also needs its own parliament or whether Westminster is adequate representation.

Pros

[1] A parliament for England would be democratic and fair. The other three regions have their own parliament and this would give England equal status. It would also nullify the 'West Lothian question' where Scottish and Welsh MPs vote on English-only issues.

[2] It would be better for Westminster. There would be more time to work on truly UK-wide issues such as the economy, defence and foreign affairs.

[3] England does have its own distinct culture and traditions separate from its UK identity, and the English deserve some degree of home rule.

Cons

[1] England is fully represented through Westminster and it is unnecessary to create another level of bureaucracy.

[2] Westminster would be marginalised and there would be a lack of joined-up thinking, especially if different parties were in control of the two parliaments. For example, education policy is not independent from economic policy.

[3] There is no language, culture or heritage that is under threat from Westminster. The English can enjoy their traditions without the need for an expensive and unnecessary new parliament. Also, home rule should be a response to a demand from within a nation. There is not the public support in England for this measure and it should not be forced upon the people.

Possible motions

This House supports the creation of an English Parliament.

This House would devolve power from Westminster to England.

Related topics

Scottish independence

Democracy

House of Lords, elected v. appointed

The House of Lords began as a second chamber for hereditary peers which had the power to veto bills coming to it from the House of Commons. The Parliament Act of 1911 removed the power to veto and replaced it with the power to delay a bill. This established the ultimate sovereignty of the House of Commons. In 1958, life peers were created in addition to hereditary ones. These appointments are made by the government of the day to senior representatives of politics, business and other areas of society. There are also 26 Lords Spiritual who are bishops of the Church of England. The setting up of the Supreme Court in 2009 ended the position of Law Lords (which had existed when the House of Lords was the highest court in the land). The Blair government started the process of reforming the House of Lords by removing almost all of the hereditary peers and replacing them with life peers. Tony Blair's government, however, was divided about how to finish these reforms. Should the House of Lords eventually be fully elected, fully appointed by an independent commission or a mixture of the two? This article looks at the arguments for a fully elected versus a fully appointed chamber. There is also a related debate about whether to abolish the second chamber completely.

Pros (elected)

[1] There is no place in the twenty-first century for any system other than a democratically elected chamber. This would bring Britain into line with other democratic nations and would also be consistent with other changes that Britain has recently made, such as elected mayors, elected police chiefs, etc. An appointed House is not that much better than a hereditary one, as it is still elitist and leads to cronyism.

[2] An elected House of Lords would also be more accountable as the members would be representing constituents. This gives a voice to the public, whereas an appointed peer only has to represent their own views. Why should their voice count more than anybody else's? And why should the public have no mechanism to remove that peer if they disagree with the views espoused? If there is a link between

Cons (appointed)

[1] The second chamber has less power than the House of Commons as it can only scrutinise, suggest amendments and delay legislation. A democratic system is not therefore required and in fact could be problematic – why should they not have an equal voice if they have been elected too? Our system is based on the sovereignty of the House of Commons and this could undermine that. Democracy is better served through allowing the supremacy of an elected chamber that is scrutinised by an appointed one.

[2] The Lords provide invaluable expertise in the committee stages and debates on legislation. They are leaders in business, science and technology, the arts, religion, education and politics. They provide a wider range of views than another chamber full of career politicians would. They are also free to be more independent

the Lords and the public, then you have a more participative democracy.

[3] An elected chamber would be more representative and less elitist. Appointments of the great and mighty perpetuate social inequalities and lead to an ageing, white, male, privileged majority.

[4] An elected House could better perform its function as a constitutional check on the Commons and the government of the day. This is true for two reasons: first, it would have more of a mandate which would give it authority and more teeth with which to stand up to the lower house; and second, it would give it greater independence as the government would appoint the commission that appoints the Lords; this would give the government an influence over the body that is supposed to be a check on the Lords.

because the party whip is less strong and they can choose to be cross-benchers affiliated to no party. The security of tenure that comes with the lack of elections also means that experience and wisdom are kept and that the peers can be more principled and outspoken.

[3] A chamber that is more representative of the public may be achieved more effectively through appointment than through elections. An independent commission could have as part of its mandate to be inclusive of gender, race and economic background. It is very difficult to achieve social engineering through the electoral system as the make-up of the House of Commons shows.

[4] An elected chamber would not perform the effective check on the House of Commons we would wish it to. One of two things can happen: either the same party controls both houses, in which case the second chamber simply rubberstamps the first without the rigorous scrutiny we want; or different parties control the two chambers which can lead to the gridlock that we see in the USA when different parties hold the presidency and a majority in Congress. This would prevent the Commons from governing effectively with the mandate it has been given.

Possible motions
This House would elect the Second Chamber.
This House would support a fully appointed House of Lords.

Related topics
Democracy
Marxism
Judges, election of
Monarchy, abolition of

Police, arming of the

Britain is one of a small minority of countries where the police force does not carry guns. Is the idea of a bobby carrying a truncheon old-fashioned and unsafe, or is it something that works and that we should be proud of?

Pros

[1] The police need to be able to protect the public as effectively as possible. There may be occasions where being able to shoot to disable a criminal (or where having the threat of doing so) provides the optimum safety to those present, especially if the criminal is armed. There are an increasing number of guns on the street so the problem is becoming more acute.

[2] We ask our police to risk their lives in the line of duty, and we should give them the best means of protecting themselves. If a police officer is faced with an armed criminal, they deserve to be armed themselves to deal with that threat. A truncheon is not sufficient defence.

[3] Carrying of guns by the police acts as a deterrent to criminals. It is important that the police should be feared, and carrying a firearm achieves this.

[4] Carrying a gun gives a police officer authority in a way that the uniform alone does not. The officer does not need to use the gun; it is the carrying of it visibly that increases their status and therefore helps them to do their job.

[5] Police officers would be given extensive training in the use of guns. There would be a strict policy for when a gun could be fired including punishment for misuse.

Cons

[1] The public are well protected by the current system. The police have a number of options for dealing with different situations which do not involve shoot-outs in which civilians could be caught. The police also have special armed divisions for when the need is there.

[2] Carrying a gun does not increase the safety of police officers – it decreases it. Criminals are more likely to arm themselves and more likely to shoot if the police are armed. An officer's gun could also be used against them. Surveys of the police show that an overwhelming majority does not support the arming of all officers.

[3] Giving guns to the police would create an arms race as criminals would feel the need to carry guns too. The more guns there are in society, the less safe we are.

[4] The police need the trust of the public, not its fear. They need communities to report crimes and aid investigations and this would be hindered by the presence of guns.

[5] If the whole police force were armed, there would be accidents and wrongful shootings and this is too high a price to pay. The proposal could also attract the wrong type of person to apply to join the police.

[6] There is no reason why Britain needs to follow other countries in this issue; it is free to follow its own best interests. There are also no advantages in standardising the police force rather than allowing for

[6] This would bring Britain into line with most countries in the world which arm their police forces. It would also standardise the police force as, increasingly, special units do carry guns.

specialisation. The current model allows armed police to be deployed when needed without having to give guns to every bobby on the beat.

Possible motions
This House would arm the police.
This House would give a gun to the bobby on the beat.

Related topics
Capital punishment
Zero tolerance

Scottish independence

In 1997, Scotland voted 'yes' in a referendum for devolution of powers from Westminster. This led to the setting up of the Scottish Parliament which has limited tax-raising powers and control over policies such as health, education and transport. In 2011, the Scottish National Party won a majority in the parliamentary elections, and their leader Alex Salmond used this mandate to call for a referendum on Scottish Independence to take place in 2014.

Pros

[1] The principle of self-determination should be followed and the Scottish people should govern themselves. The Scottish people have their own distinct culture and history; they have their own legal system and education system; their political discourse is further to the left than England's. They should be able to make all of their own decisions rather than have laws dictated to them from Westminster.

[2] Scotland has the potential to have a viable, and indeed flourishing, economy in its own right. It has strong tourism, manufacturing and services sectors and it has natural resources including oil. It would wish to participate fully in the EU and this would give it support to do so.

Cons

[1] Scotland is able to keep alive its distinct culture and aspects, such as its separate legal system, within the union. Devolution allows it a large degree of self-determination while also recognising the strong shared history and culture which exists in the United Kingdom. The Scots are not being dictated to from outside; they have a strong voice in Westminster and are often over-represented at Cabinet level.

[2] Scotland is economically subsidised by England and would be financially worse off on its own. As a smaller economy, it would also have less resilience to external factors.

[3] Devolution has been successful; independence is the natural next step. Scotland has proved it is capable of self-rule in almost all policy areas and it has the infrastructure set up. Gaining control over foreign, defence and economic policy would be a smooth transition.

[4] Scottish independence would be in the best interest of the rest of the United Kingdom. At present, Scotland is heavily subsidised by Westminster and the money saved could be invested in poorer regions. It would also be more democratic, as the current system has led to the so-called 'West Lothian question': the situation where Scottish MPs vote in Westminster on issues which will not affect their constituencies.

[3] Devolution has been successful; independence is unnecessary. Scotland has a large degree of control while still protecting the union of the United Kingdom; this allows Scotland to have a greater global influence through UK foreign and defence policy.

[4] Scottish independence is not in the interest of any of the regions of the United Kingdom, all of which would be weakened by a split. If it wishes to remain a strong world player, then the United Kingdom should stay together and keep as large an economy, population and military capability as possible.

Possible motions
This House supports Scottish independence.
This House believes that Scotland would be better off outside the United Kingdom.

Related topics
English Parliament
Democracy

Should Britain leave the EU?

Britain joined the European Union (then known as the European Economic Community) in 1973 and voted to remain a member state in a referendum in 1975. In the 1990s, the issue of whether to remain a member became more prominent and the UK refrained from further integration such as joining the euro. Much of the British press and public are Eurosceptic and UKIP (the UK Independence Party) has been growing its support, but the main political parties are all committed to staying in Europe. Do the benefits justify the political and economic costs?

Pros

[1] Public opinion in the UK favours leaving the EU, and so it would be the democratic thing to do. It would also be more democratic as it would transfer powers back to Westminster, which is a

Cons

[1] It is not clear that the people of Britain care as much about the issue of the EU as do its political parties and its newspapers. The UK is represented democratically in Europe through its directly elected MEPs

more accountable body. Leaving would restore sovereignty on the national level and bring decision making back closer to those affected.

[2] The UK is a reluctant member state. It has never been willing to join the euro, it expects to be able to negotiate endless opt-outs and it opposes further integration. This means that it does not have a strong voice in the EU in the way that France and Germany do, and yet it is still subject to the laws and regulations that are passed. The UK traditionally has stronger links to the USA and the Commonwealth, and it could use its independent position to promote its own interests and to have an influence on the world stage.

[3] Untethered immigration has put a strain on UK infrastructure. The freedom of movement that is granted under the EU has seen huge waves of immigration into the UK from Eastern Europe. This has led to a shortage in school places and has meant that there are fewer jobs available in industries such as construction. It has also meant that the UK has had to further restrict immigration from outside the EU. The government should be able to control immigration levels, but while it remains part of the EU it cannot. The government predicted that fewer than 20,000 immigrants would come to Britain in 2004 when eight new member states joined the EU. The actual number was 690,000.

[4] The UK is a net contributor to the EU. This means we subsidise poorer EU nations when the money could stay at home. Countries such as Spain have built excellent new roads with EU money, while many roads in the UK remain of poor quality. The money we give to the

and through the Council of Europe. The reality is that if the UK were to leave the EU, it would still have to follow many of the EU laws and directives without having any say in them.

[2] The UK is no longer a superpower. The EU can compete with the USA and China, but the UK cannot. If the UK leaves the EU, it risks becoming isolated and losing its influence on the world stage. The UK is one of the largest economies in the EU and one of its two nuclear powers. This guarantees its influence at an EU level while not compromising its relations with the USA or the Commonwealth.

[3] Citizens of the UK benefit from being members of the EU. Freedom of movement means that they can live and work in any EU state. There is also added human rights protection through the European Court of Human Rights. The effects of immigration have also been positive for the UK, bringing many skilled workers to the country and helping the economy to grow.

[4] Businesses in the UK benefit from being part of the largest single market in the world. About half of all of the UK's trade is with the EU and there are advantages in terms of the absence of tariffs and the level playing field created by all states using the same regulations. Being an EU member state also helps to attract foreign direct investment to the UK because of these benefits.

Possible motions

This House believes that the UK should leave the EU.

This House would hold a referendum on EU membership.

EU could also go in aid to those in greater need. If we wish to contribute abroad, perhaps it would be better to give the money to less economically developed countries where more obvious good could be done.

This House believes that the UK is better off in the EU than out.

Related topics

United States of Europe
European Union, expansion of the
Euro, abolition of the
Regional trade blocs over global free trade

Written constitution

The 'constitution' of a country is the set of fundamental laws that lay down the system of government and define the relations of the executive, the legislature and the judiciary. Almost all countries have a written constitution, of which the oldest is the American constitution of 1787. (The Bill of Rights is a set of 10 amendments incorporated into that constitution in 1791.) The UK is the exception in having only a 'virtual constitution'. That is to say, the constitution is not written down in a document anywhere. but has emerged over the centuries as the result of various different agreements, laws and precedents. Important laws that are part of this 'virtual constitution' are Magna Carta of 1215, the Habeas Corpus Act of 1689, the Parliament Acts of 1911 and 1949 and the Reform Acts passed between 1832 and 1928 to extend the electorate. An organisation called Charter 88 was set up in 1988 by a group who were concerned with what they perceived as the autocratic way in which Margaret Thatcher passed unpopular legislation with small Commons majorities and on a minority vote from the electorate as a whole. Charter 88 argues that a written constitution would safeguard the liberty of the individual against the excesses of an 'elective dictatorship'. The massive majority of the Labour government elected in 1997 and the 'presidential' or 'dictatorial' style of Tony Blair led to renewed concerns about the excess of power put into the hands of elected politicians. Vast constitutional changes made by the Labour government (e.g. Lords reform, devolution and signing up to a Constitution for Europe) and mooted by the coalition government after 2010 (e.g. more Lords reform and fixed-term parliaments) show that any government can make radical constitutional changes with no extra checks and balances in place for protection. The Human Rights Act of 1998 passed by the Labour government acts as a *de facto* Bill of Rights, but could be repealed by any parliament, so does not offer the protection of a constitutional Bill of Rights.

Pros

[1] In countries with a written constitution, the parliament cannot pass laws infringing on the rights of citizens. If it does, the courts can declare the laws

Cons

[1] This is a theoretical argument that ignores the facts. The countries with written constitutions have been just as reprobate in their assaults on individual

illegal. For example, segregation in the USA was ruled unconstitutional by the Supreme Court despite several state assemblies supporting it. Without a written constitution for the judiciary to appeal to, the power of parliament is ultimate and this means that there is no constitutional way for unjust and unpopular laws – such as the Conservatives' poll tax legislation of 1990, or the ban on beef on the bone and the banning of handguns by the Labour government in 1997 – to be deleted from the statute book. A written constitution provides a check on parliamentary power.

[2] Britain is one of only two democracies in the world without a written constitution (the other, Israel, has spent 50 years failing to agree on one). And since British law is made by governments with minority public support (generally around 40 per cent), it is all the more vital that that minority is not given unimpeded power. Charter 88 was founded in response to the particular excesses of Thatcherism, but a written constitution, including a bill of rights, is needed to guard against all future autocratic parliaments, whatever their political leaning.

[3] Liberal democracy relies on the 'rule of law', first enshrined in Magna Carta in 1215 in England to guard individual rights against the excesses of the monarch and royal officials. Thus the idea was established that the powers of government must themselves be subject to law. But the British parliament is subject to no authority beyond its control of itself. This is philosophically repugnant and politically dangerous. A written constitution would remedy this situation.

rights as those countries without one. The constitution of the USA was said to allow for slavery and segregation, and today it fails to stop the death penalty – the ultimate expression of the state's oppression of the individual. In practice, Britain has a very good human rights record – much better than most countries that have written constitutions. Nigeria and Iraq both have written constitutions.

[2] Written constitutions are ruled upon by judges; in Britain, these are unelected and tend to be pro-establishment, if not reactionary. If society is minded to oppress minority rights, the chances are that judges will also be so minded, and will interpret a constitution accordingly – just as racial segregation was said by successive US Supreme Courts in the nineteenth century to be constitutional. It is less desirable to place more power in the hands of judges (whether unelected or elected) than it is to place it in the hands of elected representatives.

[3] Of course Britain does have a constitution, albeit an unwritten and hence subtle one. British history has shown that the convoluted interaction between precedent, convention and the wrath of a vengeful electorate at the ballot box is a more effective check on politicians than any legalistic written formulations.

[4] The British political system was desperately in need of modernisation by the 1990s, and its flexible constitution allowed this to happen. A more rigid, written constitution may have left it stuck with the outdated system of hereditary peers being able to delay the legislation of the elected government. Most constitutional changes are, by convention, put to

[4] The lack of a written constitution has meant that governments have been free to assault traditions and institutions. The House of Lords was reformed by the Labour government with no clear plan and no clear mandate beyond its parliamentary majority. A written constitution would include further safeguards, such as requiring a referendum or a two-thirds majority vote in parliament. The monarch required a second election to establish a mandate for House of Lords reform in 1911, but with a weaker monarch now, there is no remaining check on a majority government's power. Other changes such as devolution have been put to a referendum, but with no constitutional requirement for a minimum turnout, only 35.4 per cent of Welsh people voted for this huge and historic change.

referendum, and if the public care, they can vote for change (as they did for Scottish and Welsh devolution) or to retain the status quo (as they did when they voted 'no' to electoral reform in 2011).

Possible motions

This House demands a written constitution.
This House supports a Bill of Rights.

Related topics

Democracy
Social movements: courts v. legislatures
English Parliament
Scottish independence

APPENDICES

The following appendices are reproduced with permission from
www.noisyclassroom.com

APPENDIX A

Style tips for persuasive speaking

- Make eye contact with your audience – let them know you are talking to them.
- Use variety – in your voice, body language and facial expressions – that way you will keep everyone's attention.
- Make sure your body language and tone of voice are appropriate to what you are saying – if you are talking about something sad, do not smile and vice versa.
- Do not move around too much – you do not want the audience getting seasick! Watch out for distracting gestures such as jangling change in your pocket or playing with your hair.
- If you stand up straight with your head up and your shoulders back, everyone will think you are confident, even if you are really feeling nervous.
- Try to sound like you care about what you are talking about – if you sound bored, your audience will be bored too.
- Try to pick interesting and persuasive language – if you just say 'good' and 'bad' all the time, it will not be as effective as picking your words carefully.
- Try to pick examples or analogies that you think are appropriate for your audience – an example from youth culture will be more persuasive to a room of teenagers than to an older audience.
- Try to have a strong opening so that you make an impression from the beginning – think in advance of a powerful way to grab the audience's attention – and a strong closing so that you leave them on a high note.
- Have a 'sound bite' that everyone in your team can use a few times in their speeches; for example, in a 'women fighting on the front line' debate, 'quality is more important than equality'.
- Be yourself. There is no need to overuse traditional vocabulary such as 'the worthy gentleman' which will sound clichéd to modern audiences. Neither should you attempt to alter your own accent; many of history's finest debaters had strong regional accents or speech impediments.
- Make sure you have a glass of water nearby and do not be afraid to use it if you have a dry mouth.

APPENDIX B

Preparation for debates that are not in this book

What if *Pros and Cons* does not have the motion you are looking for? Here are some questions to ask yourself to help generate enough arguments:

- What is the most important reason why we should or should not do this? (For example, is there a problem we want to solve, a link we want to break, a principle we want to uphold?)
- What are all of the other advantages and disadvantages? (For example, it is cheaper, it sends out a strong message, it reduces a harm, etc.)
- What are the practicalities (cost, time, staffing, getting agreement, space, etc.)? (These are particularly good on the opposition for attacking the proposition plan.)
- What are the principles? (Equality, human rights, justice, liberty, freedom of choice, etc.)
- Who are all of the different people who are affected by this or play a role in it? (Police, doctors, government, parents, children, teachers, the poor, developing countries, NGOs, transnational corporations [TNCs], etc.) Is this good or bad for them?
- Are different countries affected differently? Developing/developed; democracy/dictatorship; religious/secular, etc.
- What examples can we think of from the news recently that fit into this?
- What other examples can we think of? (Avoid examples from fictional sources and from your history lessons for the most part.)

And if you're on the opposition, you might also want to consider the following questions:

- Is the proposal moving us too far/fast in an area without general consensus (moral, political, cultural, technological)?
- Why now? Why should we move first?
- What is the current trend?
- Are there more pressing issues?
- Should we be dealing with this problem as part of a broader issue?

- Libertarian: are freedoms (speech, movement, expression, trade) being infringed?
- Authoritarian: should there be more government regulation?
- Is security at risk?
- Does the proposal tip the balance too far to one side? Is one side ignored?
- What are the international implications?
- What about accountability?
- How much will this cost? Where is the money coming from? Who will run it? Do they have a good track record?

APPENDIX C

How can I keep speaking for the full time?

When you start debating, speaking for the full time (be it three, five or seven minutes) can be daunting. Even for experienced debaters, impromptu motions can be announced which leave them thinking 'How can I speak for seven minutes on that?' Here are some tips to keep you on your feet until the double bell.

- Speak *slowly* – often when we are nervous, we speak really quickly, but if we speak more slowly, we will get better style marks and speak for longer.
- Really *develop* each argument – talk about it in detail and try and think of two or three ways of explaining it, giving different examples and analogies. If you need to make it go on for longer, imagine that nobody has understood you and you need to explain it again even more clearly, going through each step.
- Unless you are the first speaker, you can take up a lot of time in your speech with *rebuttal* – rebut everything the speaker before you has said and anything from any other speakers on the other side that you want to pick up. Rebuttal should not be dismissed quickly – like developing your arguments, make sure you develop your rebuttal to make it really clear.
- Beginnings and endings – if you have a rhetorical opening and closing, and signpost your own and your partners' points at the start and summarise them at the end – that might take up to a minute of your speech!
- In an ideal world, if you had enough to say, then you would not take more than three *points of information*. If, however, you are going to run out of things to say really early, it is better to take a couple more than to end before time. If this is going to happen, try to spread them out rather than take them in a row.
- Make sure you use the preparation time to generate enough material – see Appendix B for advice on this.
- If it is not going to be possible to do a full-minute speech with new arguments and rebuttal, you are going to have to *repeat points* that have already been made, but if you do so, try to make them sound as new as possible with fresh analysis and examples. If the worst comes to the worst and you have finished your points and there is a minute left, do a very detailed summary of your points (i.e. repeat your own points). This is not ideal, but you will lose fewer marks than by sitting down early.

APPENDIX D

Guidance for the chairperson

The chairperson should introduce the topic and the speakers on both sides. They should then call each speaker in the pre-arranged order. They could say: 'It now gives me great pleasure to recognise the first speaker for the proposition, James Bond.'

When the speaker has finished, the chairperson thanks them and calls on the next speaker. If there is a floor debate, it will be up to the chair to ask for points from the audience. They could say: 'Please raise your hand if you have any points', and then choose somebody. If the points all seem to be to one team, the chair should ask for opposing points to balance it out. At the end of the debate, the chairperson should take a vote. They could say: 'Please raise your hands if you wish to vote for the proposition. Now the opposition. And finally any votes in abstention (or undecided)?'

The chairperson should then announce the results of the debate by saying either 'The motion has been carried' or 'The motion has been defeated'. They should then congratulate the teams and invite them to cross the floor to shake hands.

APPENDIX E

Key vocabulary

Motion or resolution: the topic which is to be debated. In many formats, this is phrased 'This House . . .' in reference to legislative houses.

Proposition or affirmative or government: the side that agrees with the motion.

Opposition or negative: the side that disagrees with the motion.

Chairperson or speaker or moderator: the person in charge of the debate who makes sure that everyone follows the rules and introduces the speakers.

Timekeeper: the person who keeps time and gives time signals.

Points of information: a structured way of interrupting a speaker (see page 3 for more details).

Rebuttal or refutation: the responses made to the arguments on the other side.

The floor debate: a period during or after the debate where the audience can share their views.

Summary speeches or reply speeches: the final speeches on each side that sum up the key issues in the debate.

Protected time: the period at the start and end of a speech where no points of information can be offered.

Accepted/taken/rejected/declined: words used by the speaker when offered a point of information to show whether they will allow the interruption.

Extension: the new material that is delivered by the third speaker in the British Parliamentary or World Universities Debating Championships style.

Burden of proof: what the team feels they need to prove in order to win the debate.

Model: the details of the practical implementation of a policy.

Clash: the areas of the debate where the two sides have disagreed.

Definition: the terms of the debate.

Counter-proposal: where the opposition puts forward an alternative plan instead of supporting the status quo.